Curriculum Change in Secondary Schools, 1957–2004

This book is about curriculum change in secondary schools and shows how the quality of education has been affected by increasing intervention of central government.

Based on the story of one secondary school between 1957 and 2004, we follow the changing context of before and after the introduction of the National Curriculum; the changing role of LEAs and governors; and the characteristics since 1992 of school inspections charged with the responsibilities of policing the operation of the national tests, predictions of results, examination results, nationally set targets and compliance with detailed prescription of school curricula. This is a one school story seen through the eyes of the heads and their deputies who covered that period and some assistant staff who served during forty years or more. How did those changes affect what they sought to do as professionals? This is a story which takes curriculum as the main engine of a school's development and so takes the quality of education as the result of the relationship between what happens in classrooms and what happens in the school as a whole. It is a two-way flow. Where has it taken us? This is offered as a profit and loss account.

Norman Evans has had a lifetime involvement with institutional and curriculum change in schools and higher education and is currently Trustee, Learning from Experience Trust and Visiting Professor at Goldsmiths College and London Metropolitan University, UK.

Woburn Education Series

Series Editor: Peter Gordon
University of London, UK

First published 2005
by Routledge
2 Park Square, Milton Park, Abingdon, Oxon OX14 4RN

Simultaneously published in the USA and Canada
by Routledge
270 Madison Ave, New York, NY 10016

Routledge is an imprint of the Taylor & Francis Group

© 2005 Norman Evans

Typeset in Times by
HWA Text and Data Management Ltd, Tunbridge Wells
Printed and bound in Great Britain by
Biddles Ltd, King's Lynn

British Library Cataloguing in Publication Data
A catalogue record for this book is available from the British
Library

Library of Congress Cataloging in Publication Data
Evans, Norman, 1923–
  Curriculum change in the secondary school / Norman Evans.
    p.   cm.   – (Woburn education series)
  Includes bibliographical references.
Curriculum planning–Great Britain–History. 2. Curriculum
change–Great Britain–History. 3. Education, Secondary–
Curricula–Great Britain–History. I. Title. II. Series.
  LB2806.15.E89 2005
  373.19´0942–dc22   2005002939

ISBN 0–7130–0242–5 (hbk)
ISBN 0–7130–4062–9 (pbk)

Curriculum Change in Secondary Schools, 1957–2004

An educational roundabout?

Norman Evans

Routledge
Taylor & Francis Group

LONDON AND NEW YORK

Dictionary of British Educationalists
Peter Gordon and Richard Aldrich

Royal Education
Past, present and future
Peter Gordon and Denis Lawton

Teacher Training at Cambridge
The initiatives of Oscar Browning and Elizabeth Hughes
Pam Hirsch and Mark McBeth

The TUC and Education Reform, 1962–1970
Clive Giggs

Schooling of Working-Class Girls in Victorian Scotland
Gender, education and identity
Jane McDermid

Clara Collett, 1860–1948
An educated working woman
Deborah McDonald

Biographical Dictionary of North American and European Educationalists
Peter Gordon and Richard Aldrich

The Struggle for the General Teaching Council
Richard Willis

Curriculum Change in Secondary Schools, 1957–2004
A curriculum roundabout?
Norman Evans

For all who knew Senacre 1957–2004
especially 1957–67
with gratitude

Contents

Foreword

Senacre, the school that is the subject of this book, illustrates remarkably well all the contexts and themes which have affected secondary school communities over the last half century. The story of the school therefore uncannily reflects the reality for teachers and schools of policies created and imposed at a national and sometimes local level.

The new secondary modern schools erected in the 1950s and 1960s were created at a time of great hope. Indeed the often generous proportions of their buildings were to set a standard which subsequent generations, especially after the oil crisis of the early 1970s, did not attempt to match. So Senacre was a school designed for what contemporaries often described 'as fit for the sons and daughters of returning heroes'. Later the Newsom report *Half our Future* set out the vision that reinforces the purpose and motivation of those in schools like Senacre.

Here therefore we have a book that views education and social changes of half a century through the lens of a school and its seven headteachers. So how Senacre coped with the raising of the school leaving age, with the earlier curriculum innovation in the era of the Schools Council, and later with the Technical Vocational Educational Initiative (TVEI), not to forget records of achievement (ROA) – are all part of the school's story. There are local twists too including the continuing strange story of Kent's selective system. For example we hear of a period in Senacre's history where the school lost its best pupils at 13+ in what turned out to be a half baked and botched attempt to ameliorate the worst effects of selection.

Here too you will read of what it felt like to be in a school on the receiving end of the National Curriculum, of published league tables, of going 'grant maintained' and becoming a technology college – and later bizarrely losing that status.

Here you will read of a school which waxed and waned under the leadership of seven different characters as headteachers. The book takes you through some astonishing changes in fortune – some entirely self-created, others the combination of inner doubts and other pressures. Ofsted and HMI are usefully contrasted as the school moves from health to ill health and crawls back again. 'Serious weaknesses', 'special measures' and recovery are all told through the story of Senacre.

The publication of the book is timely in the sense that one of the impressions one gets as one reads the school's unfolding story is how much more circumscribed the freedoms of schools have become in the last half century. For all governments' talk of 'independent state secondary schools' Senacre has less curriculum freedom now than it did when it was created. Then in a spirit of trust there was an encouragement to experiment: HMI visits were rare; LEAs had few advisors. Now there is the tyranny not just of external exams and tests but of practical and detailed advice from the Qualifications and Curriculum Authority (QCA) backed by regular Ofsted inspections of schools published like the league tables for all the world to see. Soon inspections will be at a few days' notice with schools in a state of constant alert. For all the real improvement in delegation over funding through local management of schools and fair funding, the lot of the headteachers and their staff has become more pressured and confined. The rate of change accelerates as Anthony Giddens reveals in *Runaway World* – the published version of his Reith Lectures in 2000. What is clear to anyone in schools nowadays is that the impact of this rapid kaleidoscopic change penetrates the walls of a school to an extent that it did not fifty years ago.

And at last Senacre is poised to be part of yet another national initiative – this time the creation of 'federations' of schools where it is acknowledged that groups of schools cooperating in a more or less closely and formally coupled partnership stand more chance of meeting the needs of staff and pupils than a free for all among individually competing schools.

The author of the book, given his pride, natural and proper as the founder of the Senacre story, has doubts. The key issue to me is that whether such a federation is the take over of one school by others or whether all the participating schools acknowledge that they can create a worthwhile new identity, which adds value to the equal separate identities of the participating school communities.

All those who love school communities will enjoy the story of Senacre as it unfolds in the following pages.

Tim Brighouse
Chief Advisor for London Schools

Preface

A first love always goes in deep. Its tributaries can run through a lifetime. My first professional love was as head of Senacre Secondary Modern School between 1957–67. Curriculum development was all embracing. It has lived with me ever since.

By chance I discovered that some men and women I had appointed in the 1960s had served for over thirty years and so had retired relatively recently. That gave me the idea for this book.

Professor John Elliott, RE teacher at Senacre – just retired as Dean of Education at University of East Anglia and Director of the Centre for Applied Research in Education – and I had often bemoaned what had happened to the secondary school curriculum as the years went by, claiming perhaps arrogantly, but with dismay, that what was developed as a highly effective school curriculum for its pupils in the 1960s seemed to have been thrown away. Instrumentalism seemed to take over from invention and innovation. And so the idea for this book came to the surface.

What had happened to the curriculum in that one school could be plotted by men and women with long memories and ringside seats for witnessing the changes, which occurred in the last forty years, as well as being affected by them. There was first-hand evidence to bring the story to life. They agreed to help. Four of my successors as heads agreed to join in, so did two deputies who filled the other periods. The idea became writing in prospect.

Necessarily the account of the first headship is autobiographical, and has been read critically by colleagues who were with me there. Every other chapter has been cleared by those who feature in the story and were valuable sources for it. I am grateful to them all. The acknowledgement pays tribute to them. It has been a fascinating two year journey. We all hope that others will enjoy it as well.

Norman Evans

Acknowledgements

Six staff appointed during the first headship served for over thirty years, contributing 200 years between them in the forty-three years between 1961 and 2004. Two appointed in the second headship served for thirty years. Without that continuity this story of Senacre could not have been told. They know who they are. So do other staff who served in one or more headships without whom the story could not have been told with authority. These included: Chris Arnold, Gary Branchett, Brian Cannell, John Elliott, Pamela Judge, Tony Hewson, Peter Judge, Chris Norris, Chris Roberts, Quentin Skinner, Brian Thomas, Nick Wheeler-Robinson.

And of course nothing could have been told at all without the agreement, support and willing collaboration of the heads and their deputies who followed me: Barbara Hall, Paul Drayson, Margaret Yellop, Neil Hunter, Paul Leadham, Andrew Parsons, Sheila Storey, John Werner.

To all I am deeply indebted for their forebearance, patience and willingness to help tell the story of the Senacre they cherished greatly and which has given me such pleasure in writing.

I am especially grateful to Brian Cannell, Barbara Hall and Chris Norris who served the school for thirty and more years and read the entire script several times over, made penetrating comments and put me right where I was wrong. I am also indebted to John Elliott who for years supported and encouraged the attempt to tell the story. All my thanks go to him.

It just needs to be said that all contributions to the story are based on personal recollections and reflections. And if anyone anywhere finds an inappropriate emphasis, or factual error, the fault is mine alone.

Norman Evans

Chapter 1

Introduction

This book is about curriculum. It is not about curriculum theory. Rather it is about the changes which have occurred to the curriculum in secondary schools during the last forty-five years, when government interventions have multiplied exponentially. It seeks to strike a profit and loss account of the effect of those interventions on the quality of secondary education.

The book is a one school story about that trajectory of curriculum development, drawing heavily on the experience of seven successive heads and some long serving assistant staff in what began as Senacre Secondary Modern School in Maidstone in 1957, and successively became Senacre High School, Senacre Technology School and then Senacre Technology College. It was put in special measures and then climbed out of them again.

It is a one school and seven heads' and many members of staff's story. It attempts to chart the relationship between the narrow and wider interpretations of the curriculum as understood and experienced by heads and their assistant staff under the influence of ever more regulation and scrutiny. What effect did the prescriptions for the curriculum have on the wider interpretation and on the quality of educational opportunities offered?

As a single school story the book attempts to give some account of the impact of the growing pressures which came from governments' anxieties about the quality of schooling, which led to Acts of parliament, the National Curriculum, and fundamental changes to the way schools were organized and inspected, requiring them to manage their own finances, reducing the role of local authorities, making governing bodies legally responsible for the conduct and financial probity of their schools, all buttressed with detailed regulations and instructions for keeping records and making returns, with targets to be met giving both predictions and actual levels of pupil achievement. It is a story which one way or another affected all secondary schools in the system.

During this period the curriculum changed from being largely the preserve of heads of schools and their staff, where they were consulted, to becoming the legal responsibility of governing bodies to meet statutory requirements. Laisser faire gave way to investigations of the secret garden, first prompted by James Callaghan's speech at Ruskin College in 1976 which in time led to sets of precise prescriptions by central government as to what schools should teach and increasingly how they should teach it. Enshrined in the National Curriculum in 1988 it was to be policed by inspectors to ensure compliance.

In 2004 there were signs that ministers are beginning to understand the educational limitations of tight prescriptions. Some freedom is being restored to schools to take better account of the particular needs of the pupils who come to them. The 'one size fits all' doctrine seems to have run its course. But government diktat remains. So does prescription. It is yet to be seen how far the loosened grip on the centralized curriculum will lead to better education experiences and how far they will be paralleled by fewer bureaucratic demands. It is as if the bright shining light, powered by an engaged curriculum which characterized what Senacre and other schools tried to provide for their pupils in the 1960s and early 1970s, is now focused on a different secret garden, the mysterious, impenetrable thinking with untested assumptions in the Department for Education and Skills (DfEE).

There is no better way of giving a snapshot of the distance travelled by the curriculum in forty-five years than by putting side by side the work and role of governing bodies. In 1957, 2.00 p.m. governors' meetings were relaxed, even chatty, occasions lasting about an hour and a half. The head described the essentials of numbers, staffing, buildings, and anything which seemed interesting. LEA governors who were councillors were often chided for the poor service or resources made available from the education committee. The district education officer would make emollient noises. Questions might be asked about this and that but in no sense was there any scrutiny of what the school was doing.

Nearly fifty years later it is very different. Governors sit in board meetings with procedures like board meetings the world over. The curriculum lies at the core of their legal responsibilities but in the pressure of other business it can struggle to get sufficient attention. Meetings can last up to three hours, three or four times a year with sub-committees in between. Finance, staffing, curriculum, pastoral care, premises and lettings, the response to the latest ring-fenced initiative announced by the DfEE or regulations following another Act of parliament, all can appear on the agenda. Examination results are pored over to detect the smallest improvement or deterioration. League tables giving comparisons between nearby schools are discussed with anxiety. So sometimes there is hardly time for adequate discussion of curriculum, and yet it is governors' central responsibility.

Ask anyone in the street what they understand by curriculum and most will reply something about lessons and subjects. The more knowledgeable may talk about learning opportunities. They think about what goes on in classrooms, the staff, the rooms and facilities available and the way they are timetabled. Those are the boundaries which dictate what can go on in lessons.

That is a narrow interpretation of curriculum. For this book there is a wider interpretation. It is taken to mean the total range of possibilities for pupils and young people to learn. Curriculum then becomes all encompassing of what a school does, feels like, stands for, day by day – a whole school curriculum.

The story told here throughout this shift from relative informality to strict legal formality in supervising a narrow interpretation of curriculum, is about how within that growing formality, the school managed to provide the best possible service for the young people who came to it. Each head had a particular view of how to provide the best. From 1974 onwards each had to grapple with the problems arising from increasing external instructions on how to provide it. And the same set of questions remains. How far have external interventions improved the learning opportunities available? What, if anything, has external intervention prevented schools from doing that could have enhanced learning opportunities? And have the gains outweighed the losses, or the losses outweighed the gains. How does the score card read? Is it narrow and focused or wider and embracing? Where is the curriculum now?

The short answer is that in some respects it is trying to get back to elements of where it was forty-five years ago. This is indeed a curriculum roundabout. The longer answer is in the story which follows.

Chapter 2

Curriculum explorations
The first headship, Norman Evans, 1957–67

Scene setting: personal

To begin at the beginning. I do not think curriculum was even in my vocabulary when I began as a 32-year-old fledgling headmaster of Senacre Secondary School, Maidstone in 1957 (a product of a public school and Cambridge who had achieved the rank of lieutenant in the RNVR). School mastering was all I knew about education. But then the curriculum was of scant interest to the government. R.A. Butler records in his memoirs *The Art of the Possible* (Butler 1971: 92) that during a conversation about his forthcoming Act he reminded Churchill, who wanted pupils to learn about Wolfe's storming of the Heights of Abraham, that it was not thought to be the business of parliament or ministers to decide what children were to be taught. That was for the teachers and professionals who ran the schools. Such was the ethos of the time.

It lasted a long time, certainly in some teachers' minds. In 1983 Edward Blishen could write about his response to a visiting HMI intrusion:

> I believed a lesson was a private transaction between teacher and taught, and that no amount of official importance could justify such unnegotiated intrusions.
>
> (Blishen 1983: 4)

The year 1957 was a time when Kent Education Authority was fast building secondary modern schools and was looking for graduates to run them. Hence I found myself at Senacre. Like many ex-servicemen beginning their careers or picking them up again and finding themselves headmastering, I had a strong sense of optimism about the way society could change and saw working in the state system as a way of trying in some small way to help things along. So when I had had enough of public schools, I remembered that Gerald Owst, Professor of Education in the Cambridge University Department of Education had said that Kent was looking for graduates. That was the connection.

By the time I left ten years later, I had a set of curricular principles which influenced everything I have done subsequently in teacher training and higher education for the next forty years. However even then there was a faint smell, like wood smoke hanging in the air, suggesting that the Butler days were closing, and that outside intervention would come from officials and politicians.

Baggage carried: professional

If I did not think in curricular terms that September, I did have strong ideas about pupils' potential. At Bedford School, one of the great public schools, I taught fifth and sixth form English and history, with weekly current affairs lectures. In 1950 the General Certificate of Education at O level and A level replaced the School Certificate and Higher School Certificate. An important change was that whereas the School Certificate had been a grouped subject requirement, O level became a single subject examination. Over several years I realized that there were boys in the lowest examination groups in the fifth form who had failed the same examination not once, but twice. Mechanically, the treadmill took them round and round the same syllabus. It was hardly surprising that troublemakers were among them, large, growing young men that they were. Sometimes they were badly taught. I was sure that treating them differently would not only improve their classroom performance but sort out some of the behavioural problems at source.

When I found myself facing fourth-form classes of boys and girls as head of English in Sir William Nottidge Secondary School in Whitstable, I realized that I could have swapped some of them with those Bedford School boys and outshone them. Potentially they had the ability to succeed in GCE O level. It was equally obvious that they had no idea of their own potential for examination success, let alone of their opportunities in life. Nor did the state. Nor did most parents. Expectations were on a different plane. I may have been ignorant of curriculum theory but I did know something about teaching. (I am somewhat reassured to see that the English syllabus I produced there was headed 'Listen: Look: Read: Speak: Write'.)

This is borne out from a quite different source. As I was short of staff, I recruited a young man from Bedford School as an unqualified teacher after he had won an open award to read history at Cambridge and was having what is now called a gap year. Reflecting on his experience he says:

> Coming directly from Bedford to Senacre I remember how very struck I was, especially teaching the leaving class, how very able some of the children were, much abler than so many boys at Bedford who were gaining such an effortless start in life. Several of the girls seemed much the brightest of all and I can still remember faces vaguely and names exactly.

A young Cambridge graduate who joined the staff through the University Appointments Board underlined the disparity of opportunity in a different way.

> I admired their honesty in speaking their minds without the hypocritical cotton wool wrapped around most comments of my own family and friends. I found

their knowledge of the seamy side of life, even as early adolescents, far more extensive than my own. One 13-year-old girl, on my mentioning she had a ladder in her stocking, replied without missing a beat 'Well, do you want to run up it Sir?' Her mother was a local prostitute I learnt later. I began to see examples of real courage as many fought the poverty, cruelty, indifference, ignorance and neglect in their own homes and society at large. It made me realize an educational diet consisting of entirely standard grammar school subjects was doomed to failure.

But I arrived at Senacre with another understanding which I learnt at Bedford School. This was trust. No one ever asked me any questions let alone exercised any supervision of my teaching. Mervyn Pritchard, a Staff HMI for history, listened to a sixth-form lesson and then remarked that I should get off the lecturing style and find other ways to teach. That was like a wake-up call. I began to give periodic lead lessons, set an essay, collected subscriptions to create a small working library with multiple copies of some books so the boys could work independently, and held what were essentially coffee-laden tutorials in my study in a flat in a boarding house nearby. No one ever asked why the boys were not in my classroom, or why they were walking to and fro during lesson time. For the fifth forms we had walls plastered with historical summaries and stories, Shakespearean scenes and sequences and interpretations of poetry. Only one or two colleagues commented on this. The headmaster's assumption was that how schoolmasters taught was their own affair, provided that pupils' achievements were up to scratch. This was very much a laisser faire attitude. Of course there were dangers. Inevitably some masters were more conscientious than others, and in and among common room gossip of this dull form and that troublesome boy, some were interested in pedagogy and improving their teaching techniques – and some could even have done so with a few sharp reminders. And there were huge benefits. There were brilliant heads of English, history and mathematics. Top scholarships in mathematics came regularly with open awards in English and history. But the plus side was time and space to take initiatives, which promoted high levels of responsibility and the sense of authority that goes with it.

For me that translated into the need for time and space for the mysterious relationship between teacher and taught to get to work and promote learning in one way if not in another, trust within clearly understood boundaries. Hence headmastering was trying to create the conditions for the staff to do what it was agreed was to be done which meant looking beyond subject disciplines to what constituted the whole school, non-teaching staff, premises, all of it. But again for the classroom aspect of the curriculum I had no idea how to create it. It also meant as I came to understand it, that for staff to give their best, the key was time and space, encouragement, support and, where necessary, protection, when the use of time and space became controversial.

The ex-Bedford schoolboy, now Regius Professor of History at Cambridge confirms this.

My other memory is of how much latitude there was – if you like, how much trust, and hence how much discretion over what was taught. There were requirements of course, but what I chiefly recall is how easy it was to embellish those (including films, play acting in class, etc.) without anyone supposing this was irrelevant. I can still vividly remember some of those days and even wonder if they weren't some of my most fruitful days of teaching (in a teaching career that, including Senacre is now an unbroken forty-two years).

Also I realized the world I had stepped into when the head at Whitstable asked me not to call the caretaker simply by his surname. He liked to be called 'Mr' which characterized the nature of the life of that school. The caretaker seemed to have control over the use of the building. Staff, lessons, pupils were under continual, usually benign scrutiny as the head stalked the building, checking classrooms, walking in to speak to a pupil or a member of staff, interrupting lessons, all the time looking rather grim as if expecting trouble. I wanted no part of that.

I brought something else. A tutor training course in Cambridge to prepare for taking classes for the Workers Education Association taught me the need to respect what learners brought with them and to value silence as a powerful pedagogical tool. It proved to be a valuable piece of equipment.

So if curriculum was not then my way of thinking, pupil potential and what would now be called I suppose a supportive environment certainly was. How to realize the first and create the second was another matter.

It was not easy. Senacre was built to serve Shepway, a large council housing estate with road after road of more or less identical buildings, re-housing large numbers from a run-down housing area. Parkwood, another estate followed on, with a more pleasing environment. And that was the school's catchment area, with the village of Langley added. There was little social mix. As such it was perceived generally to be at the less desirable end of Maidstone. Inevitably that reputation rubbed off on the school.

Into the unknown: looking for a curriculum

In September 1957 there were 240 pupils inherited from temporary accommodation in Nissen huts in Mote Park plus the 120 new first-year ones. In addition Senacre was a parking ground for another 120 pupils due to go to another new school not yet open. They all had to be staffed and timetabled against the pattern of subjects which was established in Mote Park: English, mathematics, science, history, geography, religious education, art, music, domestic science and needlework, woodwork and metalwork and physical Education.

A letter from the District Education Officer (DEO) in February after I was appointed stated that there were thirteen new appointments to be made. There were under four months to find them to add to the nine already on the staff; three established heads of departments, two with graded posts and a deputy among them. In those days it was an applicant's dream with advertisements galore. By short-circuiting the education office's procedures there was a full complement when the school opened. Phoning, scouring applications in the divisional office, calling those who had been rejected in other schools, using connections – Nancy Martin at the London Institute of Education, the University Careers Service at Cambridge – there was never an interview in the education office. Some were interviewed in our cottage in Littlebourne. During the Easter holiday the head of boys' crafts was signed up in the Greyhound pub in Corfe Castle, and a young man was surprised on the doorstep of his home in Cornwall to see his application form for another school used as a calling card. The assumption was that candidates had other offers in their back pockets or handbags. It was a close run thing. So the nine established members of staff were joined by thirteen others. All of them but the heads of boys' and girls' PE, and boys' crafts, were young novices. There was complete freedom to appoint them. They were the most interesting people it was possible to find. No education officer, no governor played any part in it. In a way it set the tone for the next ten years. At least the timetable was covered. The first days were complicated. Having staff and pupils trampling through mud, along duckboards did not seem the best way to begin in a brand new school, so I refused to open for a fortnight.

So arriving at Senacre armed with that assumption about ability of the pupils which would come to the school, there was one clear goal. This was to find ways and means of lifting their expectations, widening horizons so that access to middle level white collar employment for many, and professional possibilities for some, became a reality, to realize their potential in both senses of the word. Doing so could demonstrate to some pupils, their parents and very importantly, the staff, that examination success was achievable, within the grasp of some of the young men and women who otherwise would leave school at fifteen at the end of their fourth year, or earlier at Easter according to their birthdays, if they wished to do so. Beyond examination syllabuses I had little idea of where that would lead.

Curriculum lessons first learnt

Action on the twin fronts of pupil potential and a supportive environment first came together in 1959. That summer was the first time there would be leavers at the end of the fourth year. If there was to be a fifth year with examinations in sight it had to begin then. As it turned out it was the pupils themselves who taught a most salutary curriculum lesson.

LEA advisors agreed that there was a probable 10 per cent overlap between those who passed and failed the 11+ exam selection. (Kent still uses the exam today.) It followed that it was perfectly reasonable for the school to take soundings for establishing a fifth year with the college of Preceptors syllabuses as an opening gambit. The DEO raised no objections. Heads of English and mathematics overcame their scepticism of using the preceptors as a stalking horse for GCE that followed on a year later which created a sixth year. A pupil-produced magazine for May 1963 shows that the 1962 examinations resulted in twenty-eight pupils with College of Preceptors statements, five with certificates and fourteen of them with GCE ordinary level passes.

Fifty-six out of the 120 families attended a meeting to hear about plans. One wrote in pencil at the bottom of a slip of paper asking for a provisional place on the fifth-form course, 'I cannot say definitely yet financial of keeping him at this time'. He stayed, and that spoke volumes about what the school was trying to do. Thirty forms came back asking for a place.

And this is where the first curriculum lesson began. Seven pupils from what at that time were called the C and D streams asked to stay. Streaming was then almost universal. It was how Bedford and Nottidge arranged things. But the idea that some of the C and D streams would not want to leave as fast as they could, was something that never occurred to anyone.

What could be done? Rejecting those young people was out of the question. It was equally obvious that sitting in classrooms all day long, going over what now are called the basic skills would not only bore them silly and be asking for disciplinary trouble, but be a very ineffective way of helping them learn more, and improve their English and mathematics. Help was at hand. Fortuitously there was a teacher in charge of D streams who had done a course in special education. Essentially a local man, he played in local teams, and was very well known in the town. He was a very good supportive teacher who did everything he could for his collection of slow learners. After some persuasion, he agreed that a programme of work experience could go some way to meeting the needs of this small fifth year group. Using his many contacts, he found employers willing to accept these Senacre pupils as quasi employees. They would keep the same hours as regular employees. They would be out of school for up to three days a week. He would visit them in their workplace and talk with the employers. There would be no formal reporting. General remarks in end of term reports would suffice. In the current jargon it was to be 'work based learning'. And so when the fifth year opened for the first time in 1959–60 it was with two forms: one for examinations and one for non-examination work.

Naturally some older members of staff were more than sceptical. But they trusted their colleague and in any case there was nothing they could do to stop it. The DEO approved the scheme in an exchange of letters. He was one of the old school of local educational authority public servants who saw their job as helping and supporting heads to get on and do their job. It was trust again and at that time he had authority to bestow it. So in effect he authorized one of the first, if not the first, work experience programmes in the country as part of secondary schools' curricula at the turn of the decade. He did so with firm encouragement, whatever he thought of the idea privately. In the same vein, he phoned later referring to an appointment to a headship in another new school. 'I thought you would like to know, Norman' he said, 'We have just appointed another boy to a headship'. Deft, subtle, supportive, warmly human, I guess intuitive of the DEO. It was what now would be called management, and something which no course can ever teach. The only managers we knew of then were in banks, Boots and Marks and Spencer.

But a second curriculum lesson was coming. It showed how little was understood about what curricular innovation could do. Before long those young people dubbed C and D stream out on work experience were asking for more English and mathematics. They came, went in and out of the school as individuals, as their work experience dictated. Their relationship with the master who ran the programme changed. It became more relaxed and their self-confidence grew. There was hardly a peep of trouble out of any one of them, and there was never an attendance problem. Careers interviews took on a different tone and purpose. Looking back it was all so simple. Find something those young men and women wanted to do. Give them support to do it and as much responsibility for doing it as possible, and everyone's life is more enjoyable.

Combined, those two fifth forms brought a sea change in the school. Those pupils learnt, knew they were learning and on they whole liked it. They had the precious experience of success. So much so that some insisted on staying on for sixth year to tackle GCE O level head on. (By the end there was an A level correspondence course for religious studies.) Parents liked it of course, those of the more and less able alike. Staff were gratified as examination success came along and as careers interviews for the less able began to take them into more interesting jobs. The DEO was delighted and so were the governors when it was reported to them.

Curriculum development was moving; an important milestone was passed but there was a very long way to go. For the next year or two it was hard to create the sense of time and space which was an essential ingredient in attempting to reach the goal of realizing full potential. The curriculum remained formal and traditional with the two fifth forms tacked on. A young Cambridge graduate who joined the school in 1959 to teach history commented that the curriculum was dictated by the books which were in the school. They were inherited from the Nissen hut days from the master who taught there and had done nothing in the two years before he left, to rewrite a syllabus. The young graduate used materials he got from the local history classes he attended as he said to do anything to interest them in the past. What goes around comes around. Forty-five years later the Tomlinson Report on 13–19 education is predicted to make recommendations which are more or less the same as that use of work experience in 1959, so much for all the reforms imposed on secondary schools by successive governments.

Climatic change

Then public affairs took a hand. The Crowther Report on the education of the 15–18 age group was a report from the Central Advisory Council for Education chaired by Sir Geoffrey Crowther (HMSO 1959). Later the Robbins Report on Higher Education chaired by Lord Robbins quoted from it to underline the significance of family background: 'The close connection between a father's level of occupation and the educational achievement of children at school. The link is even more marked for girls than boys'. (Robbins Report, HMSO 1963: 50). Tacitly it raised questions about access to and participation in higher education. This was indicative of significant changes in public attitudes to education by government and hence in influential circles. This had no immediate effect on what could be done in Senacre as a school, but it did help create a more reflective sense of possibilities.

Hard on its heels came the 1960 report of the Beloe Committee to the Secondary Schools Examination Council. It recommended the establishment of the Certificate of Secondary Education (CSE). It was conceived as 'a school leaving certificate designed to be at a standard slightly below the ordinary level in GCE, but where grade I was equivalent to a GCE pass. It is organized on a regional basis and teachers are represented on the regional committees' (Wardle 1970: 178). In all probability this new arrival on the educational scene offered far more radical opportunities than the Beloe Committee thought of, let alone intended.

The Certificate of Secondary Education (CSE)

As a benign government influence, the connection with innovation at Senacre was direct. Through membership of the Incorporated Association of Headmasters' (IAHM), as it then was, I was on the Examinations Committee for the South East Regional Board, eventually becoming its Vice-chairman. For the next seven years this connection spawned an extended family of curriculum designs in the school. The opportunities offered by CSE were seized during the planning period. Scepticism came from some quarters, but a sense of high enthusiasm ran through the meetings whatever the frustrating disagreements, sometimes with the secretary to the board and inevitably with some subject panels.

Paragraph 11 of the constitution of the board stated:

The functions of the Examinations committee shall be;

(a) To make arrangements for the conduct of examinations approved by the Board
(b) To appoint examiners and moderators after considering the advice of Subject Panels
(c) To approve arrangements for the adoption of syllabuses
    (Constitution of the SEREB for Certificate of Secondary Education approved by the Secondary Schools Examination Council, 1963)

This seemed to invite schemes which avoided some of the unsatisfactory features of GCE, and the committee set about exploiting that invitation. But first there were some salutary warnings.

If HMI Mervyn Pritchard issued one wake-up call, the first meeting of this Examinations committee brought another. Phillip Taylor, was an assessment expert in Birmingham University, employed by the ministry as an advisor to CSE planning boards. His contribution to the committee's first meeting was dramatic. He drew attention to the problems of designing examinations which were valid and reliable. He drew a straight line across the blackboard, cutting it into a two-thirds section and a one-third section. Calmly, almost conversationally, he fingered the two-thirds section and said that that was the area of any syllabus covered by questions in examinations. Fingering the one-third section, he said that this area was taught but not examined. This he explained, showed the extent to which luck featured in public examinations. They were neither valid nor reliable. If a new Certificate of Secondary Education was to be any good, it needed to do rather better than that. The committee was asked to take note if CSE was to be valid and reliable. It is not clear that that lesson has yet been learnt.

As the subject panels submitted their proposed syllabuses to the committee for approval, Taylor's expositions were increasingly influential. Rapidly a combination of continuous assessment or continual assessment appeared in planning papers and examination regulations. Texts in examination rooms, dictionaries and so on were written in. The acceptance of examinations as part of the curriculum and not some add-on to it began to creep into the scheme of things. CSE examinations were thought of as means of enabling candidates to reveal what they knew instead of running the risk of ignoring and concealing it.

That was a nasty shock. It challenged established practice, which was preparing pupils for examinations by reviewing previous examination papers to spot likely questions. The proposition that there was an inherent nonsense in teaching a third of the syllabus which would not be examined was a heretical challenge to orthodoxy. It led to far more radical thinking. It raised questions about the appropriateness of syllabus content, about its relationship with motivation for learning, about assessment for revealing – not semi-concealing – knowledge and about the educational purpose of school public examinations. Now it would be called staff development. It came just at the right time.

CSE provided an arena for tentative explorations of all those issues. The route into them was opened by the decision of the examinations committee and approved by the South Eastern Board to adopt three possible modes of conducting examinations: Mode 1 where the board set syllabuses and examined, just like the GCE examinations; Mode 2 where the school wrote the syllabuses and the board conducted examinations; Mode 3 where the school wrote its own syllabuses, and set and conducted its own examinations. External examiners oversaw Modes 1 and 2. External moderators oversaw Mode 3 at all stages. Syllabuses and marking schemes had to be approved by the board. Monitoring visits occurred during the teaching. Examination results were scrutinized by evaluators. Quality was assured.

The first CSE examinations were introduced in 1965. Included in the 1967 696,087 entries in individual subjects (Wardle 1970: 142) were English, mathematics and social science entries for some thirty-nine pupils from Senacre, with thirteen taking GCE O levels as well. Mathematics followed the traditional path of the board's syllabuses and examinations. English and social science were under Mode 3 regulations.

Licence for curriculum innovation

For Senacre, Mode 3 was break-through time. For some time the head of English, a brilliant teacher, had timetabled every form for one period a week to be in his room to select and change books. This was the reading scheme. There was no formal teaching, just browsing and talking about books and reading and writing about them. Multiple copies of paperbacks were there: Hemingway's *Old Man and the Sea*, Anne Frank's *Diary of a Young Girl, Canga*, by J.A. Vaughan, *Walkabout* by J.V. Marshall, *The Long Walk* by Slavomir Rawicz, Beverly Cleary's *Fifteen, The Bronze Bow* by Elizabeth Speare, James Hilton's *Lost Horizon, The King must Die* by Mary Renault, *Frenchman's Creek* by Daphne Du Maurier, Gabriel Fielding's (Alan Barnsley) *Birthday Kind, Brotherly Love*.

One girl's record for April to June 1967 read – *A High Wind in Jamaica, The Dog Leg Garden, Darkness at Noon, Stranger than Fiction, Walkabout, Ballet Shoes*; and a boy's – *Man Overboard, Fair Stood the Wind for France, Ask for King Billy, Clocks and Watches, Adventure and Discovery, True Adventures of Great Explorers Told Me*.

These books were the centrepiece of the curriculum. Book reviews had a purpose beyond the obvious one of encouraging writing. They led to the creation of *Senacre School Magazine*. It was A4 size typed or written, with brightly coloured covers, red, blue, green, all with the oak leaf emblem, designed by the milkman's daughter at Littlebourne. As well as book reviews there were articles of all kinds, poetry, comment about school matters, letters together with illustrations, original drawings and sketches. This was classroom lessons serving the larger purposes of a school community with reasons for doing things, which pupils could easily recognize. The problem was to deal with complaints from the county supplies department about the number of books which were written off and re-ordered.

From that central strand in English teaching it was a short step to Mode 3. Already there was the framework and content for course work assessment. There was initial scepticism. Having helped to design, draft and approve the Mode 3 regulations in the board, I knew what was on offer and saw its significance for the curriculum as a whole. But to begin with, very understandably it was hard for staff to believe what was being put in front of them. They had encountered nothing like it. For all their criticism of things as they were, the idea that the curricular future was in their own hands was more than daunting in practice, however fine in theory. Not least there was a very large additional amount of preparation to get through, syllabus, examining and marking schemes to get approved. There was also the marking of course work. But underlying it all was the attempt to devise assignments for pupils, which were calculated to engage them.

There was a social economics Mode 3 which required practical work including practical visits for observation involving Benenden School – Princess Anne was there at the time – and the local girls' Borstal, remembered by the staff member who invented it.

Not everyone was enthusiastic. The head of mathematics stuck to his position of teaching to set piece syllabuses, and very good at it he was too. Disappointingly the head of science never showed the slightest interest in the curriculum beyond his immediate teaching plans. So for those subjects the rule 'If it works, don't fix it' applied.

But the overall result was that Mode 3 extended thinking about the curriculum in terms of content of study, approaches to study and assessment so that attention focused more sharply on the learning that was going on in the school as a whole. These sort of CSE tracks for the fourth and fifth years triggered similarly radical thinking for the first three years. What had been a more or less traditional curriculum was revealed as seriously deficient under this sort of scrutiny leading to a search for better ways of enabling pupils to learn. Public examinations were taken as a given. They began to take their place as an organic culmination of the curriculum as a whole, not some prestigious addition. Time and space for the curriculum began to have literal meanings. There was some way to go in creating them for learning in a wider sense. Fortuitously that became possible as well.

Many staff relished the opportunities. As one put it 'My time at Senacre was 1962–6 so that really condemns me as a 1960s teacher and I am proud of it'. CSE was an external intervention to be used for innovation if a school so desired. As such it was a potent influence on the curriculum.

National and local influences

Meantime in the public national domain three other influences came from central government and two from within Kent, one unwitting and one intentional. There was the Newsom Report on the 13–16 age group, *Half Our Future* in 1963 (Central Advisory Council for Education (England) HMSO) which recommended fundamental changes for the secondary school curriculum and the raising of the school leaving age to 16. There was the Schools Council with heavy representation from teachers, which set about becoming a national curriculum development body. There was Antony Crosland's Circular 10/65, as Minister for Education which required local authorities to submit plans for introducing comprehensive education at secondary level. There was his Woolwich speech in 1966 which created polytechnics. Neither of those last two initiatives had any direct effect on the school. Reorganization along comprehensive lines was not for Kent but it did nurture thoughts about developing further the top end of the school and so did the prospect of polytechnics. They all helped to create a sense that secondary schooling was on the move. Kent's two influences came from Room 1, a senior pupils' common room and the extended day.

Creating space

Room 1 was something to be cherished. On 1 February 1962 work began on an extension to the school. The plans showed the head's study, the staff common room and school secretary were to be moved up a floor, with a large room over an archway linking two sections of the building. It was not designated but it became the senior pupils' common room.

It was open only to members of the fifth or sixth years. They were free to go there whenever they had free periods or before school or after until the school cleaning was done. No member of staff could walk in unannounced. The exception was when it had to be used for teaching fifth or sixth year groups. The pupils were responsible for its upkeep, tidiness and general order – no dirty cups left lying about. It was furnished with armchairs, with some tables and chairs for working. There was a coffee machine. Sometimes the boundaries were tested with someone smoking, but nothing to get excited about.

All this caused something of a furore in county supplies when faced with a requisition order from a secondary modern school marked 'armchairs and chairs and small tables for a senior pupils' common room'. It was with the greatest pleasure and not a little pride that furniture was delivered to what was known thereafter as Room 1. There was now time and space, literally. The curriculum was beginning to arrive at its proper place. Unwittingly the building programme had provided a rare opportunity.

The changes ahead proposed by Newsom, the raising of the school leaving age with all that it implied inspired a rather gushing entry in the magazine in 1964:

> An obvious example of Senacre's readjustment is the 5th and 6th year Common Room, run without any interference from staff, entirely by its occupants. Indeed, this is the first Common Room approved by the Kent Education Committee ... we look forward to the coming educational revolution with confidence. Here at Senacre we must be grateful ... foresaw this drastic change in affairs and have already geared the curriculum accordingly.

It seemed that pupils were getting on side.

Creating time

While CSE, GCE and Room 1 were going on in the foreground, in the background there was Newsom and the Schools Council. It was not long however before the background took over the foreground. Just as the two fifth forms established in 1959 changed the nature of the school, so Newsom gave a very powerful drive off a different launching pad. The school moved onto a different plane.

In 1961, David Eccles, the then Minister for Education gave these terms of reference to the Central Advisory Council for Education (England) with John Newsom as its chairman.

> to consider the education of those between the ages of 13 and 16 of average or less than average ability who are or who will be following full time courses either at schools or in establishments of further education. The term education shall be understood to include extra-curricular activities.

Note the word 'shall' in the last sentence.

When Lord Boyle, then Sir Edward Boyle, received that report in 1963 it contained sixteen main recommendations which included a comprehensive analysis of curriculum priorities, not merely of content but in the wider sense of the needs of young people growing up an increasingly complex world. The tone of the report was set by the title of its first chapter, 'Education for All'.

Paragraph 17 indicates its central thrust:

> but when we refer in this report to 'more able' or 'less able' we are conscious that the terms are descriptive rather than diagnostic; they indicate the facts about pupils' relative performance in school, but not whether that performance could be modified, given different educational approaches.

Paragraph 46 stated:

> The greater the number of people who are proved to be educable beyond previous expectations, the stronger the suspicion grows – and the teachers are among the first to voice it – that the rest may have been underestimated also and we are somehow failing a substantial number of young people. At the same time, the stronger the contrast becomes between those who are successful and those who are not, especially judged by those criteria which the world outside school most readily applies.

The paragraph goes on to discuss the differences in courses for young people all over the country and ends thus:

> It would be idle to pretend that all the rest of the pupils are satisfied or satisfactory customers.

Two recommendations are central to the first ten years of Senacre's story. Recommendation 1 was that 'an immediate announcement should be made that the school leaving age should be raised to sixteen for all pupils entering secondary schools from September 1965 onwards'.

Recommendation 5(a) read:

> The hours spent in educational activities, including the 'extra-curricular' should be extended for pupils aged fourteen to sixteen. Some experiments by local education authorities and schools in different types of extensions of the school day should be encouraged by the Ministry.

The priorities were clear. Raise the school leaving age pronto. And taking a cue from its brief with the word 'shall', there should be an extension to the school day. But note again, it is to be intervention by invitation and encouragement, not requirement. It was a different world then. The implication for the curriculum was also clear, that learning was not confined to classrooms. Schools Council Working Paper No.2 on preparations for the raising of the school leaving age was a timely stimulus. One member of staff recalls:

I remember you thrusting it into my hand in a corridor one day and comparing it unfavourably to some of the curriculum suggestions in Newsom. This is what we should be about, challenging pupils intellectually to reflect on their own lives, or words to that effect, implying that Newsom tended to convey low expectations of our pupils in its understanding of relevance.

The search for engagement quickened.

Time and space put to work

Senacre was one of Kent's six experimental schools to pioneer the extended day. This was the second local initiative which affected the school. From its beginning, like so many, the school had run out of school activities according to the enthusiasms of members of staff who wanted to join in. As well as the usual games especially cricket, there was modern dance, chess four evenings a week, local history, woodwork, and weekend field trips, the Student Christian Movement in schools, all according to the changes in the staff. One member of staff says:

I put great emphasis on out of school activities. The great majority of the staff and up to one-third of the pupils were in the school for an hour or so after school ended.

That was well before Newsom. He believed that he did more for the pupils in being around while teaching chess and cricket than through his classroom teaching. Even at the early stage of the school's life, the social purposes of education established the curriculum as a whole school concept.

Being an experimental school with an extended day Senacre was entitled to a full-time youth tutor with limited classroom assignments but with a three-fold brief: to establish contact with pupils by doing some teaching and by becoming involved in out of school activities; to develop vocational guidance and build up close working links with the local youth service to ensure that the school ran activities in conjunction with rather than in competition with the local youth service. For Senacre that meant developing the extended day as a highly organized after school session. Those teachers who wished to join in were free to do so and were to be paid a modest fee. Others were recruited for some particular activity from outside the school staff. 'Responsible for' became 'energetic promotion' by the youth tutor. Anything any member of staff wanted to develop could be included, provided it met all the obvious conditions. Activities included sailing (there were dinghies on the lake in Mote Park), cooking for boys, boy's crafts for girls, car maintenance (a piratical looking man with an earring came to take classes) – art, drama and music of course, theatre and cinema visits, tutorials for extra tuition. Field trips became more ambitious and wide ranging. One staff member remembers:

The extended day, piloted as part of the Newsom Report, was the only time in my experience when teachers have been paid overtime. We were all engaged to run classes of interest to pupils of the school.

The extended day did more than lengthen the hours of the school's official day. Almost tangibly, it expanded the concept of school, and very actively. Residential weekends proliferated. A high proportion of pupils and staff joined in one form or other of the extended day. Visits to parents to engage support became the norm. Not only was the concept of school expanded but its range extended as well.

It turned out that tackling vocational guidance was in some ways the most important aspect of the youth tutor's job. It was also the most sensitive because of the possibilities of cutting across the responsibilities of some established staff. Individual interviews became almost the central strand in the youth tutor's role. Nowadays it most likely would be called counselling, in addition to trying to find ways of engaging the full range of pupils in the extended day, as he put it:

> Sometimes, situations were revealed which could be rectified internally and it began to be seen as a non-authoritarian channel for solving some of the individual staff–pupil conflicts or tensions that arose. The youth tutor could be talked to in a way the headmaster or senior figures could not. However the delicacy of balance in maintaining the confidences of a pupil and at the same time the trust of the school was soon evident.

And this led to many visits to parents.

Other things helped to create time and space. There was a new kitchen manager. She seemed interested in more than just cooking and serving lunches. Thus encouraged, she brought the weekly menu for comment. Numbers were juggled so that all staff who took a table had a free lunch. It was a good way of combining relatively easy control with social education, to be pompous about it. One staff member recalls being rebuked by a pupil about table manners. But there was something else. It emerged that the kitchen manager liked baking her own rolls. After that more often than not there were rolls at lunch. And she discovered that I liked tea with lemon.

There is no way of measuring the effect of such arrangements. They could hardly be negative. It provided time and space for staff and pupils to talk about the kinds of things which arose from the extended day and curriculum changes if they wanted to. Altogether the extended day simply served to support, encourage, develop and extend changes in the curriculum, which had been in train before Newsom was written. It was time and space again. As one member of staff says:

> Lunch was a pleasant affair. There was family service, with a teacher sitting at the head of a table. It was a learning experience in manners and deportment.

There were other factors at work, mysterious in their influence. The caretaker stayed with the school when it moved. With his wife as a cleaner they took great pride in their surroundings, and the way the school developed around them. (He was killed, alas, by a massive heart attack in the lavatories one evening. And now in 2004 astonishingly, his daughter is site manager.) The groundsman also took great pride in the school and its surroundings. With their colleagues they were more than maintenance staff. In the unpredictable way which is so often undervalued, they were unofficial confidantes to many a pupil, and even to young members of staff who hung around after the end of school. This was so noticeable when later, to reduce costs, the county decided to replace the school's groundsman with a peripatetic team. Standards deteriorated. Goal posts, pitches, mowing – nothing was done on time. Equipment went missing. Trouble and frustration followed. An important strand in the human fabric of the school was torn out. This was a small dark cloud on the horizon, a shadow cast on things to come.

Unstreaming as catalyst

For most schools in 1957, setting or streaming pupils in A, B, C and D streams was the norm. It was hardly surprising that the restive debates about the curriculum led to questioning the validity of streaming as a teaching and learning system.

The deputy director of the National Foundation for Educational Research (NFER) presented the results of a large scale investigation. After anxious discussion it was decided to arrange mixed ability groups for a new year entry in 1963, except for mathematics where the head of department believed it would inhibit pupils' progress. It was to be an experiment, risky even, and if it did not work then streaming would be re-established. It was risky because there was no way of trying it out first before introducing it and neither was there any way of providing adequate preparation for staff. Success or failure was in the hands of the enthusiastic staff who had suggested the idea in the first place. They succeeded and work it did and in ways which no one predicted. It was staff development on the hoof as recalled by one member of staff:

> The decision is a good example of what is now fashionably called evidence based practice. But note the space left for staff judgement. We launched mixed ability teaching as an experiment by testing a hypothesis derived from large scale research in our particular school. For me it was one of the Senacre experiences that influenced my commitment to and promotion of school-based action research.

Unsurprisingly, unstreaming led to searching questions about ways of engaging pupils more actively in their own learning. Unstreaming, or mixed ability groups, confronted staff not only with the range of abilities in any group, but the way bright pupils were slow in some things and how supposedly slow pupils could excel in others. It was a short step from that to trawling for topics which would engage fully all of a group, while enabling each to perform at their own level and without stigma. 'One size fits all' simply would not do.

And so the battle for the disaffected began in earnest. This is how one member of staff saw it.

> Disaffection was particularly manifest in the humanities, RE, history and geography. If the curriculum structure had a plus it was that it enabled some to compensate for the failure to pass the 11+ exam entrance into grammar schools and to proceed with taking their GCEs. But for the majority it implied a radical re-structuring of the curriculum to motivate an active engagement in learning by making it more relevant to their lived experiences in every-day life. I was fortunate in finding a large number of colleagues teaching other subjects and the head intent on reforming the curriculum generally. I participated in a very grass roots school based movement towards reforming the curriculum generally.

Curriculum for engagement

There was a wonderful harbinger for the future. The HMI who had Senacre on his list of schools was a peg legged aging man who drove a Triumph sports car – it was amusing and puzzling to watch him struggling to get into it – who had been an assistant inspector and clearly was puffed up no end with his status as a fully blown HMI. Sometime during my first year, he walked into my study without knocking. He brushed aside my comment that in future I would be glad if he would check with the school secretary, or better still phone to make sure that I would be in. That was not his way of doing things, he said. And all he wanted to know on that occasion was confirmation of all the figures he had already from the Kent Education Committee about numbers of pupils, of staff, stage of the building construction, as a pretext for looking me over.

Years later he appeared, as rudely as before, and after talking a bit about the usual trivia he set off to visit some classrooms. Where was religious education? I told him and let him go and find it. Not long after he stormed into my study. 'Do you know what is going on?' he asked. 'They are looking at love comics. What are you going to do about it?' The answer was 'nothing'. I had no idea what was going on but knew there was some good reason for it. He fumed a bit and left. It turned out that the class was trying to work out the various meanings of love displayed in tabloids as a way of engaging with Christian meanings of love. Engaged pupils had sat before a baffled HMI. On reflection it was probable that the man's experience must have been largely of elementary schools. Curriculum development in secondary schools would not have been his strength.

As that RE teacher recalls that incident:

> I obtained a great deal of support for reforming the RE curriculum inside the school but some resistance from an HMI inspecting me in my probationary year, who thought I should be teaching the Bible exclusively. He didn't like that fact that I was asking pupils to deconstruct the view of love embedded in love comics.

The pity is that he asked nothing about RE. He would have found that successive curates from All Saints wandered in and out at will. Ethos was the school's wider version of RE.

But it was that kind of understanding of engagement, which led to the evolution of a humanities scheme. The RE teacher took the lead.

> After that I got together with colleagues from history, geography and English to develop an integrated humanities curriculum. Some teachers didn't like the trend towards reform but with the head's support they were not a great nuisance. We were confident we had all the answers. Very arrogant we were, but it enabled us to push things through.

It began gently with the same teacher taking geography and history and working to projects. This was nothing dramatic, just escaping from boxes. Year 1 began with Mesopotamia, the cradle of civilization opposite geography and the globe, place identification, latitude and longitude, major wind systems. Twelve terms later Year 4 ended up with the Thirteen Colonies and the physical geography of North America, having taken in Antarctica, Europe and Russia on the way. Another scheme ended with a complete week when pupils could choose to spend five days either on field studies in North Wales, or history and geography field studies on Romney Marsh, or historical and geographical studies of Maidstone or study of community in Maidstone.

Then there was a year long schedule on the family for the fourth year. Samoa via Margaret Mead, through Queen Victoria up to family life on Shepway estate, where most of the pupils lived. More ambitious again was 'a syllabus correlating social science and economics, psychology, history, geography and religious studies for the fourth year'. It centred on topics relating to human development, including the effect of genes and environment and the questions 'What is Man?' 'Who am I?' 'How do we explain human behaviour?' (See Appendix 1.) There was a scheme for the study of Nazism, which involved English as well. Team teaching began. By blocking off parts of the fourth year timetable for all those subjects it was possible to create time for mass lead lesson introductions to some topic by one member of staff, and then break into as many small groups as staff and rooms permitted for follow-up work; or films, plays and enactments, these presented no problem for a whole year present.

These schemes can be presented as ridiculously pretentious for 14–15 year olds. They were nothing of the kind. They were based on the belief that growing young men and women are capable of engaging seriously at their own level with topics which connect with aspects of their daily lives. Pedagogically they were based on respect for pupils' views. Organizationally they were a nightmare. The preparation by staff was truly impressive. The results were gratifying. The scheme was a deliberate attempt to offer young people access to a higher, more sophisticated level in inquiry and understanding.

Drama and art and music always were extra curricula in stage shows of one kind or another. But a play like *Peterloo*, about the 1819 massacre, written by the head of English, with its rousing, rising words 'We will overcome' sung again and again was like an extended extended day, such was its impact on the school as a whole. *David and the Donkey,* a Christmas play written by Tony Brown in 1965 had similar impact. Later it was put on in Drury Lane. These contributions to pupils' learning are not quantifiable, but powerful they are. And if it meant scrapping the timetable to let things like that happen, then why not?

Time and space secured

There were advantages for pupils and staff. The standard rhythm of the school day was broken up and made days more interesting. Some of the fourth year pupils were self-evidently fast growing young adults. Even the most imaginative efforts by skilled teachers left some of them bored, restive, resentful and cooped up, where the day was chopped up into a succession of different occasions for being bored. Many were just too large to be treated like larger versions of first to third year pupils. Team teaching went some way to replacing boredom with involvement.

Most certainly it gave staff a different arena for seeking to engage pupils with their learning. And this was vital. Discussion could become a learning tool. Not question and answer but discussion as a deliberate means of getting these young men and women to think about, comment on, explore whatever topics were under consideration. They all had experience of families and life on a housing estate. They all had ideas about what they hoped for in life. Most had something to say if they knew they were being taken seriously. It was standard adult education technique. Applied to younger adults who happened to be in school, it tried to open new doors to learning.

Then came options, arranged through blocking off fourth year boys' and girls' practical crafts and art on the timetable. There was no reason why boys should not learn about food and cooking or fabrics, or girls how to handle woodwork and metalwork tools and make things which pleased them, if that was what they wanted. Girls brought in their small sisters or 'borrowed' one from next door so that they had to learn how to keep on eye on a child while they were cooking. It was called child care. Nor was there any reason why fourth form boys or girls had to take art lessons if there were other things they would rather do. There was a constructional crafts course, which looked at population, housing distribution, the social implications of different types of house. All that led into more study time in the library.

Most important of all was choice. Options meant choice for pupils. They had a chance to begin to take charge of their own learning for part of their time in school and hence learn something about responsibility for their lives as a whole. It also meant choice for members of staff. Given the range of options and who chose them, they were free to devise whatever seemed appropriate. It was engagement down as many different routes as possible. It was time and space again.

So a combination of CSE and Newsom had fired up enthusiasm for all those efforts to re-jig the curriculum. They came out of the commitment of a group of staff that engaged in what in effect was a serious intellectual inquiry into the nature and purpose of the curriculum. Then it would not have put it in those terms. But this is where the Schools Council took a hand.

The Schools Council

Again through the IAHA, I was on some committees of the Schools Council. Either through that contact or someone hearing what Senacre was doing, in 1965 the project director of a Schools Council/Nuffield Foundation Feasibility Study on the humanities heard of the humanities programme and came to visit to see for himself. Subsequently the Senacre scheme featured in the project's published report, Working Paper 10, 'The humanities and the younger school leaver'. It included a detailed account of the school's integrated work on the family. It had some influence in the subsequent evolution of the Schools Council/Nuffield programme, the Humanities Curriculum Project led by Lawrence Stenhouse, not least because Stenhouse recruited to his staff John Elliott, the RE teacher who had had an interesting brush with HMI. The Nuffield Foundation had another inquiry, 'Society and the young school leaver: a feasibility study'. Its project organizer also came to visit bringing with him an education editor from Penguin Books Educational which, alas, came to nothing.

With that kind of public recognition, confidence was high when it came to producing Mode 3 schemes for CSE. English, social economics and technical crafts followed. By 1967, at the end of the school's first ten years, over 50 per cent of the fourth year were remaining for a fifth year and a dozen or so for GCE ordinary level a year later.

The curriculum: home grown

The bulk of those developments evolved without any direct outside intervention or external support. A combination of Crowder, Beloe, Newsom and Robbins fundamentally affected thinking about the curriculum. These were government commissioned reports on what it took to be vital national issues. But action on the recommendations was left to individual schools and local authorities. What intervention there was came from LEA advisors who made some helpful comments. But in no sense were they anything to do with the curriculum developments, which Senacre put in train. That was done by a group of exceptional, enthusiastic staff who seized opportunities to devise new ways of engaging pupils.

Intervention begins

When intervention did come, it came from the LEA. It was neither helpful nor supportive. A new county education officer arrived from being a deputy to Alec Clegg, who at that time was something of a visionary as a CEO. There was a wonderful story of the chairman of his education committee walking down the corridors shouting 'Clegg, Clegg, where are you?' Perhaps it was that relatively benign authoritarian style which the new man brought with him. It impinged on the school in four ways: dealing with gypsies; work experience under Newsom; the first fully blown LEA inspection. The fourth was just tiresome.

An edict came from the new CEO that in future all interviews for appointments at head of department level or higher had to be conducted with governors and an education officer present. That simply complicated matters. It interfered with timing of interviews – a vital matter – with the risk of losing good candidates. It introduced a degree of formality which could set the wrong tone. It felt like a personal insult or withdrawal of confidence. Was this Yorkshire travelling south or just a way of the new CEO being assertive, maybe under pressure from his committee? Speculation ran wide.

Language speaks. The old style DEO retired at about the same time. Under the new CEO, district education officers became divisional education officers. Hierarchy took over from geography, as the new DEO soon found out. The occasion was gypsies.

Gypsy controversy

The Conservative member for Maidstone East was bothered by press stories about gypsies' troubles in his constituency. He came to see for himself. The school attendance officer was in a panic. He could not get some gypsy children in a caravan in the woods near the school to attend. Sensing trouble, with tedious and really rather pointless litigation, I set off through some quite deep snow to find them. There a bizarre three-way conversation took place. He told her to 'tell him', never speaking directly to me. I tried to get them to understand that it would save them and the school a lot of trouble if they registered their children, had them attend, however erratically and that would be the end of the matter. I doubted the children would turn up. However it turned out that that family was related to a girl with a badly cut leg who appeared at our front door in a nearby village – she worked in the bottling plant of a Maidstone brewery – distressed because she could not find her family's van and her Gran. It had moved during the day. We bound up her leg and called the police, who drove her around until they found the van. Somewhere in the background there must have been Gran. The gypsy children duly arrived the next day. Gran must have said so.

Soon so did others. I told the new DEO about the teaching problems and that the only way of coping with this group of around ten was to bring in a part timer, experienced in the teaching they required. He agreed. Weeks later he was on the phone with an angry, furious voice. He had been ticked off comprehensively by the new CEO for approving an appointment which had not been authorized by the county office. Unfortunately, hierarchy had taken over and centralization had begun. Common sense and initiative seemed at a discount.

Work experience interrupted

LEA hierarchy also worked in a different way and very unhelpful it was too. Newsom suggested work experience for fourth year pupils. Somehow the county got to hear of the work experience programme which had been running since 1959 for fifth formers and of its possible extension into the fourth year. This was in 1964. A sharp letter from the CEO arrived, demanding an explanation for running an unauthorized programme, saying it had to stop. A copy of DEO's approval letter in 1959 went with the reply. There was no answer. But the programme got stopped in its tracks. Henceforth everything had to be done through the careers office. It took two years of correspondence, visits, and negotiations before it could be reinstated. It was maddening that what was taken to be a vital element in the revised fourth form programme in preparation for the school leaving age going up to sixteen was scrapped. It meant that about 250 young people went without that choice. In some ways it was a foretaste of what was to come, the postponing of the raising of the school leaving age. Centralization and intervention was getting serious.

There was more to come, not so much intervention as revelation. When the work experience option re-opened, it seemed a good idea to have placements in the offices of the county education officer. Not long after two girls began there the CEO sent a letter complaining that they had a poor grasp of what now would be basic skills and were not suitable for his offices. The reply went along the lines of saying that was just the point – they were there to be helped to improve. Again, there was no reply, and this was depressing. Benenden School made no such complaint. It sent girls in return. It seemed time was running out.

Curriculum arrested

The discouragement of all that was palpable. Everything was being planned deliberately on the assumption that the school leaving age was being raised to sixteen. The omens were not good if bureaucracy was such a clumsy midwife. It was a preventive rather than a facilitating intervention.

The last intervention was like an orchestrated version of that problem. It was a good idea. A week when LEA inspectors – advisors had become inspectors, another linguistic clue to the new style of regime in the LEA – from each subject headed by a new chief inspector (another introduction from Yorkshire) spent a week in the school. It was not to be anything like a formal inspection ending with a written report. It was a consultative exercise. The CEO asked if I would agree to Senacre being the first site for this interesting LEA initiative and it was hard to refuse. But I told the staff that as a consultative exercise they should say whatever they chose and treat it as a set of two-way conversations.

The final meeting was in my study with six or seven of the team, there to question and discuss not inspect. After some general remarks came some trivia about too much time wasted, not enough on this or that, but no thoughtful observations about standards, and nothing at all on the overall intentions in the curriculum. The significance of time and space did not connect with them. The members of staff were disappointed having spent a week on and off talking with them, finding little appreciation and no support. I was more than disappointed, exasperated, let down rather. It was a bit like ships that pass in the night, talking along parallel lines. It was clear that there were different views on the curriculum. They were nice enough people, but as with some visiting tutors from training colleges, it was unlikely that many would have been appointed to the Senacre staff. However it was a good idea. Indeed if other local authorities had followed suit, perhaps later some of the direct interventions by the Conservative government would have taken a different direction.

Curriculum found

As it was, after ten years, the school had arrived at a curriculum which attempted to come to terms with the problems which arose inevitably from a compulsory secondary school education ending at fifteen, which was barely twenty years old, and providing for pupils from a fairly tough new housing estate. It sought to engage them through content and pedagogy. It did so through capitalizing on the imagination and enthusiasm of a remarkably talented group of staff. A ten year period of curriculum innovation ended with about one-third of the time in formal lessons for English, mathematics, science and PE, one-third team teaching on humanities and social science topics, and one-third on options of the pupils' choosing. No one then talked about time and space as the essential condition for engagement. Curriculum theory was short. Practice was rich. The result was richer.

It all prompts a wry reflection. In 1999 the then Secretary of State for Education and Employment, David Blunkett, produced a rationale for revising the 14–16 curriculum set out in two documents (*Developing the School Curriculum*, QCA publications, 1999 and *Learning to Succeed: A New Framework for Post 16 Learning*, DEE 1999, Stationery Office). It was 2002 before revisions to the National Curriculum worked their way into schools. It had taken fifteen years for common sense to break in, but Blunkett let it in. Henceforth the National Curriculum would observe more or less the three one-thirds structure that Senacre had arrived at in 1967. What went round came round again.

Years later in 1979 when I was engaged (!) in the problems of introducing the assessment of prior experiential learning to higher education I read this.

> Experiential Learning refers to learning in which the learner is directly in touch with the realities being studied. It is contrasted with learning in which the learner only reads about, hears about, talks about or writes about those realities but never comes into contact with them as part of the learning process.
>
> (Keeton and Tate 1978: 4)

It was that principle which informed, albeit blunderingly, efforts to devise appropriate schemes of work for pupils. Just as important, it was on the job, in-service learning about curriculum development for the staff who just took opportunities in front of them and moved on further. One who joined the school in 1962 reflecting on his interview day says:

Our initial interview day was carefully managed and I gained a favourable impression – no doubt hoped and expected. The staff seemed friendly and professional. The pupils appeared well turned out and helpful. We were allowed time to wander around at lunchtime with student guides and pick up the feel of the place. I remember being somewhat non-plussed to be invited to play chess by a diminutive fourth former who then proceeded to beat me in three moves, muttering not quite under his breath, 'No imagination, no imagination'.

You could say that it was the staff and pupils who recruited him. A young man who joined the staff in 1965 said:

> The contrast (with a traditional girls school) at Senacre was violent. Not only was it the norm to find a relatively full staffroom at least an hour after school, but various knots of people would actually be discussing their day and how they could co-operate on future lessons. For me there was an immediately constructive and warm atmosphere, which undoubtedly propagated the energy and creativity of a fairly young staff and led to a vibrant and dynamic curriculum. There was a sense of enthusiasm, challenge, support and co-operation – even of belonging which was standard in that staffroom at that time. I remember remarking to my wife 'the staff here wants to work'.

Therein lie some of the dynamics of curriculum change

The failures

It would be a grossly misleading to give the impression that Senacre was unique in being deliberately experimental with the curriculum or more than averagely successful. Nor was it that the entire staff was behind all the innovations or that everyone experienced the place like that. The three or four old guard were relatively benign, passive observers. No one tried to be actively obstructive. And although not every new appointment brought an energetic enthusiast, making sixty-six appointments of people usually in their twenties or early thirties over the ten year period offered plenty of opportunities for recruiting supporters. That offered the standard recipe for effective institutional change: identify internal champions; use new appointments to recruit the like minded to work with them; outflank opposition; support the enterprise. It was a rare opportunity.

Of course then there were outright failures, especially with individual pupils, probably more than we knew and that is part of a larger failure. As will be attested throughout this book, Senacre was at the rough end of Maidstone and it was thought of as a difficult school because of its catchment area. Inevitably there were discipline problems with individuals, unsatisfactory absences and outright truancy. But in the late 1950s up to the mid-1960s it all seemed containable. Disaffection was reduced but it was not defeated.

As far as absences and truancy were concerned the deputy and the head and latterly the youth tutor would go separately to the houses of the missing pupils, and if there was no answer push open the back door and shout 'Anyone there?' There was a tricky occasion when it became obvious that the absences of a boy and a girl coincided. Sheepishly the boy came downstairs. Back in the school after some questioning he muttered, 'Well I did have it in her'. There were no more absences. The gypsy incident makes the point dramatically. The way the curriculum evolved meant that there was a strong strand of support from a large number of staff for pupils with all kinds of difficulties. Marital problems at home brought untold emotional difficulties to sons and daughters. A few parents resented efforts to check on their children's attendance and turned up sounding violent and threatening, particularly if incest – abuse is the current euphemism – was suspected and the school was trying to protect the pupil. Once at a senior pupils' dance I was threatened by a difficult boy the school had taken in – other schools refused to have him – first with a broken bottle waved in my face and then with a chair hoisted above my head. Pipe smoking proved an effective calming influence on me, if not the boy. Later I went to see him in prison in an attempt to show him that not all the world was against him.

But all that is minor compared with the contemporary sophisticated pastoral systems. Senacre had no system. It had a preponderance of staff who understood that life was rough and sometimes nasty for some pupils, and in a completely unorganized way, often acted as a support system, facilitated to some degree through the curriculum arrangements. But it was a failure not to have grasped the social significance of developing an organized pastoral care system.

It was only a partial failure not to have succeeded in bringing mathematics into a reforming mode. The head of department was a brilliant teacher; one of those remarkable people who appear effortlessly to do nothing, and yet ensure everything goes smoothly with never a flicker and ends up with enviable results. He was too good to tinker with. Science was a singular failure. If ever there were opportunities for excited explorations it was there and there, they were not. It was a failure not to have found common ground with the LEA inspectors for the curriculum. And there is no doubt that it all gave some members of staff a hard time.

But the biggest failure was something else, parents. Regular meetings consultations on a year basis, referring to parents' remarks in the report books, which were completed every term, drew in some. Home visits for suspect absentees rarely resulted in active cooperation. Nothing seemed to stir the interest, let alone win the support of more than a faithful minority.

The one event which did work was pupils' and parents' day. It was one of the few things imposed on a very sceptical staff. Prize days were irrelevant, a waste of time. The idea of pupils' and parents' day was different. Jackie Gillott, the broadcaster and novelist, John Armitage, London editor of *Encylopaedia Britannica*, Alex Dickson, originator of Voluntary Service Overseas and Community Service Volunteers, Stuart Mcclure, editor of *Education*, the county education officer himself, they all came for a day. They had to arrive at about 10.30 a.m. and spend the morning going round the school, in and out of classrooms escorted by pupils, to ask questions, look at displays, talk with pupils, read work books, until lunch time when they sat at family service tables with the rest of the school.

For the afternoon the brief was to give a talk making connections with what they had seen and heard during the morning. There was no uplift nonsense but straight talk about why learning was important but with references to what they had seen for themselves of the pupils' own activities. Two senior students gave their own version of thank yous. I gave a short account of the year. By 4 p.m. it was all over.

Parents flocked in and it was full house every time. But we never did find a way of capitalizing on its success. There was a parent teacher association but at a fairly feeble level. Not enough energy was invested in that side of school life to have made parental support into a powerful contributor to curriculum development. Times were different, but the failure remains.

Nor was there sufficient time arranged for the staff to talk with the guest, which was a serious professional development failure; even so, according to one member of staff lamenting on developments since then:

> It was an annual event and one which involved an enormous amount of work and preparation by staff and pupils. Everyone was involved. Now everything which would cut into curriculum time is verboten.

It was a failure of imagination not to have been able to exploit those days fully. And it was the youth tutor who moved strongly to put school–parent relations on a firm footing. He says:

> Senacre had done relatively little to bind home and school together. There were academic reports, occasional summonses for parents of difficult pupils to appear at school etc., but no philosophy of seeing home and school as a vitally interacting union responsible for the overall education of the child and no clear two-way lines of communication.

It took a year before he had moved the school in this direction and by the time the next head was in office the Oak Leaf Club was a going concern as a parent teacher association.

There was a failure too with governors. They were good people and meetings never got beyond reporting of what was happening and perfunctory attempts to put pressure on the county for this or that. The astringent presence of the former head of the girls' grammar school gave some sense of support. But there must have been ways of involving them, which could have benefited the school. Maybe it was because there was so little they could do at that time that spending energy on such matters was never a serious consideration.

The big plus

The 1950s and 1960s were an unusually fortunate time to be in secondary education and a head, unique even. Curriculum ideas could bubble, be tried out, rejected or accepted as experience dictated. There was the exhilaration of having a sense of being at the fore of developments. There was great professional satisfaction, which for many was infused with a true sense of vocation. There was trust. As one staff member puts it:

> There was no objection to staff going off site during free periods or even going home if these occurred at the end of the day. It was another generous gesture which was willingly reciprocated by staff when school or pupil need arose.

The attempt was to honour trust as well as exploit it. There was freedom to create time and space for that precious chemistry to get to work – teacher and taught. No regulations told the school what to do, save include RE in the syllabus. But it was before the excitements of 1968, with student protests, some schools in uproar, and the social anxieties which went with them, all whipped up by the press. It was a cultural climate which was bound to change. Nearly forty years later it is almost impossible to conjure up what it was like to be in schools and teach in that cultural climate. By comparison, we had an easy time of it.

It was a satisfying ten years' worth of curriculum development. It began by seeking, in a rather undirected way, and ended with a sense of arrival. Without being able to articulate it then, what had happened was an attempt to see the school as a whole as way of promoting learning; what now would be called in the jargon a learning institution – with the kitchen manager, the caretaker, the groundsman and the cleaners, as well as the teaching staff all playing their part in it. Within it, the curriculum was a means of providing a range of learning activities both formal and informal, designed to engage all pupils across the ability range that came to the school. And it served the staff as well. It was a learning time for many. Five colleagues went on to become heads, and so did four Room 1 students. One became a deputy head, another a college lecturer, another became an HMI, two became professors of education. Amongst many, there was a camaraderie, born of a shared belief of being engaged in something significant, educationally as a vocational commitment. Six of the staff stayed for over thirty years.

Throughout the ten years there was a rising sense of getting a serious grip on what it took to engage with disaffected, disheartened, sometimes disorientated students, as well as doing the best for the most able. In was a curriculum which unashamedly was infused with a social purpose. It had nothing whatsoever to do with social engineering. It was trying to open doors to opportunities on a take or leave it basis.

In retrospect those years were something like a play within a play. The outline script for the play was written by the actors themselves as they ad libbed their way towards curriculum achievement. The play within the play was scripted by outside intervention which led to a peak, being followed by the beginnings of a trough, all within that first headship. And that, as it turned out, was to be the pattern which runs right through this curriculum story: peaks and troughs; drama continuing. Outside intervention wrote more and more of the curriculum script from then on.

In 1967 intervention was minimal. The school had moved steadily away from a narrow curriculum to a whole school version. In the view of those who helped create it, it seemed to do its work satisfactorily. Beloe and Newsom were powerful facititators. There had been a hint or two that deliberate intervention was lurking, but nothing to predict what was to come.

Chapter 3

Curriculum development with a difference

The second headship, John Werner, 1967–74

John Werner, the second head of Senacre, (public school, Oxford, teaching in a comprehensive school in Yorkshire) also 32 years old as it happened, had a very different kind of introduction. No mud and unfinished building awaited him, but there was the problem of a broken down car. He drove into Maidstone, house hunting. His old car:

> developed a minor fault on the outskirts of the town and as we were stationary with the bonnet up, a police car stopped and sorted it in a friendly fashion. The policeman then asked why we were visiting the town and when I said that I was coming to Senacre School he rolled his eyes, and gleefully relayed the information to his companion in the car, and wished me luck.

A school on Shepway was viewed with suspicion in the town.

He lighted on something else, a logbook. This was new to the school and he cannot recall where it came from, why or who required it to be kept. This was one of his early entries about the school as he found it:

> a vibrant school on a good site, with a remarkably committed, skilful and creative staff. Apart from the obvious advantages, this made it easier to attract the right kind of people to join us. Visitors from the outside seemed appreciative and stimulated by our approach. However, I sensed that the LEA viewed us with apprehension but maintained a support stance and gave us professional space.

The hands off regime continued, and so did the excitement for staff.

The second head knew about the curriculum and where he wanted to take it. The whole school conception of the curriculum would expand. If the first headship might be characterized as the traditional finding its way into the progressive, interpreting it as opening access to a more engaging curriculum, the second was the other way round. The progressive was trying to re-mould the traditional, with a heavy emphasis on social care. He felt passionately about that.

The context for the curriculum

Asked what his aims were he says 'If asked to summarize our aims I would say that we wished to make pupils feel respected and to respect others, to be active members of a community, to want to learn and do so successfully'. He went on:

If respect for the individual pupil is a cornerstone of policy, it follows that staff must be afforded professional respect. I hope that this happened in two ways. They were much involved as much as possible in policy making and afforded as much freedom as possible within the overall strategy to run their departments and pastoral systems. For example, I wished to introduce the Kent Mathematics Project. This individualized work let the pupils work at a particularly appropriate pace. However the highly respected head of department did not wish to take this approach. He carried on as before but the second in the department did use the project.

That of course is a continuation of the attitude of the heads of mathematics and science who wanted to have nothing to do with the possibilities offered by Mode 3 in CSE.

That concern for professional respect prompted the head, says a colleague:

To make staff meeting 'democratic' in the sense that an elected representative of the staff chaired meetings and all the issues were decided by a vote. It was not too long before the head made it clear that vote or no vote he had to retain ultimate right to decide on issues as he carried ultimate responsibility. Fair point.

Predictably of course this was to the liking of the 'young bloods' as one staff member described himself at the time but not to the liking of all. Some old hands with experience and seniority were unhappy with such experiments, and watched uneasily to see what effect they would have. However, that 'democracy' speaks of a principled approach to a collegial style.

Taking together those earlier two paragraphs, one for pupils and one for staff, alongside the comments from staff, it also speaks of a strong emphasis being put on creating a supportive, caring school community as the arena in which the curriculum could be given opportunities to flourish.

This is borne out by other stories. This one is from the head about an assembly. Speaking against casual, unthinking racism, especially against the Irish, he thought of a brief joke. Two Irish builders started to build a tower that seemed to go on for ever. Eventually they realized that they had the plan the wrong way round and it was a tunnel. He asked why the builders had to be Irish. The joke could have been about two stupid builders. At this point there was a loud yell. One young boy, known as no shrinking violet or goody goody shouted out 'My Dad's a builder. How dare you be rude to builders, how dare you call them stupid'. The head was speechless. However in telling the story against himself he was illustrating a profound point: how difficult it is sometimes to do the right thing right. It also refers to something else. That young boy must have felt secure and sufficiently self-confident and therefore respected to make any such remark in public to the head of his school, even if he was showing off.

One of the deputy's stories is similar, one is different. Both are about assemblies. At one conducted entirely by pupils, the topic they chose to discuss was a belief in God. Suddenly the question was flung out from the platform to the back of the hall 'Does the headmaster believe in God?' Following this I was quite startled to be asked the same question myself!

The other was about a Christmas variety show. The head of English had written a spoof Queen's speech centred on Senacre, which the deputy was to read. Somehow she lost the audience. The pupils got noisy and bored. The producer intervened and got her off the stage. Mortified, at the beginning of the next term she decided to use the experience as a theme for an assembly – giving people a chance. She explained that they had not given her a chance to read the speech and then she read it to show them what they had missed. It was a very good one. She says 'I would never have been able to tackle that but for the atmosphere at Senacre'.

Clearly there is a therapeutic strand at work. But it is important as an example in straightforward pedagogical terms of the benefits of admitting error, of accepting a certain measure of vulnerability. No evidence exists, but it is a fair bet that that deputy was held in higher respect than before and some pupils were given something to think about with an immediacy which they had not encountered before. That deputy said:

> working at Senacre certainly challenged some of my firmly established views of school life, whilst at the same time it offered greater scope for the introduction to methods which I felt to be important. After about twenty years' experience as a teacher I found the differences at Senacre so great that during the first few months I came very close to resigning.

The openness and lack of hierarchy contrasted so strongly with the experience of her previous school that she was not sure she could last, it was so different. 'It surprised me that at Senacre both junior and senior members of staff expressed views on an equal footing'.

She was not describing difficulties in dealing with disciplinary issues. It was giving an account of the problems of adapting to an unfamiliar way of doing things. Now retired she says she feels quite homesick with her recollections of Senacre. What she says makes obvious the connection with possibilities for curriculum development. It was the ethos of the place.

It was within the sense of ethos that the head introduced a year system to replace the house system.

> The year system reflected better the realities of school organization and so was better geared to supporting pupils in the way we wished.

For some colleagues this seemed like undervaluing sports and team games and inter-house competitions. It was not that the head was against competitive games, though he opposed an overemphasis on sporting prowess, but the role of sport changed within the school as a consequence of introducing the year system. Games and sport as an organizational structure were abandoned. The year system was calculated to strengthen the pastoral provision. But this organizational change was perceived as introducing a significantly different emphasis within the school by a staff member who, two years into this headship was involved in a shake-up of the pastoral system and became a head of year instead of head of house.

> The new head was appointed at a time when serious questions were being asked about the effects of competition on children ... seemed a firm supporter of the view that competition was detrimental to children's development. Inter-house sport largely disappeared, as did the arts competition. The house system became redundant and was replaced with a year system with the accent firmly on pastoral care and behaviour management ... Because of the type of school and the nature of the catchment area pastoral care had always been accepted as a vital concern. With the formal adoption of a year system it was placed firmly on a par with the academic life of the school.

That then was the flavour of the school during its second headship of seven years which informed the context for the formal curriculum. The ethos was a curriculum in itself. It set out to provide a care and maintenance service for staff and pupils alike. It tried to comprehend everything which went on in the building. It succoured a form of personal learning to complement what went on in classrooms, laboratories, art and design technology workshops, music, drama and PE. Social purpose remained a driver which at any rate was the intention.

> A young lad had problems in fitting in with his classmates and his teachers. We discovered that he loved gardening, and by agreement he came with me once a week, on a voluntary basis, to help in the garden of some friends of the school who had difficulty in maintaining their own garden. I feel sure that because unusual measures were acceptable at Senacre, they contributed to good relationships with the pupils, which in turn added to their willingness to learn.

That is how the deputy interpreted the connection between the care and maintenance attitudes the school deployed, and the curriculum.

But all the while pressures from the outside world were adding to the problems of devising curricula which would hold pupils to their tasks of learning.

> For the first time we began to notice the impact that television would make on pupils' attitudes, behaviour and language. *Till Death us do Part* caused an outbreak of 'You silly moo'. It was startling: bad language and invective had not been the norm till then, but things went downhill fast!

Curriculum innovations

With that as the context, it followed that while careful attention continued to be paid to the well established fourth and fifth year and its examination tracks, more attention would be paid to the needs of pupils in the rest of the school. The emphasis for development shifted.

Mode 3 Certificate of Secondary Education

To some extent the curriculum simply developed naturally from what was there to begin with. There were Mode 3 programmes in CSE for English, social studies and design technology. The head was an enthusiastic supporter of Mode 3 which he had first experienced in his previous school. 'I found this was an exciting development as it gave the teacher an appropriate professional role and encouraged one to develop professional skills and wider thinking'. There are continual references in the school log, to meetings about Mode 3 attended by the head and head of English, meetings with moderators, with other heads to consider policy matters arising.

This enthusiasm was continued by the newly appointed head of English. He too had had previous experience of Mode 3 also in Yorkshire, so there was plenty of support for continuing to find ways of exploiting the opportunities it offered, although he had to endure the snide remarks from a traditionalist: 'the freedom Mode 3 gave to cook the books'. To add a dimension to the department he set up a Senacre bookshop by arranging a discount with the local bookseller to encourage browsing. Later it was a casualty of budget reductions and the small subsidy was withdrawn. The second master for metalwork and woodwork found that the work he wanted to develop to extend into three-dimensional art did not fit in with existing CSE syllabuses. So a creative crafts and design Mode 3 course was invented. Later it was changed to technical crafts. In the best classical style, teaching determined examining and not the other way round.

The head of Humanities continued the social economics course with topics like the consumer or work covering trade union disputes, types of shops and 'hidden' sales techniques, all calculated to appeal to students' interests. Later reflections were 'that it was a little dry at times and success could depend too much in my mind on recall skills like listing the differences between a department store and a multiple ... not sufficiently issue or problem centred.' The setting up on a Mode 3 social studies course based on the Humanities Curriculum Project topics followed. Combining RE with Mode 3 created the problem-centred curriculum he wanted. Curriculum thinking continued apace. New to the school that head of Humanities says:

> I found it hard going at Senacre and I worked very long and hard on finding films and interesting materials to enhance these topics, but it often seemed to me in those early days a case of 'casting pearls before swine'. We were an

extremely inexperienced (new) team ... with only two existing staff to hold things together.

There now follows a reflection on a fundamental element in curriculum development.

I have no doubt that (his predecessor's) courses worked well for him – but they did not really work for me. The moral was and is that in those far off days of curriculum freedom, what really worked was that which you had a hand in creating and/or framing – and that you felt confident about, intellectually and in terms of delivery. And that is where the Humanities Curriculum Development Project came into the frame. There certainly were teething troubles, but I would claim that in a couple of years we were getting together a curriculum package to be proud of and which pupils were responding well to – making good progress with. We understood the key importance of the neutral chairman, which so many teachers elsewhere just could not see, let alone take on board. We learnt to use 'silence' effectively as teachers – rather than dive in and out-talk pupils as most teachers do. Pupils soon learnt that discussion was very much their responsibility with the teachers as procedural guide rather than the fount of all wisdom ... we put strong emphasis on individual responsibility for learning on topics like law and order, work, poverty and wealth, family, marriage and personal relationships, war and peace, community and environment, mass media and communication. Team teaching was now constructed around these topics rather than the course I had inherited.

The school was a pilot for Peter McPhail's Moral Education Project, another Schools Council initiative. A new Mode 3 was designed for history.

CSE grade 1 was the equivalent to a GCE O level pass. Contentious questions of quality were raised, inevitably, vociferously by some of the traditionalists who thought that an overlap between levels of work done in grammar schools with work done in secondary modern schools was, as now would be said 'dumbing down'. Anyone who knew at first hand the thoroughness with which home grown Mode 3 courses were considered before boards approved them, the battery of examining techniques and the scrutiny of results by external moderators would be hard put to sustain criticism of quality. Indeed as so often in changes within education, it seemed the complainers sought to impose requirements on those they complain about, which they would not dream of applying to themselves.

The professionalism of assistant staff as curriculum designers, teachers of subjects, assessors of course work and final examinations was taken as a given. It was given its head. As a young master put it 'Halcyon days when we were allowed to use our own ideas and strengths to advantage'. A senior colleague reflects critically of that time, 'There is no doubt that we were trusted and "given our heads" by the head and Senior Management who certainly did all they could to facilitate our requirements – especially over suiting of rooms and timetabling'. It can be noted that no one had heard of senior management then and is an example of how jargon creeps.

The entire CSE approach to the curriculum was based on the premise that teachers knew their pupils' capabilities better than anyone else, and that by devising ways to enable them to reveal what they knew, rather than using examinations as a one shot system, they produced a more accurate account of the achievements of those pupils. This was intentional revelation not accidental concealment.

The curricular organization for the humanities course in years 4 and 5 (social economics, English and religious studies) is set out in Appendix 2. The head reflects wryly: 'The chief inspector expressing surprise that our exam results were as good as they were'. There was no surprise here; it was the same one who led the LEA consultation in 1967.

Mixed ability teaching

The head believed in mixed ability classes for teaching and brought a new emphasis to it.

> I was very keen on mixed ability and promoted it. Unfashionable though it now is I am still keen on it as a starting point. ... the idea that a great deal of time is spent at the end of each year moving pupils up and down between streams or even sets is still an anathema to me.

Pupils were organized in mixed ability classes except for mathematics when he arrived. But there was a dramatic development introduced by the deputy.

> When I was appointed to Senacre I found that the school had adopted mixed ability, and I came to the conclusion that it was important to change my method of teaching. At an external meeting I learnt that French and mathematics were classed as sequential subjects and therefore unsuitable for teaching in mixed ability groups. I could not agree and devised a mixed ability French course for my class which ran for three years.

She set about planning to teach French to a mixed ability group as an arena for trying out the effectiveness of individual learning – and work it did. Using cassettes supplying vocabulary and pronunciation, sometimes with instruction in English, explanations of units of grammar or constructions, visual aids, work sheets, study cards, each pupil's progress through those materials was individual. That was the fully resourced programme. Her pupils did as well as those in a streamed class, as she wrote in an article, 'Mixed ability French' in the *Times Educational Supplement* on 27 April 1973:

> This experimental French course has shown me that the teacher can have a different but equally valuable role, not simply as an imparter of knowledge. Through carefully guided individual work, pupils are learning *how to learn*

independently and have proved themselves capable of tackling problems, which traditionally a teacher would feel himself obliged to explain step by step. The teacher is thus freed to be more available for answering questions and advising over particular difficulties. Other advantages become self-evident. There is more opportunity for oral practice, although instant correction of mistakes is not always possible; pupils do not have the problem of having missed work through absence and not understanding on their return; new pupils can join the class even if they are complete beginners.

It was not surprising that she was asked to give talks in London, Manchester and Brighton and that HMI turned up to see for themselves how such a scheme could work – and as the head comments:

> it (mixed ability class for French) showed that pupils of all abilities could access a modern language – and enjoy it. You can imagine what a beneficial effect it had on staff that a deputy head who was not a trained specialist in the subject was able and willing to put in the creative effort to achieve this.

This was 1973. Nowadays much of it seems old hat, but for curriculum development it marks itself out. A master joining the school from a traditional girls' county secondary school said of streaming:

> I should say that I had had enough of fear as a motivator ... the most execrable fear it promoted seemed to me was the fear of relegation to the B stream ... seemed to me a contradiction of higher principles so I rebelled! I was sold on mixed ability – in principle ... it was very hard work for the teachers, because they had to invent, deal with and practise words like 'differentiation' and 'pupil expectation'. It is *a* technique which works well in some circumstances, not *the* technique which will revolutionize education and solve all its problems.

Interdisciplinary studies

At the end of his first year the head wrote in the logbook:

> It has been a fascinating year. Getting to know each other took a little time. New ideas have had to be digested. The appetite for them is undiminished but an awareness that change must grow out of stability has increased. My aim must be to give clear definition wherever possible to allow growth with security, and keep staff. At the same time necessary changes in the curriculum and staff pupil relationships must be made.

Interdisciplinary studies was the first step in curriculum change. It was introduced for Years 1 and 2 (7 and 8 in current parlance). English, history, geography and art were merged into a single programme, abandoning the arbitrary division of learning into discrete subjects. In part the intention was to ease the transition from primary to secondary schools.

Currently this is a highly relevant topic. In summary, the 1997 Labour government managed to improve the standards of achievement in primary schools but achieved little general improvement in the first year of secondary schooling. Roughly the problem identified was and incidentally remains, that in some cases Year 7 pupils made little progress during their first year, because too much of the work was a repetition of what they had done before. While differing in some respects, the IDS scheme in Senacre was broadly in line with that thinking and so can be seen as an early, even radical attempt to ease the problem.

That transition has always been contentious. Every August or September there is a crop of articles in the press, radio and television on the topic, all trying to allay parental worries about the move from primary to secondary school. Not only is it the size of the building which confronts many a young 11-year-old with a range of unfamiliar experiences but it is the sheer number of pupils, their age range and the number of teachers to be encountered all within a single day, which can be daunting for some. For some settling in is a problem. For many, carting large satchels full of books and impedimenta becomes a daily obstacle race to get to the right classroom at the right time and with the necessary bits of equipment, plus the anxiety about being ticked off for bad timing or forgetfulness. Those early weeks in a new secondary school can be very stressful for some. Parents can find it even more stressful when they do not know how to make sense of what their sons and daughters are saying. Complaints to the school were not uncommon.

So the theory underlying the introduction of interdisciplinary studies for those first two years was to ease that transition by reducing the number of unfamiliar elements to the school day. By grouping subjects and a class staying with one teacher for a significant part of the day, a familiar part of schooling continued. As one member of staff put it:

> It made a lot of sense in as far as individual lessons should not be seen in isolation – but to be more meaningful if viewed as part of a themed learning experience ... of course in the real world all subjects are interrelated and make more sense taken as a whole. In a school timetable pupils would be asked to switch from say Mathematics (possibly fractions), to geography (could be Africa) to history (maybe Stone Age man) etc. ... in half hour to forty minute slots. Learning would appear rather disjointed. IDS worked on the theory that general 'topics' could be covered in different subject with far greater efficiency.

This of course was an entirely different way of thinking about the secondary school curriculum. A head of department was appointed to develop this different approach. Primary trained, she brought the experience with her of working the curriculum in this way. Some staff were not enthusiastic believing that to adopt this approach in a secondary school was asking too much of young pupils.

The problem as I saw it, was that younger children, bearing in mind it was aimed at Years 7 and 8, the first two years, needed to have skills in time management/research, and interpretation that would probably only be present in the college/student age groups. Also that method required resources and staffing at a very high level.

And

project work became the primary vehicle for study, but children were given no research skills or organizational skills and staff were not convinced by the results.

Moreover the layout of the school premises did not reflect the ease with which such schemes could be used in primary schools.

IDS had some things in common with the Humanities Curriculum Project, more of which to follow, and was in sympathy with mixed ability teaching groups. As another member of staff put it:

it should have been a system which I applauded and which was successful. It was neither. I think that 'politically' HCP worked because it was pioneered by colleagues who knew each other and who were known in the staffroom, and because they cooperated to 'make the running' between their own disciplines. IDS was by definition more all embracing and tended to create somewhat embattled new specialists desperately trying to involve more established traditionalists who were very protective of their territory.

In retrospect the head is clear:

there was insufficient preparation and evaluation applied to IDS ... the crucial fault was insufficient in-depth preparation for the staff in contrast to the innovations in mixed ability teaching and the humanities.

That was not the end of the story. Later:

The initial rawness of IDS was quietly adapted into something more palatable to other staff and recognizable as a more junior school approach to teaching and learning.

Even so, the head reflects on another aspect of this curriculum development: improving contact with primary schools. 'At Senacre I did not make real links with primary schools although I worked hard at this in my next post'.

Early in his second year the head circulated a consultative document, setting out his own approaches to the improvement of the curriculum, to promote better learning and teaching. It was a deliberate attempt to engage staff and win support for the planning for both mixed ability groups and interdisciplinary studies which he intended to introduce. The introductory paragraph read:

> This is an attempt to put forward some preliminary principles, if possible with one or two working examples prior to a full staff discussion before next year's timetable is devised. (Appendix 3)

Reading the head's subsequent doubts, it is an interesting example of attempts to foster a collegiate approach and harness it to a particular direction for curriculum development, while at the same showing some of the difficulties of introducing fresh initiatives and trying to head off objections.

The Humanities Curriculum Project

Directed by Lawrence Stenhouse, the Schools Council/Nuffield Foundation Humanities Curriculum Project (HCP) was a deliberate attempt to develop a curriculum which would engage young people aged 14–16 with an eye and a half on the raising of the school leaving age.

The project created materials on controversial topics and put them in the hands of teachers for classroom use. The materials presented different aspects to each topic, included evidence to support them and sought to extend explorations by inquiries in the community. Discussion was the mode of learning and teaching. Teachers were to act as neutral chairpersons. HCP was designed to elicit responses from the pupils to the topics they were not accustomed to think much about and help them understand how to justify their opinions. The approach was to apply what was known about a problem, and try to acquire additional learning to fill the gaps to solve it. Pedagogically it turned much upside down. It was predicated on the concept of the teacher learning and discovering with the pupils and it offered an organized step towards adulthood.

Stenhouse insisted that teachers needed to be trained to run HCP successfully. They needed briefing on how to use the large packs of materials his team compiled to support the work on the topics which were selected. War and peace was one. Teachers acting as neutral discussion leaders had the task of teaching by dialogue so that pupils learnt to think about controversial issues, having their own contributions taken seriously, all as a means of engaging them as learners with contemporary problems of society. Senacre's humanities staff had a thorough training. They were invited to contribute materials for the 'war and peace' pack and then were part of the evaluation team to report on it. It was written by John Elliott, the RE teacher who had so displeased HMI.

As with IDS, nothing was simple. Not everyone liked HCP. Something of the same subject protectionism got to work. As one teacher on the edge of HCP said about a 'war and peace' topic:

> I did not enjoy relinquishing my autonomy in the English classroom to 'service' humanities. Rather than having the opportunity to explore a theme

independently, assignments were imposed. I remember that my pupils were asked to write a letter home from the trenches. This was so far outside the pupils' experience.

However another said:

> One of the best discussions I recall surrounded an issue of war and peace. It was based on an incident from Nicholas Monserrat's novel *The Cruel Sea*. Should the captain of a Royal Navy minesweeper be sent to rescue a merchant ship torpedoed by a German U boat, sink the U boat, with the risk of the depth charge blowing up the survivors from the merchant ship, or just pick them up and let the U boat go free? 'What would you do?' the pupils were asked.

The new head of English was dropped in at the deep end. He found:

> This at once threw me into close working relationships with colleagues outside the English department, interdepartmentalism being an important strand that underlay the Stenhouse and indeed the Werner philosophy.

He noted quickly the drawbacks.

> The discussion element was difficult to sell to pupils, some of whom appeared uneasy, feeling themselves exposed, even threatened by the intellectual formality and rigour of the occasion ... being badgered to think for themselves, tease each idea to a conclusion and then squeeze the pips or even worse propose a new alternative discordant viewpoint was entirely alien to their previous educational experience. 'Oh no sir, not that again.'

Nobody said that Stenhouse was easy. However even with the drawbacks there were positive benefits for the staff and the curriculum as the head of English put it.

> The English and humanities departments were brought into a close and beneficial alliance and to an understanding of the ways in which each thought and worked. The breaking down of subject barriers enabled pupils to continue uninterrupted with a particularly interesting piece of work over a much longer period of time than the conventional curriculum permitted. The unity of purpose, made visible by inter departmental cooperation, provided them with an incentive. CSE results were as good or better.

And the proof of the pudding lay in the eating. CSE was the predominant exam, notably in the Mode 3. The results were good. There were some GCE entries but the entries were small in comparison with CSE. However, GCE examination results improved and were very good in English and humanities subjects. The experience of teaching in this way developed skill levels in teaching which probably would not have developed without the methodology of HCP itself.

The HCP approach was all of a piece with what Eric Pearson, a staff inspector attached to architecture and buildings branch wrote in the day and joy of 'discovery' in primary school development.

> Education is an active process of learning by exploration and discovery ... Knowledge is only absorbed and interpreted insofar as its relevance is understood.
>
> (E. Pearson 2000: 274)

This was not a problem confined to Senacre. The in-service programme never succeeded in involving a sufficient number of schools in HCP to influence the entire system. The postponement of the raising of the school leaving age did not help. Nor did the creeping anxiety in government about young people dealing with controversial matters. (Their exclusion later from the Youth Training Scheme was yet to come.) In Senacre the pedagogical approach is still used by some long standing experienced staff and not found wanting. As that head of humanities put it 'I think that the humanities package that we had put together was ideal for the raising of the school leaving age (ROSLA). The rationale is given in Appendix 4.

Creative arts

Creative arts was another innovation. It was much discussed at the time, nationally. Introducing it the head said 'the triumvirate creative arts would have been simply to give more coherence and clout to an area of the curriculum which I considered did not always get its fair dues'.

In a sense it was all of a piece with IDS and the humanities. Art, drama and music were all put in a group of blocked off periods using fewer periods than those allocated to the three subjects separately. Because the three in charge of the subjects were outstandingly talented and highly committed teachers the scheme worked well enough.

As with the other innovations there were mixed feeling for some. The art master had some misgivings about the extent to which pupils were being denied the opportunities which specialist art lessons provided. But there was also satisfaction.

> 'ARTS' have always been linked – as expressions of mankind's greater sensitivities so it was natural that creative arts was established. Art, drama and music formed a natural bonding (later to include English); all were a means of expressing emotions and feelings. In this system I was allowed to work with some senior pupils under the option scheme to take their purely artistic studies to an individual higher level – especially as some wished to take individual careers linked to one of the previously mentioned subjects. I had many happy, productive years as a member of the creative arts team.

Creative arts concentrated mainly on senior pupils – which I thought was the right way round, allowing the junior pupils to gain the necessary skills (basic) to be able to manage time, materials etc. for better effect. So Years 1 and 2 (7 and 8 today) followed a normal subject based timetable in these subjects.

For drama the master says:

> I never could understand why drama was regarded as a sort of spare time subject while art and music were traditionally essential components of a standard curriculum … timetabled. Drama no more sought to produce competent, qualified actors than music, musicians, or art, artists, PE/games footballers, so the common purpose of the subjects was agreed to develop the imaginations and creativity of the student. These three disciplines were not necessarily limited to the discrete disciplines and we three teachers often found ourselves pursuing similar ends, or studying similar periods, out of kilter with and exclusively of each other. … It made more sense to consult more fully and to cooperate continuously. Half a year was blocked for at least an hour for teaching on a thematic basis, with a plenary session followed by some exercises or stimuli-slides/tape, video, film talk, followed by group discussion to pursue their responses through their chosen medium. Groups rotated so that pupils did not stick with one medium or teacher. Teachers became facilitators (a sort of midwife principle) and would fulfil the needs of their syllabus as the wishes and needs of their pupils suggested. There would usually be a coming together at the end of themes where work achieved could be exhibited or 'shared'. In due course the system expanded to include the whole year and we were allocated extra staff (often part-time) who responded variously to the concept. Some thought it a doddle; others thought it much too difficult. We attracted interest and support from science, PE/dance over the years. We would usually tackle two or three themes a term.

This raises an interesting curriculum question: the separation of drama from English on the timetable. The head of English says:

> It was a great help to have the extra burden of drama teaching (and play production) removed from my shoulders and timetabled as a separate subject in the capable hands of a drama specialist. Drama in many schools I discovered, limped along as a poor relation.

That view may have been influenced by another. Over time he built up a team of English specialists.

> Only a team of specialists had the knowledge and enthusiasm to spark ideas from one to another and create that important sense of momentum with unity.

He counted himself lucky to be able to do so for he learnt that:

> Some heads believed in the maxim – English is a common language so every
> teacher is a teacher of English implying that English presumably with the aid
> of a course book, could be taught by anyone as long as direction and oversight
> came from a specialist at the top.

Nothing is new. That is exactly what the headmaster of Bedford School said in 1950.

Mathematics

The head wanted to find a way of enabling more students to succeed. The Kent
Mathematics Project seemed a way to do it. It was an individualized scheme where
students could work at their own pace.

Again as with IDS and HCP all was not plain sailing. The head of department
did not use it, preferring his traditional and very successful way of teaching.
However his second in the department, who became head of department, liked
and used it, and went on to reach consummate success through it. The two schemes
ran side by side. Since both were outstanding teachers it is almost a case of method
being irrelevant where teachers have the charisma to take students with them. For
a non-specialist it did not seem to offer much. But then non-specialists often find
it difficult to budge from the straight and narrow where they feel confident.

> At its worst, without close monitoring of pupils' progress and application
> there could be twenty-five pupils working with little pace or urgency, through
> booklets with answers in the back. It could allow pupils to coast. It could
> allow pupils to ground themselves. Introduced at a time when the majority of
> teachers taught firmly from the front, rather than whirling around like
> Dervishes as they currently do, the teacher could become even more remote,
> rather then central to the process .

Activities

The enterprise course was a way of mainstreaming some Newsom ideas. It was
hotly defended whenever there was any attempt to reduce its time allocation, or
later abolish it. Blocking off a half day for the fourth year forms and organizing
differing activities for them was an established feature of the curriculum. But the
enterprise course was a notable development. A full Friday was blocked off every
week for Years 4 and 5. The course was aimed at disaffected fourth and some fifth
year students and had a weekly activities day. Fridays saw small groups rotating
around trips to fire stations, power stations, telephone exchanges, coal mines,
factories, with all the usual and unusual outdoor pursuits including horse riding,
flying, boating, golf and walking orienteering, rock climbing. There were also

personal challenges – how far can you get on a 'rover' bus ticket? The teacher who ran the course recollects:

> My own feelings about the course included: that there was an overt attempt to introduce youngsters to the real world they live in – warts and all – at least it was not just PE which could take pupils out of school on a regular basis; that some of the more 'in-between' activities could be legitimized; and some of those activities traditionally associated with middle/monied classes could be experienced by all. I got a tremendous buzz out of organizing it: making the necessary phone calls, briefing and supporting staff, and sitting in the staffroom on a Friday afternoon/evening, sometimes watching the minibuses return safely from a series of expeditions I had set up some months before. It did a lot for personal development of staff as well as pupils.

This was a huge undertaking, involving outside agencies, and generous staff allocation to ensure safety without compromising the independence of students which was the fundamental purpose of the scheme. It was a high risk undertaking too which could not have happened without the explicit, strong support and backing from the head.

> Looking back it is astonishing what we were able to do – even what we got away with ... this seemed like a breath of fresh air in the delivery of education – a deliberate, and as experience showed, a largely successful attempt to make school a place pupils wanted to be.

By carrying forward the Newsom concept of the extended day the school was offering a hugely varied range of educational activities which was inspirational in practice for staff and pupils alike. As another put it:

> you could as a professional, try things out and take risks. Sometimes things worked: sometimes they did not. But overall that time of professional adventurousness offered far more pluses than minuses in terms of learning for teachers as well as pupils.

And there was hilarity. One staff member recalls that the head:

> gave his elderly Morris Minor to the school. We taught children to drive in it around the playgrounds as an extended day activity. I even tried to teach (a staff colleague) to drive. He rammed the girls' changing rooms. Can you imagine this happening today?

No wonder the extended day was such a success. And it all spills over into timetabling. Curriculum change and reform is not easy and innovation is never without risks.

Timetabling for innovation

At its simplest, timetabling is a matter of relating priorities to juggling teaching spaces, staff and pupils so that everyone is in the right place at the right time. The trouble is that each subject, each specialist teacher presents particular requirements to do the job of teaching as it should be done, and inevitably they are incompatible. When everything is done about blocking off periods for groups, tinkering with numbers of periods allocated to each subject, and twisting the arms of some teachers to teach what they really do not want to teach, some staff members for some subjects and other staff members remain dissatisfied either for the needs of their subject or for what they see as the well being of the students.

This was normal. Normality became more difficult to sustain because of a number of outside pressures. There was the problem of providing a curriculum tuned to the needs of the fourth year students who were going to be required to remain for a fifth year. There was the issue of the kind of world of work they would enter. Computers, it was being warned, would replace dull repetitive work. Education for leisure was added to the curriculum as a strong component.

Newsom ideas and the enterprise course featured prominently. Pressures on the timetable intensified. Some subjects needed time but not in large blocks because pupils lost concentration. Other activities needed large blocks of time if they were to function at all. Practical and creative subjects complained that short bursts of time were no good to them because they could not get the equipment out and put back again in time.

The attempted solution was to organize the day as a succession of twenty-minute periods. No one used a twenty minute period, but combinations of two, three or four could accommodate all requirements. (See paragraph 5 in Appendix 3.) It was a valiant effort but did not work. A deputy head had to spend all one Christmas holiday undoing the timetable and re-shaping it to ensure smooth running of the school.

The extended day

The extended day notion continued to earn its keep. A new youth tutor was appointed but its mixture was more or less unchanged. It offered opportunities for both staff and students to follow their own bent and developed relationships between staff and students and adults from the outside world, relationships between staff and parents who served as both teachers and learners. Undoubtedly it widened the curriculum. But as before the extended day contributed to that widening in quite a different way. As a licensed outrider to the formal school system, with no form, no registration to look after, the youth tutor promoted, facilitated contacts of a different kind from the regular school routines with both pupils and parents. He became an additional conduit of connection to try and cope with disciplinary and attendance problems. As such, he was something of an invisible prop to the curriculum.

As with all bright ideas, the problem is to keep them shining. Now people talk about economic sustainability. For the school curriculum, sustainability is the great problem. Staff change and students' interests change. So renewal is a constant, never ending task. On the whole the school succeeded in re-inventing the extended day as required. For a time it reached out to the intentions of community schooling where resources and premises were made available to the local community in the hope of encouraging a sense of mutual responsibility.

Governors and parents

The head believed he had good relations with his governors, respecting them as individuals. He went so far as to experiment with having parent governors attend staff meetings: 'This was not a happy experiment' as one staff member recalls. The head now thought they were too compliant, saying that now he would look for governors who would be willing to be trained, be more questioning, more willing to come in to school as a matter of course. Perhaps it is not surprising that at that time some governors were uneasy about the appointments of a Sikh and a black South African. One respected governor said 'I can understand you appointing one, but why two?' How times have changed!

Similarly with parents in retrospect the head felt some unease.

> Reference is often made to what used to be known as 'the secret garden of the curriculum'. I would go further and suggest that, at that time, parents were kept at arm's length far more than now and were not really consulted about major changes to any part of the school. The system gave out the message 'Trust us, we are educators'. Of course it is more difficult to involve parents in a deprived area but it is essential to do so.

The youth tutor put it differently in a report on his activities:

> Very few schools in Kent have a really successful parent teacher association – most have none and others have a wishy-washy structure which may look good on paper but is valueless in practice. It seems to have been widely accepted, almost by default, that teachers are now required in conscience to fulfil many of the obligations previously regarded as falling within the province of the parent (inculcating conceptions of honesty and of reliability for example). This is a noble gesture as far as it goes, but will become a self-perpetuating evil if we don't tackle the problem at source and involve parents directly, actively and vigorously in the process of accepting full responsibility for their children's development and choice of future.

Those are strong words. They were written in the late 1960s and are also prophetic. Since the 1980s there have been strenuous efforts to turn that gesture into convincing action. But there is frustration all the time as more and more is loaded on to schools, surfeited by more regulations and their teachers who are then blamed for matters outside their control.

Uniform

All the curriculum innovations represented deliberate attempts to move away from more traditional approaches to students. Abandoning uniforms was all of a piece with that thinking. It was another attempt to find additional ways of engaging students in learning. As the head put it:

> I wanted to innovate but had not thought of myself as anti-traditionalist. I believe that tradition should be a living thing, susceptible to necessary change as the world changes but without changing its basic values ... I did not question the traditional usage, values or principles of education, but felt that if you make education universally available you have to change the way you deliver it.

At that time there was a view that uniform restricted students' personal and individual development and so it fitted uneasily alongside other innovations, designed to improve what schools could offer to their students. The Beatles were in and flower power expression of individuality was high in young people's consciousness.

As with other innovations, not everyone on the staff was an enthusiastic supporter of this new policy. The deputy says she recalls 'attempting to do things to rule', expecting girls to dress correctly wearing skirts on a school trip. The head suggested gently that trousers were warmer, particularly as it was winter. Some younger staff members were enthusiastic.

> I'd say that the non-uniform contributed to students' willingness to give new procedures a try. But I wouldn't say that I was particularly aware of any improved motivation of uptake. My generation of teachers was excited by all innovation – we were maturing but still young enough to be keen and to be accepted by senior students, who were also wearing flared trousers, funny haircuts and platform shoes.

It is worth noting that the decision to abandon uniform was the result of a majority vote in a staff meeting, against the strong wishes of the minority.

In retrospect the head was not so sure that abandoning uniform was a good idea. He began by thinking that maintaining uniform used up too much time and distorted staff–student relationships. He did not believe that uniform helped students to learn to dress appropriately for different occasions. 'I recall a parents' meeting where a parent asked me whether girls were allowed to wear trousers. I said that they were and that all parents had been so informed. 'I know' he replied, 'I just wanted to hear you say it'. Later he thought:

> The abolition of uniform was not done carefully enough. With the benefit of thirty years' hindsight, such a step should have been preceded by discussions with parents and primary schools and a pilot evaluated. For instance fifth years could have had it as a privilege ... there should be a better way of

teaching appropriate dress and one that did not require so much chasing. However in practice I believe it did harm our reputation. I recall a comment that our pupils looked like a football crowd as they came out of the school but I cannot remember who said it. I came to realize that it (uniform) gave a sense of identity, and to the community a sense of security that the young people were in control. It still bothers me that in so many other countries these things are achieved without uniform.

Other staff found it bothersome. One commented that this reached such a pitch that they were not anxious to say where they taught. Another remembers proudly telling the village grocer that he was going to teach at Senacre. 'Oh the Borstal' came the reply. Reputations are so fickle. They stick easily. Abandoning uniform as a curriculum reform was rather like IDS. Introduction without careful preparation spelt trouble.

The wider context

There is no doubt that some parts of the catchment area of the school encouraged such views. And there is no doubt either that the various changes to the internal organization of the school and its curriculum during the second headship made it stand out in the public eye as different from others. And it is almost certain that the abandonment of uniform blinded some of the public to the purposes of the innovations: external perceptions obscuring internal reality. And there is no doubt either that those external perceptions bothered some members of staff when, inevitably, they ran up against them in their day-to-day lives. This may be an example of the same events being experienced differently by different people. The senior master comments 'I do not think there was a discipline crisis at Senacre'. But seen from the outside, the impression grew that discipline had slipped. As mentioned before, reputations are indeed fickle. They affect staff and thus the curriculum.

However, like the first, the second headship was in a school where the catchment area was determined by the LEA. Automatically each year some 120 pupils arrived from the same half dozen or so primary schools. Only those parents who made a fuss managed to register their children at a different school. The spirit of the time meant that other heads would be extremely reluctant to admit children from outside their own catchment area. So parents and their children became a captive cohort. And since by intention, during the second headship, Senacre was markedly different from other secondary schools in the area, it is easy to see how public perceptions affected the reputation of the school.

But times were changing. All the curriculum innovations which were introduced during the second headship, like those of the first, were essentially home grown. Neither HMI nor the LEA made any significant contributions, save support for the humanities projects. The only clue to the LEA taking a close interest are entries in the log for an LEA inspection spread over a week in mid-February 1970 by six inspectors. This was followed by the chief inspector, the assistant education officer for secondary schools and the school's local inspector attending a governors' meeting. And very important, the head remembers

> The LEA did not interfere. Indeed the Divisional Education Officer supported me strongly on the one occasion I had serious trouble with two members of staff. Yet I am sure he did not agree with my philosophy and so I was particularly appreciative of his support.

But the context for secondary schools was changing. Nationally interest was sharpening. There were experiments going on all over the place. Countesthorpe College in Leicestershire was one such example. It had opened in the late 1960s and set out to be deliberately adventurous. The local press and the MP took an interest. There was a huge row in 1973 when it was discovered that some pupils had been set to work on a sociological survey of the sexual mores in the locality. Margaret Thatcher, then Secretary of State for Education and Science asked HMI to provide her with a report. A full inspection was mounted lasting ten days involving twenty-one HMIs. The report was highly critical about wilful damage, lack of supervision, disruptive behaviour but was balanced in its comments on good student/ staff relations, some high quality teaching, but slack discipline. The national press took up the story and made a meal of it, contributing to a rising unease about education generally. Its effect was to discourage curricular experiments and to ask awkward questions about different approaches in classrooms (McClure 2000: 187/8).

The Countesthorpe episode occurred against a background swell of trouble about primary schools. In 1967 the Central Advisory Council chaired by Lady Plowden which had been sitting since 1964, issued its report *Children and their Primary Schools* (HMSO 1967). It was based on a very extensive research programme. A random sample of some 3,000 teachers in primary and secondary schools were sent questionnaires to supplement the research data. In the late 1960s Plowden became something of an authorized text for those who questioned the effectiveness of didactic methods of teaching for young children and who wanted primary education to take greater account of the sociological factors which influenced so heavily the possibilities of them benefiting from what the schools had to offer. Under its influence primary schools' curriculum and pedagogical methods became something of a national export, with workshops and conferences and consultations occurring regularly in the USA and elsewhere, drawing heavily on Leicestershire and Oxfordshire.

However anxieties surfaced about the standards of achievement. They were articulated in the *Black Papers*, which castigated so-called progressive methods and which gave rise to stories about bad schools, but blamed all this on the permissive society which brought with it loose morals, the pill and indiscipline in schools. Again the press lapped it up and made a meal of it (Cox and Boyson 1975, Cox and Dyson 1977). All this was stoked up by press reports following the student revolts, sit-ins, and so on in 1968 which brought disruption to universities and was part of a wider international anti-authority stance.

So towards the end of the second head's tenure the general climate for education was darkening. The likelihood of intervention in the curriculum was looming up fast. The question then was to what extent intervention would enable schools like Senacre to continue to be true to what they considered to be their responsibility. As the deputy head put it:

I have always seen the needs of pupils, (both as individuals and groups) as guidelines for curriculum development, as opposed to standard academic expectations, which can well be achieved as a result.

That was echoed by the head.

When I look back at the school I do not see my time there as curriculum driven, although we did make some innovations. It was the ethos and pupil-relations, very much attempting to build on the foundations laid, that I believe were the hallmark of the place.

Prescient for the future

Almost sadly, wryly with hindsight he added:

The curriculum in place was a sound basis and absence of external pressures was a bonus. There was true professional freedom. Later experience suggests that, as a profession, we abused, as well as used appropriately, that freedom and as a result have lost a great deal of it to the detriment of the pupils and the nation. Fortunately it was a time when the tradition of professional freedom for the head and innovation was very strong. I hope I made good use of this professional freedom, but I have also come to believe that, given this freedom and the power it brings, a head needs a different kind of support and supervision than any I received.

Between 1957 and 1974, seventeen years of the school's first two headships, the stream of curriculum innovation and development flowed strongly. It was supported by a strong contingent of staff who throughout those years provided a precious continuity of thinking, reviewing, revising and indeed stability. However by 1974 strong external forces were looming. Kent Education Authority had preserved its grammar schools, whatever the pressure from government or local people to reorganize along comprehensive lines. A change in government in 1974 probably saved it from an ultimatum, but it led to a compromise system: the Thameside Scheme which was bound to change the curriculum. It was primarily a political and administrative intervention, a harbinger of what was to come. The head sensed it and disagreed with it. As with the first head, the time had come to move on.

Of some things there can be no mistake. There was strong continuity: the curriculum had a social as well as an academic purpose informed by a deliberate widening of it. The way it was expressed differed, but the thrust remained the same. The change from a house system to head of year system was a fundamental reorganization of the way the school worked and laid firm foundations for the future, particularly for the way the pastoral care of pupils developed. And whatever those changes would set in train, the strong continuity among the staff meant that in varying ways something of the influence of those seventeen years would continue. It was not always easy, as a young teacher (then) recalls.

> I well remember staff meetings continuing at the pub into the late evening where we argued on educational theory. It was almost like a continuation of college – remember many of us were fresh out of college. But this feeling (enthusiasm) was not universal. HCP, IDS, staff council, mixed ability teaching, enterprise, creative arts, abandonment of school uniform, head of house becoming head of year, it all came in a hurry. There was an alternative, reactionary viewpoint, which watched the experimentation with grave misgivings. What this faction lacked in numbers it made up for in experience and seniority. The head did not have an easy ride.

Nevertheless:

> A relatively young, highly motivated staff, given an autonomy most teachers can only dream of now, and with very limited bureaucracy, was a heady mixture. I look back on this with no small measure of pride at my own teaching at that time.

Perhaps that captures something of the sense in this story up to 1973, of a deeply satisfying professionalism, with a strong strand of vocationalism by a member of staff who had been in the school for eight years and later became its deputy head. Intervention was minimal but there were hints of what might be coming.

Chapter 4

Curriculum intervention begins

The third headship, Margaret Lynch, 1974–83

There was a fairly sharp change of direction for the curriculum during the school's third headship. Partly it was the result of a very different style from her two predecessors. Whereas for them Senacre was their first headship, each beginning aged 32, with relatively little experience, the third, aged 51, arrived as a very experienced and successful head of a difficult girls secondary school in Deptford, south-east London which was about to be combined to create a large prestigious comprehensive school. Maidstone was also her home town. She came along a different route. As a sign of the times, her official title displayed on the school's signboard by the entrance from the road was 'headteacher'. Her two predecessors were 'headmasters'.

There were three influences at work behind the change of direction. Partly the change was because she was something of a traditionalist and disapproved of mixed ability teaching and interdisciplinary studies. Her view of what a school was there to do in some ways differed. She took great trouble with individual pupils with a strong sense of pastoral care but the emphasis changed. She disliked the influence of a voluble parent/teacher association.

Partly the change came because a more traditional style was just what the LEA wanted: to implement new arrangements for admissions to secondary schools – the Thameside scheme – of which more later. Indeed staff believed and the head herself dropped heavy hints, that she had a firm brief from the authority when she was appointed to return the school to traditional ways of teaching and turn away from the 'progressive'.

Another reason for the change was the result of the very successful creation of a physically disabled school facility. Both of these changed not only the direction of the curriculum, but introduced a different emphasis to its content.

In some ways the traditional was bound to be in her bloodstream. She had worked at the Air Ministry during the war, then did her teacher training and must have begun teaching in the late 1940s, not long after secondary schooling for all was first introduced. Then, most of the newly constituted secondary schools took over the curriculum for the top end of all-age elementary schools with a leaving age of fourteen and did their best to adapt it to provide for 15-year-olds – often aping grammar schools. That was likely to have characterized the training course she followed and the teaching practice that went with it. English was her specialist subject; she had been a head of department and loved the English canon. Indeed staff mention that she used to move around carrying piles of books, many of which they say were inspection copies, not returned. So it can be no surprise that the third head nurtured a fairly traditional form of curriculum in her second headship.

Change of style

Unfortunately these speculations cannot be checked at first hand, because Margaret Lynch died soon after her retirement in 1983 on medical grounds. But as a head of a difficult secondary school in south-east London in the late 1960s and early 1970s, she is bound to have been only too well aware of the controversies and high drama which were enacted at Countesthorpe. When the scandal of the William Tyndale primary school blew up in 1976, she would also have known about all the troubles it caused for the Inner London Education Authority. In short-hand terms, dissention among the staff, the head, the governors resulted in the normal curriculum being ignored to such an extent that staff were suspended. There was a full inspection. A new head and new staff were appointed, and a public inquiry was conducted by an eminent QC. Once again arguments about school organization and teaching methods were lapped up eagerly by the press. That was enough to make any head wary.

There were mounting frontal attacks on education. The *Education Black Papers* raised the temperature. The left-wing teachers at North London Polytechnic were accused of bias in their teaching of economics, sociology and history. The shine had worn off the Plowden Report on primary schools. Professor Neville Bennett wrote *Teaching Styles and Pupil Progress*, which questioned the validity of some teaching methods.

It is clear from the kind of woman she was that she would be determined to ensure that no such troubles would ever take place in a school where she was head. Indeed she would have seen it as her prime responsibility to do so. It would also be understandable if she was sceptical of anything which seemed loose and freewheeling in the curriculum.

Whereas the first two heads were described by assistant staff variously as 'a man of enormous enthusiasm and vision' *and* 'the secret of the success of Senacre in those years was the autonomy granted to a visionary head with a talent for appointing interesting staff ... ran a tight ship', the third head was seen as a 'formidable lady', 'highly intelligent, steeped in English literature – she could recite passages from Shakespeare and *Under Milk Wood*'. And 'she was quite dictatorial, but like all good teachers she had the interests of all pupils as the basic fundamentals of her philosophy. She liked to be in control', 'she had a huge sense of humour', *and* then 'discipline was perceived to be restored. Uniform was reinstated and homework given status ... although this was not a period of intensive curriculum change and development, the reputation of the school grew'. The evidence for that growing reputation is rock solid.

She was a heavy smoker, walked with a stick, wore a wig and suffered from chronic arthritis. During her time at Senacre she had two hip replacements and concealed her constant pain with an iron self discipline. Somewhat unkindly a more junior member of staff described her as having 'an old world junior headmistress approach' which did not always bring out the best in some of her staff. Yet there are curiously contradictory stories about her conduct in staff meetings. As one staff member put it

> Staff meetings in the school were still few and far between. Staff sat around smoking, passing notes, doing crosswords or dozing ... painting nails and others would finish knitting. But then ... X as yet inexperienced ... upset Miss Lynch by something he said. Without warning, she suddenly threw back her chair, flung down her cigarette and bore down on him, waving her stick, threatening him and calling him *chummy.*

And she was a character. Another colleague recalls:

> An outbreak of silly 'chicken scratching' by pupils occurred [chicken scratching was the self-infliction of patterns and scratches created on their arms by a sharp point on edge]. Miss Lynch ordered a full general assembly at the end of the school day. She marched in with a large book under her arm, and proceeded to read out medical items as 'school law' from it (it was in fact the staff room dictionary). She then promised that anyone in future caught inflicting such action on themselves or anyone else would be sent to the school nurse for a medical.

Assemblies were different too:

> When she took assemblies it was always an interesting time. She dealt with moral issues using her vast experience of life, travel and literature. Often they were delivered in a variety of dialects and accents. She had the habit of suddenly looking across at a member of staff during an assembly and say, 'Isn't that right Mr so and so?' You certainly had to be alert.

The head of English recalls:

> I soon discovered that trying to argue with Miss Lynch was like wrestling with a good humoured jelly fish – a waste of time, generally, as she was fixed in her own ways and tended to dismiss others out of hand and as an English specialist herself she approved of my department and let us go our own way. She was an avid reader of fiction and did much to transform the library and fill it with books of wide appeal, supplementing the work of the official librarian.

Evidently her contribution to the curriculum in terms of finding ways of promoting learning through the library was direct.

There is a logbook entry for 7 May 1981 about a complaint made by a parent to the county education officer and others and a letter to the *Kent Messenger* about a book from the school library which was on the county list, hinting at some obscenity, without any reference to the school. The entry ends with: 'The book has been withdrawn from the school library and Mr ... so informed'.

What that entry does not say was when the parent was not mollified by being told that the book had had a good review, the head of English recalls:

> Sensing a public relations disaster in the offing, she invited him into the school to bear witness to the burning of this 'vile' book. As she solemnly recounted this tale to me, our eyes suddenly met and she burst out chuckling. Like her other big gestures, she saw this as a farce in a good cause.

A change of style was unmistakable. The curriculum was bound to change with it.

Curriculum change begins

The head made voluminous entries in the logbook, a kind of detailed diary of each school day. This in itself is a commentary on the scale and scope of a head's responsibilities at that time, so unlike the present. It must have taken hours of writing time. An entry for 3 September 1974 shows clearly the broad direction the curriculum would take for the next nine years. It records the first set of meetings the head had with the staff in her first term in 1974. It reads:

> Meeting for senior staff, general discussion etc. staff departmental meetings both for subject and pastoral departments. Staff council at which the head stated that she was opposed to 1st, 2nd, 3rd year pupils making unaccompanied education visits as had been the policy heretofore. The legal position of the head was that of full responsibility for the welfare of all pupils – in the case of 4th and 5th year on Newsom activities it is sound educational policy for external activities to be encouraged that develop initiative and responsibility. In the case of younger children, the dangers, especially of accidents, whilst unaccompanied, outweigh the educational advantages which might accrue. Staff therefore were told that permission for these unaccompanied visits was withdrawn and the head would not be responsible for children off the premises, with staff's knowledge in contravention of the new policy.

Staff too had early indications of a different approach being taken. For 9 September 1974 an entry reads:

> X seen regarding climbing over the fence into school on Sunday. X as youth tutor works the extended day, but the caretaker has complained of staff, being

in the building until well past midnight and into the early hours of the morning. Subsequently, cupboards have been found forced open and the maintenance of school security becomes difficult ... the secretary's cupboard had been forced open some time in the week end 7/8. All staff to be told that cupboards are not to be forced open and that reasonable time must be observed for the vacation of premises and the operation of securing the school against intruders. This should take account of evening school and the extended day but give a reasonable period for staff involved in these matters to vacate the premises having filed their records, etc.

It states on 10 September: 'All staff told of the above'. It was as if she had decided to administer a short sharp shock to the school's system. No doubt it was that approach which prompted a middle-ranking member of staff to say:

MML was undoubted good for the school and did what was necessary to convert it from 'progressive' to 'competitive', the requirement of the day. But my feeling was that she did not fully appreciate her staff or their respective professional experience and predicaments. She behaved like Methuselah, treated us like senior pupils, addressed us 'wee babies' and was obsessed (appropriately as it turned out) with the changes the future would bring and the apparent irrelevance to them of our collective and individual pasts.

But came the punch line: 'Despite all, however, things might have been a lot worse without her ministrations'. By the end of her headship that view was well proven.

Two remarks perhaps sum up the change of style. One staff member says 'it was like being on probation again' and another recalls 'she always felt it necessary to correct some pupil or other when she entered a room'. Another referred to 'Molly's own shibboleth by which she was to be come known: RIGHT! There was instant silence, more or less, and a kind of order prevailed'. It was somewhere between authoritative and authoritarian perhaps, clearly there were implications for the curriculum.

Curriculum change

The former head of humanities had become senior master. He refers to a document he issued at a staff meeting in November 1974, which asked questions about the approaches to pupil learning at its beginning (Appendix 4): Of it he says:

it gave heavy hints or forebodings of her intention to undo integration of subjects and mixed ability. And ... I do recall another meeting when, following a pronouncement I queried her decision with a voice quivering with anger and anxiety. I remember my absolute frustration and discomfort over the whole business.

And he was correct. The head of English remembers going with the senior master to argue for the retention of mixed ability teaching.

> She received the paper courteously, ... listened to our arguments without taking offence though our presentation was sometimes passionate. But at the end she was dismissive, regretfully, as a bank manager (in those more cautious times) might reject an overdraft requested from an unreliable client 'for your own good'. She knew better and she was implacable. That was her way.

Within twelve months all that was gone: no mixed ability teaching, no inter-disciplinary curriculum. 'Steady she goes' was the watchword. The change was eased by the promotion of the deputy and that senior master to other schools and the arrival of a deputy as an outside appointment

That document amounts to a serious approach to an institutional self-study. As such it indicates an impressive level of professionalism in the 1970s, and a highly sophisticated understanding of the practical application of some educational theory. As a potential action plan for the curriculum, the Office for Standards in Education (Ofsted) would be hard put to improve on it, thirty-odd years later. Some of the staff agreed with the senior master.

> Approaching 40 (as most of us were) with quite a large and growing family put me in that band of men aware that something had to be pulled out of the career hat soon. It was therefore very un-nerving to have the professional carpet pulled and most of one's experience and values negated or contradicted.

The change of direction for the curriculum is made explicit in an entry for the first staff meeting of the head's second year on 2 September 1975.

> 1st, 2nd, and 3rd year curriculum which includes subjects: history, geography, social studies and RE, formerly operating as a 'blanket IDS'. English has a separate place on the TT and is taught by English specialists. Other subjects are taught by specialist teachers with linking syllabuses. Fifth form continuing options already started in 3rd Year. Fourth form begin subject options for CSE, etc. Leavers' course introduced.

This is how the deputy described the new arrangements.

> We adopted a curriculum which we felt was apt for all the students whether leaving at 13 (that refers to the Thameside Scheme) or remaining at Senacre. Thus all students did English, mathematics, science, craft and design technology, geography, history, religious studies, French, art, music, drama, physical education and personal and social education. We also felt that a forty period week with eight lessons a day was the best vehicle for such a curriculum, particularly as it allowed doubles, or blocks of four at any time in the day, so to speak. We did not want mixed ability classes, nor rigid streaming, so we

settled for broad banding by ability – in our case 3 bands with considerable flexibility for movement between them. Each department was free to organize their own groupings within each band. The mathematics department, however, wanted streaming across whole year groups which we were able to accommodate.

There were three options for the 4th and 5th years. Each was allocated 4 periods each week and had some humanities, and then either practical subjects or art and RE or more humanities.

The mathematics master who took over as head of department said of options:

> deliberate attempt to give children some degree of ownership of their own education. Choices often reflected parental aspirations rather than the child's real interest or talent. Children chose courses because they wanted to remain in friendship groups or they liked a particular teacher (there are worse reasons). Sometimes they chose those courses they felt would involve least academic effort. For all these reasons firm guidance was often necessary.

Options never are easy to deal with. That quote illustrates some of the difficulties of trying to engage pupils through offering choice. And very significant for the future, that logbook entry included:

> First physically handicapped pupil enters school … appointed temporary welfare post to comply with regulations.

That had huge implications for an additional element in the school's curriculum as it evolved.

That close meticulous attention to detail in some directions shines through the logbook and characterizes the style of leadership at work. It was an energetic, direct, hands-on everything with few things escaping attention. 'She liked to be in control'.

The Thameside transfer scheme

The broad banding decision was central to curriculum change, and was a deliberate preparation for the introduction of the LEA's Thameside Scheme. The scheme, introduced in 1976 must have been under discussion within the LEA for some time, even before 1974 when there was a change of government. The scheme was to change the 11+ selection for determining those who went on to grammar, technical and secondary modern schools to a 13+ system. All pupils leaving primary schools were to go to the nearest secondary modern school – now to be called 'high schools' – for the first two years of their secondary education. It follows that because Senacre's curriculum had been different in essential ways from the other secondary schools to be involved in the scheme, the LEA may well have considered that its pupils might be at a disadvantage at the 13+ stage. Comparisons of admissions with pupils from other schools might be difficult and that could pose complicated administrative problems. Hence when remarks were made about the new head's role such as 'widely known from county level was to bring the school back into line again and raise its standards' and 'was appointed in 1974 to turn things round which she did very quickly', it looks as if the LEA had used the appointment of the school's third head to ensure that Senacre would fit easily into the Thameside Scheme without contentious arguments. It was a fundamental intervention in the school's curriculum. However it was clear that the head's thinking about subjects, the way they were taught and ways in which pupils learnt best, supported the change of direction in the curriculum so that Senacre could be integrated successfully into the scheme.

Broad banding was introduced for the first three years to include history, geography, social studies, RE, English. Mathematics had always been setted or streamed with other subjects taught by specialists. The school therefore reverted to a curriculum which was broadly the same as what was on offer in the first two years of the grammar schools. No doubt the scheme looked administratively watertight on paper. In fact educationally, it leaked as badly as the 11+ it replaced.

An entry in the logbook for 28/29 August 1977 reads:

> GCE and CSE results as forecast, very poor. Too many pupils were sent (30 per cent) to upper schools in operation of the Thameside Scheme. Reports from upper schools of results of some of pupils sent are also very poor – these pupils were not of calibre to benefit from academic GCE programmes and yet would have provided much needed incentive for CSE pupils at Senacre.

That is repeated for 31 August when the educational validity of the scheme was queried. A member of staff in their mid-thirties recalls:

> In simple terms, this seemed to arise out of a realization that there were a few pupils who were late developers – and anyway why was 11 the magic age at which to decide people's academic potential and commit them to it for life ... from a social point of view the Thameside Scheme was about as much a disaster as it was from the academic point of view.

All that happened was that the 11+ problem was moved up two years to 13+. From the late 1950s it was well known that the 11+ selection system contained a 10 per cent overlap between the bottom stream of a grammar school and the best pupils in a secondary modern school. Nothing in the Thameside Scheme did anything to alter that balance. Overlap would continue at selection.

Clearly the head agreed broadly with the curriculum changes which the Thameside Scheme required. But that does not imply that she was content with the educational results of the scheme. Indeed the log records that on 17 March 1976 an elected staff representative attended a teachers' meeting concerning re-organization of secondary education in Maidstone and reported:

Three schemes were proposed (a) a straight through 11–18 comprehensive school system, (b) 11–16 comprehensive schools followed by a sixth form college, probably the old grammar schools, and (c) a middle school system the details of which I forget but it was very complicated. The chairman while stressing that the meeting had no voting powers accepted under pressure, to at least allow a show of hands. The results were interesting. Kent schools, at least in the Maidstone division, overwhelmingly supported a move to a comprehensive system. They also, by a large majority favoured the sixth form approach which would allow sensible use of the existing grammar schools with their experience of A level work. Even the grammar schools' staff prepared to countenance any change could see the sense of it. No one considered the middle school system seriously. It was so complex it would take months, possibly years to implement and almost certainly involve enormous extra expense. We were later informed that Kent had decided to adopt the middle school system. With a general election probably less that a year away it is not difficult to guess their motives.

The head does not record her views. She was at the meeting so it seems reasonable to question the extent to which she supported the middle school scheme proposal on educational grounds. Whatever the administrative benefits for the local authority, the educational benefits were questionable. It was an intervention which ignored the judgement of professionals. This time it was the LEA. Next time it would be central government.

What was fundamental to the changes both educationally and administratively was that the catchment area of the school was changed. It was enlarged. Two hundred and twenty pupils now came from a far wider area and therefore from more primary schools than the 120 as before. And barring successful protest by parents who did not want their children to go to Senacre, at that time those 220 numbers were guaranteed. But competition between schools and the fight for numbers were not far away.

The deputy head was clear that the success of the operation rested on the head of year system.

> We were most fortunate to have some very strong staff in these positions who became the real engine-house of the school ... and X who not only improved discipline almost overnight, but who also made a vital contribution of the whole ethos of the school whether it be in academic or social spheres or whatever.

Some consequences

Some consequences of this change in the system for transfer from primary to secondary schools were predictable, others were quite unpredictable, all of them having a long term curricular significance.

The pupils

There was the curriculum of the school itself, and its immediate impact on pupils. Now there was a clear division between schemes of work for the first three years and for the fourth and fifth years, which benefited some but made life more difficult for others. A member of staff responsible for the scheme says:

> A fully comprehensive intake certainly enhanced expectations and morale. However, the loss of 25 per cent of the year group at the end of Year 8 was unsettling. Friendships were broken; pupils had to be regrouped for Year 9, and Year 9 as a doldrums between lower and upper school became pronounced. This apathy and lack of motivation and engagement with the learning process was only redressed by the introduction of SATS.

The future head of the upper school observed that 'later this effect on Years 10 and 11 added to the difficulties in meeting target standards'. Another put it thus:

> Eventually the separation occurred – although a surprising number of 'selected' pupils actually chose to stay at Senacre. It was then necessary to rebuild the confidence and the fractured self-respect and social groups of the unselected. To this end my own attitude implied 'Right the guests gone, now let's get down to family work'.

That reference earlier to SATS is important. It is refers to a positive influence which came later on from government intervention in the curriculum.

But for standards and targets it is possible that the effects went wider than that. Grammar schools lost their first two years. That space had to be filled. So when the head noted in the logbook that low standards meant too many pupils were being transferred from Senacre, it was implying that the ability range was being widened in grammar schools and narrowed in the ex-secondary modern schools.

Conversely, a fully comprehensive entry was bound to lead to improvements in standards and achievements during Years 7 and 8. If 25 to 30 per cent were to be bound for the grammar schools there could be no doubt about it. The public perception of the school was bound to change for the better. The entry saw to that. This was first direct intervention in the curriculum. Educationally, it produced a mixed bag of results.

Size

Numbers increased. The third headship began with 600 pupils. The Thameside Scheme meant that instead of a four form entry of about 120 pupils, 180–220 became a seven or eight form entry. By 1980 there were some 1,000 pupils in the school. That was bound to have far-reaching effects on capital investment in the expansion of the building as well as organization and staffing, and disruption. Logbook entries on governor's meetings are littered with complaints about the way building construction was making the everyday life of the teaching day almost impossible. The pupils were in the corridors. The bell system was disconnected so members of staff were issued with whistles and refused to accept responsibility for pupils' safety because a stairwell was hazardous. For 13 June there is a full page recording a visit by the chair of governors' to prepare for a governors' meeting the next day. It is important to remember too that the school leaving age went up to sixteen in 1972–3. It was a large expansion just about doubling the size of the premises.

In the middle of all that was the problem of asbestos. For a whole term the school was evacuated to a nearby empty primary school while blue asbestos was removed from the ceiling of the assembly hall.

Staff

The staff found themselves teaching pupils right across the entire ability range. This had huge influence of the pedagogical element in the curriculum.

> The prospect of accepting the full range of ability in the first two years was daunting to some teachers, though they'd hate to admit it. Whether they had the acumen or not, they certainly did not have the experience of teaching at this level. I was amazed at how quickly the new groups devoured my material. The pace of teaching accelerated. Did the less able get left behind? Not in drama. I don't think so. It was certainly possible to tackle more abstract and cerebral work, but the less able were perfectly capable of working on ideas once their contemporaries had introduced them.

That was one view. Another was 'the first time we had the experience of a fully comprehensive intake and we liked it'. This is talking about a vital dimension to curriculum change: the capacity of staff to teach so that all pupils could learn.

Like it or not the style of teaching and so learning changed. One experienced master who had been in the school for eight years wrote of marking:

> Different abilities needed different applications of encouragement, praise, correction, discipline and so on. But the grading had to be fair and relative to some absolute standard. Formerly, English staff had become pretty accurate and consistent at 'impression marks' and had achieved excellent results using it as a flexible encouragement. Now grades must be harder and faster, must relate to the entire (national) ability range and to a final exam grade. Pupils would quickly recognize that their own level seemed to have a ceiling. This obviously encouraged despair in some, complacency in others. The broad bands tended to become narrower and narrower.

As if to underline that another says:

Schools were asked to provide evidence for their recommendations and surprise, surprise, increasingly some form of internal examinations results were used. Under pressure from the grammar schools this process reverted to the final year of primary education. The circle was complete.

But of course there was another effect on staffing. A fully comprehensive entry with pupils staying for two years was an attractive proposition for more highly qualified staff than when there was just a secondary modern school entry. This clearly contributed to the rising reputation of the school. Rising academic standards in those two years with the other three years benefiting accordingly, meant that overall the public perception of the school changed for the better. The formal curriculum is one thing. It only comes alive when teachers teach it. So to that extent the 13+ scheme helped to lift the school's levels of attainment. If the curriculum had become more traditional, learning and teaching had strengthened. However, this was to work in reverse when the Thameside Scheme was dropped in 1992.

Parents

There was an entirely different school–parent relationship to chart, not least for its effect on the curriculum. The public posture of the school changed. In uniform, pupils of Senacre with an ability range from the brightest to the slowest were perceived to behave in a more orderly manner. And inevitably with an all-ability entry, standards of achievement were seen to rise in those first two years. It was no surprise that the reputation of the school rose. But as with other reputations it was fickle, as time was to show.

Because of the wider catchment area inevitably there were vigorous protests by some parents at the distance their children had to travel to get to the school, especially from an area which considered itself socially superior to the housing estate surrounding the school. It seems that those protests died down when parents realized that with 25 per cent of pupils from Senacre going on to grammar schools the chances for their children improved. In some ways it was the equivalent to contemporary efforts to moving house to get entry to a particular school. They were on to a good thing and, predictably, they exploited it.

Consultation evenings formed part of the procedure. They swamped the staff. A logbook entry for 1 March 1978 says:

Parents' Evening for first year, 7–9.30, over 300 parents … some complaints re inability to see all staff but overwhelming response made seeing staff impossible … had over sixty parents who wished to speak with her and would not confine their discussion to 5–10 minutes. Parents seemed very happy with pupils' education and progress – no complaints on that score, but rather the reverse.

Indeed the consultation element in the scheme inevitably tended to bear down on the curriculum.

> There was strong pressure from many parents, of course, to ensure that their children 'achieved their true potential'. Junior schools had invariably made valedictory predictions, and if these were not fulfilled, parents were not happy. Consultation evenings became minefields. Obviously parents wanted to know the truth, but equally we were instructed not to make forecasts.

The head of English endured one parent who was:

> ... furious that I had demoted his daughter from A to B, was all psyched up for the occasion. Though I explained why this had happened, he attempted to bully me into submission ... He reeked of booze and his wife kept tugging at his arm in fear that his obstreperous behaviour would have the opposite effect and stiffen my resolve. There was, in fact no need for concern as their daughter was clear for promotion. But the rules forbade me to say so, so I had to sit there and taken it on the chin. (TH)

As could be expected, attendance at parents' meetings shot up, parental support strengthened. However this did not automatically mean a strong PTA. Some staff noted however that the head trimmed its sails when she considered it was becoming too influential and abolished it in 1976.

Numbers

By the early 1980s the numbers in the school rose to nearly 1,000, with students coming from quite far afield as a result of the school's growing reputation. But the transport problem did not go away. And it heralded dire consequences for the future. The logbook records at the beginning of the school year 1981–2;

> First year numbers more depleted than warranted by falling rolls because of payment for transport. Letters from parents to school and DEO confirming this – saying that Senacre was first choice but new cost of transport prohibitive.

Since first year numbers in effect control the staffing of a school for the next five years, this was just the sort of utterly unpredictable factor which could affect a school's ability to support its curriculum. As it turned out, although no one knew it at the time, it was a warning shot across the bows of what was to come, when huge efforts by senior staff set about recruitment in earnest. But it also concealed something else. By 1983 as well as an absolute decline in numbers, those numbers included only a fraction for whom Senacre had been their parents' first choice. And that was despite the catchment area being determined by the LEA as to which secondary school their sons and daughters would attend. That was a time bomb waiting for the next head. Competition was building up.

If there were pluses they were at the expense of very large additions to the work of the staff. The prediction that the scheme would be complicated and expensive proved accurate as the requirements mounted on schools to enable the system to work.

Procedures

Fortuitously the introduction of the head of year system to replace the head of house system had in some ways prepared the school for conducting the necessary educational procedures to deal with the Thameside Scheme. The system was strengthened with head of year assuming disciplinary responsibilities as well as pastoral and academic ones. It was another example of unforeseen consequences of a previous decision.

As part of the Thameside Scheme, a year head stayed with the group in the junior school for the two years and had the job of working with junior feeder schools in relation to incoming pupils. In effect this was a curriculum innovation. For a year head this meant:

> Talks with staff of those schools to obtain background information in addition to the record cards (off the record things).
> Talks to the children (in their own school) to dispel fears, tell them about OUR school requirements and organizational details and to answer questions.
> Collect record cards for sifting information.
> Arrange to interview parents with children at Senacre (form filling, general health requirements, equipment required) etc.
> Arrange a day at Senacre to sample a limited timetable.

The year head sorted all that information into tutor groups of pupils, usually eight groups of twenty-four, each with a mix of abilities, different feeder schools boys, girls, friends where possible. All this information was logged along with reading age, IQ, NFER tests, subject report grades and test scores and subject recommendations for grammar schools. This produced some sort of ranking order using a weighting scale for subjects – more for mathematics, English, science and French, less for history, geography, RE – which was discussed internally before being presented to the head for final comments. Interviews with parents followed to explain the school's decision. An independent body held appeals. All was submitted to the LEA, which issued the official letters of allocation.

As the deputy head described it;

> We developed what we felt to be a sound, objective selection procedure for the 13+, involving the use of objective tests as well as results and recommendations from all subject areas based on examination as well as course work

assessments. The year head collated all this information before making initial recommendations which were then considered at deputy head level and modified in consultation with the year head before going to the head for final approval. Parental interviews always followed our agreed procedure.

This was a huge additional load for a school to carry, almost prophetic for the heavy loads to come. But it also brought some benefits. Relationships with primary schools were transformed. Whereas during the first two headships that relationship was rather perfunctory, during the third it became organic. This was to be of critical importance for the future. And there is no doubt that the standards of achievement rose for much of the school, if not all of it. It was however complicated and expensive as predicted.

Balance sheet

All in all the Thameside Scheme seems to have been politically inspired, and while it brought some considerable educational benefits to the secondary modern schools, as well as administrative benefits to the authority, it merely confirmed the sheep (few) and goats (many) division while postponing it. In the process it is arguable that the curriculum requirements of the first two years to make the scheme fully operational, worked to the detriment of the many. The 'doldrums Year 9' symbolizes the difficulties for a school trying to provide continuity in the curriculum for the many. Without continuity the difficulties just multiply for securing pupils'engagement in their learning, let alone their becoming willing learners. And educationally it landed the school with additional problems once government targets became a fundamental curriculum preoccupation.

What could not have been foreseen was the withdrawal of the scheme sixteen years later during the fifth headship. That was more disruptive than introducing it. Withdrawal came when great emphasis was being put on parental choice for schools, so the school had to invest heavily in pupil recruitment to fill its places in addition to trying to improve learning and teaching. By then, budgetary controls governed by numbers made it more difficult to plan ahead.

So it is not unreasonable to suggest that on this occasion education became the servant of administration whereas before it could be claimed that to some extent administration had been the servant of education. It was official intervention in the curriculum in capital letters, written in black. Introducing a scheme which altered fundamentally the secondary curriculum and then withdrawing it fifteen years later was an unfortunate way of trying to improve the education service.

A gossipy view of some long serving staff members is that as long as the 13+ was in operation the school could attract very good teachers but all that stopped when the scheme was discontinued in 1992. After that it was difficult to recruit good staff because anyone applying for a post from a Kent school to one outside the county was at a disadvantage, being without experience of teaching in a comprehensive school. Were that to be true it would be an interesting example of an unintended deleterious consequence of an administrative bureaucracy overriding professional educators. It was shooting yourself in the foot, no less; and in the closing years of the twentieth century, it might have had something to do with the number of secondary schools in Kent which were in special measures.

What is quite clear is that the intention during the first two headships of using a whole school interpretation of the curriculum to try to connect with students in the social realities of their lives was replaced with an attempt to convert the school into an academic waiting room for some and a destination for most. That was the changed emphasis in the curriculum.

The national context

In March 1976 James Callaghan became prime minister of what became a minority government. He latched on to education as an issue which would connect with the public. In October that year he made his speech on education which is enshrined as the 'Ruskin speech'. In a sense this was an ordinary person's guide to trying to improve the education of children and young people.

> There is nothing wrong with non-educationalists, even a Prime Minister talking about ... (education) ... I take it that no one claims exclusive rights in this field. Public interest is strong and will be satisfied. It is legitimate. We spend £6 billion a year on education ... He went on. It is not my intention to become enmeshed in such problems as whether there should be a basic curriculum with universal standards – although I am inclined to think that there should be.
> (Maclure 2000: 196)

After that it was almost inevitable that strong intervention from the centre would come at some time. But he went on:

> to the critics I would say that we must carry the teaching profession with us. They have the expertise and they have the professional approach. To teachers I would say that you must satisfy the parents and industry ... for if the public is not convinced then the profession will be laying up trouble for in the future.

If he was signalling the way things would go in the future, the style of intervention which followed for nearly the next thirty years was hardly what he had in mind at that time. But whatever his private thoughts, the Ruskin speech was the first public move by a national government towards explicit intervention in schools' curriculum. By referring to it as a private garden, it signalled that privacy was on the way out. Home grown curricula would seem a thing of the past.

A round of public consultations followed, the 'great debate', and the head was involved. The logbook records that on 19 July 1977 by invitation of the secretary of state, Shirley Williams, that the head was to participate in the final meeting of the 'great debate' in December at York University and had already attended a session with the secretary of state and senior HMIs and half the other participants. A few weeks before there is an entry about attending a meeting at Springfield, the offices of the LEA, about heads' accountability. LEAs were feeling the pressure from the centre.

That is not surprising given the plethora of papers which began to flow from the Department of Education and Science. The Green Paper, 'Education in schools' followed up the 'great debate' in 1977 as a discussion document on curriculum, standards and examinations. Circular 14/77 also in 1977 asked LEAs to give an account of how they were managing the curriculum. HMI produced 'A view of the curriculum'. Then came another consultative document in 1980, 'A framework for the curriculum' written by civil servants, which was considered too prescriptive by teachers and LEAs. It was followed by a less prescriptive document in 1981, 'The school curriculum' which was then followed up in 1983 by Circular 8/83, which asked what LEAs and governors were doing to follow up what was laid out in 'The school curriculum'. Step-by-step intervention in the curriculum by the centre was the next stage after the Ruskin speech.

So it is not coincidental that from 1977 onwards LEA inspectors were in and out of the school continually. The chairman of Kent education's schools' committee and LEA inspectors are noted as attending governors' meetings. Governors visited more often. Anxiety in central government about the state of the secondary curriculum in particular was bothering HMIs and this led to pressure on LEAs to sharpen their supervision. So the head was well informed of what was afoot.

Newsom muted

Meantime the curriculum for Years 10 and 11 was explained to parents of those pupils who were remaining at Senacre. The common core of subjects continued. Each pupil was to take English, mathematics, science, humanities, a practical subject, an aesthetic subject and physical education and three courses taken from three option blocks. Each option block had four periods. A leavers' course was introduced which was an extension of the enterprise course which had been established during the previous headship.

> It was a rotational course designed to give pupils a range of educational opportunities, to develop initiative and promote character building. Creative arts and work experience were included. There was an extensive sports programme which included ice skating, 10-pin bowling, rock climbing and sailing. A particularly innovative part of the course was a trip to London when pupils were given a small amount of money and then had to see how far they could get and what sights they could see for this money.

All this in curriculum terms demonstrated the value of having a youth tutor who could concentrate on finding new ways of engaging pupils in learning which were not restricted to classroom activities.

The extensive range of away visits continued. A random list includes, the Council for World Citizenship, HMS *Pembroke*, the Science Museum, the Imperial War Museum, Women's Royal Army Corps headquarters, Wembley, the Harlem Globetrotters, *Fidelio* at Glyndbourne, Marlowe at Canterbury, Kent Mountain Centre in Wales. Special studies weeks continued as well with groups camping or youth hostelling, touring Holland and studying special topics. So parts of an outward looking curriculum held their place. Fifth formers succeeded in examinations and scored well in obtaining employment.

There is a wry reflection on the work experience programme of one day a week at work for some thirty difficult young people within the enterprise course and its successor the leavers' course. This was an adapted version of the 1959 work experience which was banned by the LEA in 1964. Then it was for slower pupils who wanted to take advantage of staying at school for a fifth year. Now it was for 'difficult young people', an instructive curriculum shift. The substantial work experience programme was a fortnight blocked off at the end of the school year when the timetable was suspended. Then the programme expanded in its modified form. A senior master who was responsible for careers from the start, took on what his predecessor had begun and had the same range of local connections. As a senior colleague put it:

> he seemed to know everyone of any consequence in Maidstone's business community, largely through Bearsted Golf Club! This proved invaluable in creating a new work experience programme. Our children could be found in most of the larger stores in the town, in offices in Springfield, assisting in the town hospital, acting as drivers' mates on delivery vans, working in garages, on building sites, in virtually any light engineering works in the area. (It is worth remembering that these were the days before the public adopted an American love of suing at the least prospect of financial gain.) Most spent one week in Year 10 though some went on a day release basis over a large part of the year. Many were given firm offers of employment as a consequence of their performance on work experience. Many were given part time jobs. I remember one girl of modest academic attainments who was offered a post as a dental receptionist as soon as she left school, so delighted was the practice with her general manner ... both boys and girls were given taster courses in the army ... both were involved equally in the programme. For some the experience motivated them to make the most of their opportunities in school; for others it confirmed their view that the classroom was no place for them.

That senior master had been inherited by the first head and was a close colleague of the man who first got work experience going in 1959. This is a good example of the value of continuity for the curriculum.

Creative arts continued much the same with art, music and drama collaborating. It was given a boost at the turn of the decade by creating a head of creative arts and aesthetics. An aesthetics course was born, which was an intellectualized version of creative arts, emphasizing receptive skills rather than productive ones.

It followed logically from these arrangements that the school became organized as a lower and upper school. The Thameside Scheme with the 13+ selection system fitted in neatly. A humanities and social sciences course was devised for the upper school. It became 'a vehicle for personal social and health education (PSHE) but the programme was not formalized. 'In Year 9 it was in the hands of the year head and form tutors. Essentially it was dependent on the enthusiasm and responsibility of those staff involved'. But the integration of English, history, geography and religious studies to produce a coherence within and across them faded away, with discrete subjects returning to their old departmentalization.

All this was explained to parents as a survey of curriculum opportunities for the next two years at the annual options meeting. But the doldrums problem with Year 9 continued, and within its imposed boundaries the school did its best. Again the deputy head stated:

> Year 9 was always something of a problem, particularly in terms of discipline and possibly with regard to feelings of 13+ rejection, much exaggerated in my view, but curriculum wise it was simply a continuation of Years 7 and 8. At the same time it was seen however as a preparation for Years 10 and 11 and time was given over to careers work and to giving students and parents as much information as possible about curricular choices in Years 10 and 11. Our parents evenings were always well attended (all years) but our option evening in Year 9 particularly so.

At the other end the remedial department taught low-attaining pupils basic skills in place of English lessons.

> Pupils with low reading ages were withdrawn from lessons for remedial attention. So these children spent much of their time on an impoverished curriculum, concentrating on the basic skills of literacy.

The logbook records on 7 July 1981 'LEA inspector to talk about Schools Council Project on Schools History'. This is the only reference to any national or LEA curriculum initiative save for mathematics.

Certificate of Secondary Education

These years culminated in the Certificate of Secondary Education and the General Certificate of Education ordinary level. Mode 3 CSE continued and was prized. The head of mathematics records his belief in the educational opportunities offered.

> CSE was fully developed and considered by many to be an excellent examination. In mathematics it allowed for a considerable variety of approaches to

both the teaching of mathematics and the choice of subject content. This was brought about by the establishment of a number of examining boards, each with its own approach to examining mathematics and each producing two core papers covering the basics and a third paper chosen from a ring that included papers extending the basic topics, papers on navigation, papers on Boolean Algebra. It was possible to select an examination for those who had reached their limit of their understanding and interest or by a different selection an examination suitable for those wishing to pursue their studies in the subject. If you really could not find anything to your liking you could even write and submit your own examination paper either for the third paper, Mode 2 or the entire three papers, Mode 3. Each year in post examination area meetings the papers were analysed and discussed and recommendations went back to the boards.

That marked a substantial development for the mathematics curriculum. Mode 3 continued for other subjects, English, religious study, social science, history. Inevitably those developments brought additional administrative work. An indication of that is given by the head's invitation to the head of technical crafts in 1981 to become examinations secretary as well. Presumably this was a way of reducing the administrative weight on her own office. He says 'In those days the job was relatively simple, though lacking the assistance of ITC, being essentially CSE where all subjects were dealt with by a single board, and a small amount of GCE'. He held that post until retirement in 1999.

For the formal curriculum therefore the third headship saw what appeared retrospectively as a school with a two part phased curriculum: Years 7 and 8 in the lower school following what was increasingly like the first two years of a grammar school. The upper school had a 'doldrums' Year 9 and continued to develop some of the curricular strands which had emerged after the publication of the Newsom Report. Gradually the curriculum became more formal and restrictive so that the whole school flavour of it weakened.

Curriculum innovation

In one respect however, the curriculum was developed in a quite different way and as it grew it, had a great influence on the school as a whole. In 1974 Margaret Thatcher as Secretary of State for Education and Science set up a committee of inquiry into special education under the chairmanship of Mary Warnock. Legislation based on the Warnock Committee was a long time in coming but in the 1981 Bill the new multidisciplinary procedures were established using 'discovery, diagnosis and assessment' as the report had it.

Perhaps her own chronic arthritis prompted the head's initiative in seeking authority to develop specialist provision in the school for physically disabled children in secondary education. Perhaps she picked up clues from heads' meetings. Perhaps it was prompted not only by the establishment of the Warnock Committee but the general interest in the media in that topic. For whatever reason, the head devoted a considerable amount of her energy, time and attention to the development of a first class facility. It must have been the notion of integration, urged by the Warnock Report which inspired her. As her deputy saw it:

> Miss Lynch was the driving force here, so that Senacre became the chosen school in the Maidstone area for the integration into mainstream education of those with a physical handicap. A teacher (scale post) was given responsibility for overseeing their day-to-day welfare. Classroom assistants were provided sometimes with a nursing background. These students had their own base but emphasis throughout was on 'normalcy' so that they were encouraged to remain with their peer group as much as possible.

Physically handicapped

So that first entry in the logbook in September 1975 recording the arrival of the first physically disabled pupil was as a landmark in the school's development. As with so many other things it indicated the close attention to detail, a constant concern about this addition to the schools provision: 'arrangements for physiotherapy on Monday afternoons to Mote Part Day Centre. Ambulance to collect. Water therapy to be fixed later', all in the logbook for that day.

Over the years at a rough count, the head attended as many meetings concerning the physically disabled as for any other series of meetings whether heads' committee or panel meetings for the 13+ entry scheme. There were visits to special and primary schools to prepare pupils and parents for the transition. There were panel meetings which in effect were assessment meetings to decide which pupils should join Senacre. There were consultations with therapists and the assistant inspector for the physically disabled. There were consultations at Springfield with the LEA about the necessities of provision for integration.

Over time there were visits to the school by members of Surrey education authority to see for themselves what integration of the physically handicapped meant and how to do it. St Mary's College Wimbledon visited to ask the same range of questions.

But the strongest indication of the head's commitment to the provision for the integration of the physically disabled was her national role. In 1978 and 1979 she attended six committee meetings at the Department of Education and Science. And in November 1980 there was a conference entitled 'Children with special needs' held in the Institute of Education, University of London, under the chairmanship of Baroness Young. The head attended as a delegate to represent Kent education authority. Later she was awarded the MBE.

As the numbers grew so did the head's pressure increase on the county for an adequate number of welfare assistants. The building extension had to have ramps to offer easy access for wheelchairs. Memos went to the county architect. An LEA inspector arrived to see what proper facilities were necessary for the physically disabled to join in home economics and needlework. The assistant inspector was in and out frequently. The district inspector spent an entire day shadowing physically disabled pupils as they went through their normal day at the school, moving from room to room, while the rest of the school went on around them.

Apart from the problems of coping with growing numbers of young people, some incontinent, and keeping the facilities and staffing up to scratch, there were unexpected problems. An entry in the logbook for September 1979 records that some parents were trying to use the full-time attendance of a nurse in the school for consultations about their own personal ailments, a sort of adjunct to the GP's surgery. That was soon stopped.

The very notion of integration of physically disabled pupils in a regular secondary school made many a member of staff anxious. In the event it turned out to be a valuable addition to the school and its staff and its regular pupils. One member gave the background.

> During 1981, the Warnock committee brought about the closure of many special schools on the premise that, as far as possible all pupils with SEN should be educated in normal schools. Schools were given budgets to cope with this. Large amounts of money were poured into schools for the support of these pupils, but at the time there was no accountability. Eventually when the government wanted to know exactly how much money was being spent, the Code of Practice was brought in. This bureaucratic nightmare was to have a huge impact on a later head.

The National Foundation for Educational Research featured and came in for criticism. Some second year Senacre pupils participated in an NFER science test. The logbook for 17 June, 1987 records:

> Among the pupils was a pupil confined to a wheelchair ... this surprised the NFER representative and we were equally surprised to learn that this was the first occasion on which the test had been administered to a physically handicapped pupil.

A week later another NFER staff member visited Senacre.

> The presence of a PH child in the 'sample' has added a new dimension to the thinking of NFER ... and somewhat tartly ... It also suggests they have not fully understood the implications of the last two Education Acts. In addition it also suggests that special schools have not formed part of their samples when undertaking general educational testing.

This was within a month of the head's retirement, sharp to the end.

As for the day-to-day effect one staff member records:

It is interesting that in the late seventies Senacre, of all the schools in the Medway Towns, was selected to integrate handicapped pupils. Ramps were built. A lift was installed. Nursing staff were employed. Over the years, we, staff and pupils got used to wheelchairs careering along corridors; we grieved more than once at more than one tragic death and we witnessed amazing courage. I believe it to have been one of Senacre's greatest success stories and, sadly, one if its least publicized.

And another describes integration itself.

Physically disabled pupils were introduced to the school after the building had been modified to accommodate them and allow them full access. It is difficult to recollect that the staff were apprehensive about their ability to cope with this development and even more apprehensive about the reception that these children might receive from their able bodied peers. Such fears were totally unfounded. The pupils were integrated very happily and successfully. Whilst a spotty face, large ears or plumpness might incur ridicule and a rough ride, these children were welcomed sympathetically and enthusiastically.

The head's successor paid tribute to all that work.

One of the most interesting features of Senacre, already well established by my predecessor, was the work in the school of educating of up to twenty children with severe physical disabilities. They provided an enormous challenge in our seeking to meet all of their needs, both physical and emotional; they were in themselves responsible for changing some of the cultural values of their peers and I would suppose they may have been more than partially responsible for our survival when we were threatened with closure by the LEA ... work was outstanding and rarely received the credit that they deserved in opening up a new world to all of us.

By that time there was a fully staffed and equipped suite of facilities which would have been the envy of many a doctor's surgery or for that matter, an NHS day care centre. In a curious sort of way it seems appropriate somehow that that suite for the physically disabled was housed in what used to be the secretary's office, the head's study and staff room when the school opened some twenty-five years earlier. What was barely acknowledged then, the wider needs of the SEN, had become a central element in the school's curriculum.

Sometimes there is reference to the invisible or hidden curriculum. There is no way of measuring the effect on able bodied learners of the form of integration that the physically disabled brought to the school. But it is absolutely certain that in mysterious ways, the presence of those physically disabled fellow pupils will have influenced some of their peers, in ways which nothing else could have done. For some, that hidden curriculum would have become learning manifest. The deputy head writes:

> I was lucky to be able to 'research' this integration in the late 1980s ... I interviewed all the PH students (16) together with a representative sample from the rest of the school, crossing all years and abilities. Certain problems were highlighted like 'favouritism' towards P.H. students in that they were rarely punished, etc. but the integration was clearly seen to be a great success, benefiting both the PH students and their peers. It was advantageous to the school, too, in terms of profile, as well as in more practical terms like the availability of nurses.

Curriculum: half way marker

After twenty-seven years, how was the curriculum? The physically disabled was an outstanding example of how innovation can expand the experience of schooling. But there may have been a general curriculum price for all that devoted work. The head was unwell. Two hip operations are enough to sap anyone's stamina in their late fifties holding down the job of a head. Shortly before her retirement she was off sick with serious chest infections. The two deputy heads had to a large extent carried the school, ensuring that it ran like clockwork. One became acting head twice during her tenure as well as during the term before the new head arrived. As one colleague says:

> I think it fair to say that she was no lover of administrative tasks and the school depended on hard working deputies to keep things on course. I think in the modern jargon her form of management would be labelled as the 'charismatic style'.

The sum total of energy used up between the three of them left little time over for reflecting on the curricular and the organizational issues which lay ahead in such a fast changing world where there were ominous signs from government of future change. Moreover, numbers remained a problem which was getting more severe. Without sufficient pupil numbers there was little that could be done about the curriculum. And competition would replace specified catchment areas. With her eyes firmly focused on the changes which she knew were coming, curriculum development was not a high priority. The preservation of stability was the priority. It is no surprise that there was little innovation.

It was not that during this third headship the curriculum stayed still. The first three years reverted to something like a pale imitation of a grammar school curriculum. Formality tended to creep back into Years 10 and 11. Some Newsom style approaches to learning continued to develop for those years. CSE and GCE O level remained firmly in place with mathematics joining the Mode 3 band of enthusiasts. And by integrating physically handicapped pupils in the school the head did something utterly different. Another dimension was added. But for the majority the curriculum narrowed.

Seen retrospectively, it is difficult to disagree with senior staff and as will be seen, with the next head, that over all of it lay the baleful influence of the Thameside Scheme. It made the task of providing the best for the majority even harder. And to the extent that it inhibited some forms of curriculum development tuned to the domestic, social and economic circumstances of the majority of its growing young people, it was an example of official intervention at its worst. Essentially this was a period of consolidation to fit external requirements with the remarkable exception of the provision for the physically disabled. Although many did not agree with the head's view of the curriculum, generally she was held in high regard. As a senior colleague puts it 'She deserves a place of honour in the Senacre story. "Eccentric" is far too dull to describe her'.

So by the end of the third headship, the main body of the school was in a twofold division of lower and upper school which changed the nature and flavour of the curriculum. Then it changed again with the integration of physically handicapped as a third division which was the expression of the head's very strong sense of public service. These nine years of office set a course for the curriculum which would prove highly significant for the school's future, laying a structure which was able to withstand the eruptions to come. There was no doubt either that the curriculum had narrowed, or that declining numbers were threatening. It was relative calm before a raging storm.

Had an intervention account book been open, it would have registered losses: narrowed curriculum, falling numbers; gains: secure academic structure, distinctiveness of provision for physically disabled.

Chapter 5

Curriculum change as trouble shooter

The fourth headship, Andrew Parsons, 1983–88

This headship saw a different style of leadership again. Staff meetings at eight forty-five on Monday mornings became the norm. After being in the school a fortnight the head wrote of a staff meeting in the logbook:

> Without a 100 per cent attendance at that time. This was followed by a visit to the entrance to the school to check pupil promptness. A large number of pupils still moving into the school at 9.00 a.m. There appears to be an obvious need to question existing standards of timekeeping at all levels.

This was the concept of authority as the foundation for a collaborative style overall. As a colleague remarked of the transition from one head to another:

> Miss Lynch served Senacre well but just as she had stabilized the school and seen it through to the beginning of great changes in education it was now time for another style of head to thrust us into the heart of those changes.

'A breath of fresh air', said another.

The fourth head, aged 38, came along a different route again. Senacre was the fifth school he had served, the two preceding ones being in Kent, working for the first time in non-selective (secondary modern) schools. As head of lower school in Ashford, Kent, he had increased an annual intake of pupils from 180 to over 300 through building links with primary schools. So he knew about numbers and the need for strong contacts with primary schools. As a deputy head he had experience of the running of a school.

The circumstances of his becoming head were different too. As a deputy he was well aware of documents coming from the department about curricular revision. Sir Keith Joseph, the secretary of state for Education displayed mounting frustration that his consultative initiatives produced little action. When Kenneth Baker succeeded Keith Joseph in 1986 dramatic change was inevitable. His headship began in very different circumstances from any of his three predecessors.

Andrew Parsons was appointed in 1983 but assumed the headship in January 1984. During that autumn term of 1983 he established himself, putting down the roots for a growing period when school development, never mind the curriculum, was in for a fraught and fractious period. It was fraught, because the effort to secure the school's quota of entries at 210 required huge effort by senior members of staff to combat uncertainty about the future. It was fractious, because the local authority intervened in a quite different way, which led to an all-out confrontation with the school. That was the background to the story of the curriculum to be told during this fourth headship.

From the start, before he took up his appointment officially, he stamped his tenure of office with an entirely different style of leadership. He visited the school on several occasions when the deputy was acting head. Towards the end of the term he held a full staff meeting and delivered a tough message. He had nothing but praise for the standard of teaching and the commitment of the staff, but he had concluded that not enough attention had been paid to the circumstances in the outside world where the school found itself. 'Foreign affairs' had been neglected. The school was threatened. He had discovered that entry numbers were down to 120 instead of 210, which projected, meant a school of 600. Worse, a substantial number of those who did enrol came as second choicers rather than with Senacre as first choice. Even so at that first staff meeting the head announced that within five years Senacre would be the most popular school in the area. And all that had to be seen in context of the effects of the Thameside Scheme as the head saw them.

had the system been a serious forward step into a comprehensive structure, (he had experienced comprehensive schooling in Yorkshire before moving to Kent) then it might have some justification, but by 1984, it was clear that there was no momentum for further change and the system had stagnated into a mismatch of provision which was hardly enjoyed by colleagues in upper schools or in the high schools themselves. In truth the first two years were enormously enriched by a full ability intake, but the removal of the more able 25 per cent after two years had an impact that went well beyond academic studies. In essence, the student leadership was taken out. Sports teams were denuded of their talent, theatre and arts groups were decimated and many high schools were left with a bunch of young adolescents, many of who felt themselves left behind, left out, second best and failed.

Not that the rebuilding of student morale was the most pressing of problems at Senacre. The staff of the school had for many years devoted themselves to becoming a good secondary modern school with well tuned systems, structure and teachers in place that ensured good quality programmes of studies for the slower learning child. The staff were very well settled, had a real sense of belonging and purpose and were well respected for what they were perceived to do by the community. But by 1984 the first winds of change were already whipping up pressures and changes were underway that were to dominate my time in the school and take the school to the very brink of closure. In simple terms, the local community was happy that Senacre was a good enough secondary modern school. They were not convinced that the school could provide the routes that they were offered of a selective place at 13 and they were now constantly being reminded by other secondary schools that they had considerable choice in selecting a secondary school that met their need.

That was a mixture of cool calculation, based on a clear educational rationale set in a pragmatic political (little p) sense of the circumstances in which the school found itself. Three weeks into his headship an entry in the logbook looks at Thameside educationally:

> Private thoughts might be that this scheme of transfer at 13+ is at the most difficult age for those who go and in particular for those who remain.

It was the numbers problem the third head faced but in an even more threatening climate. As with most large housing estates teenage young men and women grew up and left. Birth rates dropped. In absolute numbers there was a marked decline. That fickle element 'reputation' was weighted heavily against the school simply because of where it was located. And like many reputations it lasted a long time, not always deservedly. The transport problem remained. Other schools had begun to recruit in Senacre's previous patch, and all this was against a constant stream of announcements by the government about parental choice. As the head saw it:

> Senacre was relying on the scraps of numbers when other schools had taken their fill and with general falling numbers in Maidstone, the scraps were falling fast.

So dealing with recruitment of pupils was the essential task the new head set himself. He did so with a different style of leadership which was deployed with great energy, as a senior colleague described his beginning.

> This was a man of enormous charisma, vision and energy. During his first month in office, he interviewed each member of staff about their role in the school. Initially their interviews were viewed with apprehension and suspicion, but it soon became clear that the head wanted to get to know his staff and wanted to listen to what they had to say. From the outset, teamwork was stressed. – this was to be no didactic leader.

Or as another put it reflecting on those interviews:

> I found Andrew Parsons a very likeable person who really cared for his staff and was interested in them as individuals.

Changing the context for curriculum change

This head had a very clear view about what had to happen to the curriculum. It needed to take more account of the world the school lived in, and he set about it in earnest. First the school had to begin to think about itself differently.

It would be fair to say that the school had hardly helped itself. My new colleagues had a very real sense of vocation and displayed huge commitment to their work. They were aware that numbers were falling fast, but they didn't see that they were in any way part of the problem or that they had many of the solutions in their hands ... My task in arriving at the school in my late thirties was to identify and build on the strengths so that the people of south Maidstone had to learn to trust us to meet the needs of all their children. We had to learn to open ourselves up and to sell ourselves to the wider community.

And they did it. Proudly the head says 'The reality that within four years we would grow our intake numbers towards being "full" again at 210 was a tremendous witness to the strength of purpose of my colleagues'.

Curriculum change to contribute to that wider cause had to be tackled, while the department was prodding LEAs to be more active in engaging with curriculum matters in schools. Accountability was becoming a serious issue. Time for national consultation seeking a national consensual approach to curriculum change was shortening fast. And as the head began to buckle down to the task one senior staff member recalls:

When Andrew Parsons began to work with the staff to manage change one wise old teacher remarked dryly, 'Werner (the second head) in slow motion'.

But first there was uniform again. The previous reforms did not seem to have lasted very well. The head records his visits to the school before taking up his appointment:

It was perhaps that very commitment to teaching that had blinded some colleagues to the dress code adopted by many students at the school ... it was clear that student dress had been well modified by many of the senior students to include rolled up jeans, red football socks and what were then known as 'bovver boots'. It was clear that any potential parent would have some difficulty in seeing beyond the facade of dress and while I have some reservations about the importance of school uniform, I have also been clear that if a school has a uniform policy it needed to respected by all. I was also clear that in an area where every school had a uniform policy, it was extremely difficult to stand alone.

Letters went to parents and on the first day of term:

With one exception every student was smart and presented an image of the student body that no longer conveyed the threatening aggression associated with their former dress. There was one stand off with one student which lasted until first morning break ... with that broken, the school could settle down to its main function and we were no longer considered the scruffs of Maidstone

... In many ways, the action over school dress conveyed to colleagues and the community much of my education philosophy.

Clearly the school uniform regime established at the beginning of the former headship had not worked in the longer term.

With punctuality and outward appearance dealt with, the school did indeed settle down to its main function, student learning. The scene was set for curriculum change. But in the strange way that sometimes adversity can be turned to advantage, strikes hit the school within days of the head arriving but:

> The professionalism of the staff was always evident. We had our action days but they were well managed and often gave me the chance to meet with whole year groups in the hall. We came through the experience with mutual respect and with a united sense of purpose that together we could achieve much. That experience emphasized the mutual recognition that we had to change, created a climate where the concept of a 'managed school' could be opened up in a way that rarely needed to be confrontational.

Perhaps the head is playing down his difficulties. As one senior colleague observed:

> it was a dreadful time to be a teacher at the chalk face. In this loadsamoney era, teachers' pay had slipped far below that of similar professionals. Our local MP described teachers as 'lazy and incompetent'. We had a contract thrust on us specifying the hours we should work (most of us already worked much longer hours). Not unexpectedly, the response from the floor was 'sod it then'. I felt sorry for the head (and I know he felt sorry for himself) having to promote change in a wretched atmosphere of unrest that was none of his doing.

That kind of intervention was unlikely to promote the changes the government was seeking. And for curriculum development as the essential means of improving the quality of education offered, it was almost as if the centre was unaware of how masochistically and self-destructively it was behaving. This was intervention at its worst.

Preparing for curriculum change

Change had to begin in the classroom. First the head had to get rid of the idea that the teacher was still deemed to be 'king' in the 'kingdom' and the head visited classrooms by invitation ' ... when I walked into a classroom the teacher would stop teaching and would not expect to begin again until I had left'. He goes on to say:

> my first visits to classrooms confirmed two features of education in the eighties. The first was that there was some absolutely outstanding teaching going on in

isolation. The second was that the environment in which teachers sought to teach and children to learn was unbelievably drab. I don't think that Senacre had seen much fresh paint since its opening.

For the first he had to find ways of getting collaboration between individual subject specialists to replace 'teaching in isolation'. For the second he recruited willing staff, persuaded the LEA to provide funds for buying paint and brushes, rolled up his sleeves and got down to painting and decorating. This had happened before, but this time it had a strong drive behind it:

> Within a year we had some parts of the school looking worthy of being places of learning and our falling rolls provided space to revamp other teaching areas to provide computer suites. With well attended open evenings we were able to celebrate with our students, their parents and prospective parents much of the pride in good teaching which had always been a feature of the school.

That cherished pride led the head to reflect on the huge contemporary emphasis on measured performance that has become an increasing feature of the school over the last ten years:

> today there is a huge contrast with my work at Senacre. The school, in common with all Maidstone High Schools took its responsibilities towards the selection process at 13+ very seriously and took considerable care to ensure that our judgements were secure and defendable. We entered students for the whole range of public examinations at 16+, but I felt no obsession with results and certainly there was no attempt to collate and compare our results with those of our neighbouring schools.

So the scene was set for a 'managed school' to take a grip on what is too easily thought of as the curriculum: what goes on in explicit learning and teaching. But as with the first two, the curriculum was thought of explicitly as how the school as an entity set about providing for its learning and teaching. Punctuality, school dress policy, premises which spoke of a serious approach to teaching and learning, all helped propel the drive for curriculum change, underpinned as it was with a collaborative approach.

Mechanisms for curriculum change

The logbook entry for 5 January 1984, the head's first staff meeting includes, 'and explained the introduction of a school notice scheme'. This developed into a regular news sheet which served as a communication system to keep staff informed about the various doings in and around the school. An entry for July 1985 reads:

> My last entry into this log. It is now increasingly obvious that our weekly 'school notes' are a very accurate reflection of what is going on within the

school and will be a very adequate log of the school. In future a copy of the school log will be the annual collection of school notes held in file in the office.

From the beginning 'isolation' was high on the head's list of changes. Converting isolation into collaboration was a prerequisite for introducing the necessary changes to the curriculum. The school notes system became a vehicle for pursuing that goal, a tool to encourage collaboration. Like the first two heads the fourth cherished the freedom for innovation:

> that very freedom gave the school enormous scope in developing and experimenting with the school curriculum. In essence, good schools were constantly involved in asking questions about what was taught and thinking teachers had always reflected upon their teaching styles. Senacre had a well established history in curriculum innovation and I inherited a curriculum structure that had been well honed over many years. The concept of a national curriculum with tight guidelines in a wide range of subjects was still a million miles way but Senacre had never in its recent years been at the extremes of curriculum development.

How to use the freedom was the question.

> My senior colleagues could offer me all the experience that I could hope for. I also needed energy and senior colleagues who were prepared to break out from the traditional role of leadership as a start. I found what I needed in three colleagues who were already fixtures at the school … all had proven themselves time and again to children, colleagues, parents and the wider community. They were now to impact in a way that would free me to look at curriculum structures and develop our relations with our partner primary schools and the wider community.

Initially this did not go down well with some staff.

> Universal wry staffroom perception that there were 'too many chiefs and not enough Indians' … how was it that a school of 650 pupils had functioned well under a head, a deputy and a senior teacher, but now with around 850 pupils required the equivalent of four deputies plus hangers on?

It was always thus. However necessary, change is always hard to steer so that the changes result in what they are intended to achieve. In this case some at least of the changes worked. Not all staff were as critical.

> My impressions of his leadership was in many ways similar to that of a managing director … as legislation, budgets staffing etc. took up so much time. The senior management team (SMT) were each given the task of looking

after one section of the school's daily running schemes – and reporting back to him at regular meetings.

One of the three was appointed as a director of studies. This enabled the head to try to extend his influence through an agreed understanding of the role of head of department.

> Some had a very tight control over their department, knew what was being taught in each year group, made themselves responsible for the day-to-day discipline in their areas and were constantly pushing for more and better resources for themselves and their colleagues. There were others who had very little idea of what their immediate colleagues were doing and saw the role of head of department as recognition for their good teaching and loyalty to the school over many years.

He issued a three-page discussion paper on the role of a head of department at Senacre High School, listing items which he hoped would be seen as a 'compromise between the idealist and the prescriptive position'. As with the more senior appointments this was resented, only more so by some. The problem was that resources were in short supply so while tightening up departmental procedures was reasonable, even welcome, it all felt like dumping additional burdens on hard-working staff. Place those inevitable tensions against the impression of teaching going on in isolation from others, and the role of the director of studies begins to take shape.

Curriculum refocused

The very freedom prized by the head over curriculum matters, could lead to a lack of coherence across the range of subjects unless very firm guidelines ran down to heads of departments and so to their staff. So the varied interpretations by heads of department posed awkward curricular questions.

> All students studied mathematics, English, science and technology, but what they studied prior to and outside their public examination courses was often left to the whim of individual teachers or in isolation by departments.

Quickly he introduced a senior school curriculum review in the form of a questionnaire with six headings and the instruction 'Please look at your senior school curriculum in terms of:

Our agreed aims of the school.
The range of pupils taught.
Any known proposal for 16+.
The style of teaching used.
The place of your subject within the senior school timetable.

Heads of Department were given six weeks to make their returns. Simultaneously working parties were set up on aesthetics, social/moral/careers education, pre-vocational education/work experience, leisure activities and the Hargreaves Report, on which more later. Each posed issues which the head did not regard as being satisfactorily dealt with and asked for suggestions. Those working parties also had six weeks to complete their task.

He also thought that the curriculum was overcrowded. The range of options was reduced. Humanities came down to a single period. In January 1985 the revised timetable was set out in every detail in another paper, which would be in operation from September, the beginning of the head's second year. Curriculum development was going full blast.

The onset of GCSE sharpened things further. Expectations were lifted for both staff and students. A survey showed it. One girl completing the course in 1988, the first year that GCSE was offered as a public examination, made that clear.

> In some circumstances I feel that the new GCSE exam has affected the way that I (and other members of the school) have been taught in the classroom. For instance, I feel we have been given a lot of work to do. This is classroom in school and at home.

Work overload gets a drubbing. Assignments pile up as different teachers set them and when students made complaint she says:

> I find that the remark that comes back from the teacher is 'poor you' or 'well it will keep you busy won't it?' As they do this, we poor kids don't get any freedom to ourselves so it is really pointless and a waste of time for us having half terms and holidays.

Despite that rather extreme way of putting it she was glad of the result.

> I think that I am glad that in English I am being entered a 100 per cent course work with no exam at the end if it. I also feel that we should just have course work with no exam at the end in all of our lessons.

She goes on to put forward a range of education and psychological reasons for that view which would not be misplaced in any current argument about the problems of standards. Another refers to problems not of their making:

> In geography our work and field work books were late in coming so we got behind on writing up about our field work. A lot of people got behind because of this also some class work.

Not that that meant that students thought their learning opportunities were reduced. One girl writing at the end of the GCSE course said:

I feel that both boys and girls have been given equal opportunities in their course work. This is because at the end of the third year we were given a sheet which had different options on it which we could take if we wanted. On this sheet were new subjects we had never done before. Girls could take woodwork, metalwork etc. (the subjects boys took), and the boys could take cookery and other subjects girls take.

She went on to give an interesting commentary on why boys did not take child care or typing because of a stereotyped view of girls as potential mothers who stay at home, adding 'I think that really in this case, boys not doing childcare and typing is really the school's fault' (DR).

Referring to what was perceived as the head's view of the curriculum, one head of department thought the arrival of GCSE was not all clear gain. He commented on reduced time for integrated study followed by some of those who found considerable difficulty with formal classroom work:

I think probably the head began to see that the way to go was along the more traditional route offered by GCSE so that we drew back from the integrated approach.

Indeed the replacement of GCE and CSE with GCSE encouraged such a shift. Inevitably at classroom level, that was a step towards a narrowing curriculum.

By the time those students were writing those remarks the director of studies had been in post for four years. Re-focusing was well advanced. The head, good at delegating, let the director of studies get on with tackling some of the flaws in curriculum provision, but always with regular reporting sessions so that he knew what was going on:

Since much of my time was devoted to changing culture, building reputation and fighting battles with the LEA, significant curriculum changes were limited. In part this was because schools had moved on from some of the wilder excesses of the past, in particular because I was happy that our children received a well taught and balanced curriculum. The National Curriculum was a feature of the future. The authority had developed an aims and objectives document but heads were quick to discover that such documents when completed received little more than a polite glance and were then filed away and the document received the derision it deserved. The lack of a co-ordinated thinking at LEA level about the secondary curriculum, or indeed any curriculum, would hardly be a surprise to those running schools at that time and contrasts so much with today where the local authority is expected to have a thorough knowledge of the performance of each of its schools and to be able to employ strategies to assist schools that appear to have lost direction.

That view of the LEAs aims and objectives speaks directly to the pressure Sir

Keith Joseph was applying to LEAs through his consultative papers, urging schools to be more active in curriculum matters and devote greater attention to standards. As an example of an LEA attempting to intervene effectively, Kent was not very encouraging. However the arena of freedom for designing school based curricula as in the past was being hedged-in ever more restrictively.

Curriculum expanded

Nevertheless that continuing freedom enabled the head to make significant changes:

> The two areas where I was able to make significant curriculum impact was in the senior school recreational programmes and in implementing the first freedoms offered by the introduction of the Technical and Vocational Initiative (TVEI).

On the first he stated the following:

> I had long been convinced that general programmes of physical education for our older children were dire and served only to convince girls in particular that they should give up on any physical recreational activities was soon as they could. I was convinced that we could do better. The message of the eighties about more and more leisure time contrasted with the usual diet of PE where the fit triumphed and the meek inherited boredom and developed a distaste of all things sporting. Once again I was blessed with a curriculum leader of the very highest caliber … put together a whole afternoon for students in Years 10 and 11 that provided a very wide range of recreational and sporting opportunities. I was convinced that everyone could find some valuable learning experience that they could take into their future life. I taught sailing, learnt to wind surf and to ski. Others might find satisfaction in dance or drama … it gave me enormous satisfaction.

That is a telling example of how to use the freedom to enhance and extend learning opportunities for students. To block off one-tenth of the school's weekly timetable for two years of students was nothing less than a massive innovative change. Curriculum development was alive and well. The widening concept did not give up.

The head comments that he does not know if the programme continued. The odd thing about that remark is that more or less the same programme was running in the school during most of its first seventeen years. It is as if there had been an interregnum to re-establish the reputation of the school through reverting to a traditional form of curriculum before imagination could be brought into play again.

TVEI was a different matter. It was a huge driving force for curriculum change and well supported through the local authority and government. It was a programme introduced by the Manpower Services Committee when David Young, now Lord

Young, was its chairman. At the turn of the decade there was rising concern about the gap between academic and practical skills forms of learning which led to challenges to the traditional structure of the curriculum. The Schools Council produced its 'The practical curriculum' just before the secretary of state closed it down. And David Young persuaded Keith Joseph to back the Technical and Vocational Initiative which was then funded lavishly. It was run through the Manpower Services Commission (MSC). Unfortunately as with so many government initiatives, the MSC had fastened on to a vital element, in this case the gap between academic and vocational learning, without having any coherent concept of how the initiative might influence the curriculum as a whole or a policy to implement it. So TVEI led to only patchy developments where enterprising schools and imaginative teachers seized the opportunities presented by the funds available. Senacre was one such school:

> When schools became aware that the TVEI initiative was to put real money into our hands, it quickly gained support from heads ... a few tens of thousands of pounds might now seem small beer ... it felt like manna from heaven.

The first computer suites were created and equipped to enhance the technology rooms. Another first class curriculum leader, widely respected in the area, devised programmes which in time led to the school becoming a technology college. And if the head was dubious about the intended overarching aims of TVEI, he grasped anything which would benefit the school. Additionally, all in the line with his collaborative way of working he saw great benefit:

> It forced secondary schools to work together in consortia to put forward proposals for spending and that in turn brought the school management teams and heads of departments together to talk curriculum.

This was another example of how a permissive form of benign external intervention in the curriculum could be positive and successful. It had the particular merit of encouraging collaboration with other schools and colleges. For TVEI however, it was an intervention at the invitation of the school. It was not a top-down imposition.

However it is important to record that Brian Nicholson, the next chairman of the MSC, argued strongly against the National Curriculum when it came, and for the partnership exemplified by TVEI. It retained the trust of teachers and a vision which integrated the 'academic' with the 'vocational' which even now remains to be realized. In these terms the National Curriculum arrested curriculum development disastrously.

Another initiative was of a quite different order. It was the result of a controlled experiment of something similar to the interdisciplinary studies introduced during the second headship. And for the same reasons, the head relied on his earlier experiment with having Year 7 pupils taught for their core subjects by one member of staff.

I was convinced that too many children found the sudden change in learning styles very difficult to cope with and that the transfer year was often wasted whilst children adjusted. The results were interesting and supported my view with scores in mathematics and English being on average higher in the experimental groups than in the control groups. On arrival at Senacre I remained convinced that this was the way forward, but encountered the same problems as in the experiment. There were no colleagues with the wide range of teaching skills and subject knowledge to move forward with the initiative and with falling rolls we were not able to recruit a number of colleagues with good primary experience. A number of us led by the director of studies were convinced that we needed to work with Year 7 children on basic learning skills. If a feature of primary education was the strong link between the class teacher and the child, then in one sense it was also its potential weakness. Most teachers have a preferred teaching style and we noted for some time at Senacre that many children struggled for a while with a wide range of teachers who delivered their teaching in a variety of ways. A secondary teacher might, for example, ask students to read two or three pages of text, and to make notes in preparation for the next lesson. An interesting enough approach for those who knew how to read for a purpose and to identify and extract the salient points. But for many of our children an exercise too far. The director quickly put together a programme and all Year 7 children had a lesson per week on study skills.

The impact of what the head describes as his own and his colleagues' limited skills in teaching the subject restricted what was achieved. But the underlying pedagogical principles were a fully worked out version of what had been tried some thirty years before and for the same reasons, improving transition. First there was mixed ability teaching and then came interdisciplinary studies during the second headship. This time there was thoughtful preparation of a programme which could be handled by existing staff. The benefits were wide ranging.

It gave a clear enough message to our primary colleagues that we were taking transition seriously. When they were persuaded to visit Senacre and saw for themselves that the school was a place of quality learning, the battle for hearts and minds was won. I knew that primary heads had enormous influence over the choice of secondary schools and I knew that our primary partners would now be carrying a positive message.

The deputy agrees:

Links with primary schools were developed and became very strong. Our view was that those headteachers of schools working with us were more likely to encourage their pupils to choose Senacre when making a choice for secondary schools.

But that was not the end of it. A thorough going consultation programme was set up. Parents of first year pupils were asked a series of questions; their answers were reproduced in an attractive publication called 'As others see us (the unexpurgated version)' and made available to parents of the next year's incoming pupils. To a professional the questions and answers are obvious and taken for granted by any good form tutor. But that misses the point. This programme was the flip side of the initiative in the taught course on basic skills, a deliberate attempt to induct into the school young people leaving primary schools, helping them adjust quickly to a different learning environment while at the same time seeking to secure parental support both for their children and the school. The introduction to the pamphlet included:

> It is from a position of honest intent and confidence that we invite comment on a child's first four weeks at Senacre. As you read the parents' comments you will see ... that this confidence, arising from the relatively intense scrutiny of individuals necessary at induction, is justified. The comments are at worst, anxious, at best glowing.

And then almost teasingly, feeling for support later on in the school life of a son or daughter, many of the parents would have older pupils in the school:

> Would a relevant questionnaire in Years 2, 3, 4, or 5 be offered with the same confidence, or elicit the same interest and involvement from parents?

That was curriculum support with a human face, offered almost seductively.

A similar document called 'Welcome to our school', with a set of comments from first year pupils complemented 'As others see us'. So parents of incoming pupils had in their hands what other parents and their children had to say about the difficult and often traumatic transition from primary to secondary schools.

> Rumours – true and false – 'I heard that it was very big with many corridors but it isn't as bad as that'. 'I heard that you might get thrown into the biology pool. Until my English teacher told me that we hadn't got a biology pool I thought it was true'. 'I heard that they had a good sports hall and sports equipment. Yes this was true'.

There are comments on every subject:

> Mathematics: 'I thought algebra was horrible but now I think it's great'. 'Our teacher is lively and sometimes makes things a joke. She explains things properly and makes sure you know what you are doing'. Music: 'Music is probably my favourite lesson. Mr Hall gives us a subject and with his help we can make good songs and music'. '... Senacre has a massive selection of instruments which cater for everyone'. 'English: English is very different.

You do fun things and you don't work out of a book all the time'. And homework: 'I think it's good but I don't like doing it'. 'I think homework is a good idea because it helps you use libraries etc. and you can work at your own speed'. And 'Take our advice. Come and enjoy yourself. It may be a big school but you will find your way around in no time. The teachers don't ask you to do the impossible, they say "Do what you can" and "The first day is bound to be nerve wracking but not to worry. Here are lots of people to help and guide you around if you get lost"'.

The deputy saw that style of consultation as critical:

> Market research generated mostly by the director of studies, provided valuable information upon which management decisions would be made. I believe it also gave those being asked questions a feeling of awareness in the shaping of the school. It was the 'someone's prepared to listen to my view' syndrome.

What this approach to first year pupils amounts to is playing to a version of the curriculum which sees the school and its surrounding community comprehensively, embracing the concept of learning as a collaborative enterprise. It is curriculum development going full bore.

In passing it is worth noting that in 2004 the government and the Department for Education and Skills is still grappling with the same problem. Its efforts to raise standards in primary schools have been quite successful. Standards of the first year in secondary schools remain unsatisfactorily low in many schools. Essentially it is the transition problem all over again.

Putting together the introduction of a recreational leisure programme designed for growing young people, the Technical and Vocational Initiative at one end of the school, and basic skills at the entry point to the school, meant there was a pincer grip being established on the curriculum as a whole.

There are two other interesting aspects to the refocusing. Both were to do with recognition. The school had never had a prize day. One was now introduced, not as an annual event but as the culmination of a reward system which operated throughout the school as a way of acknowledging achievements of every kind. Celebrities were persuaded to attend and a good time was had by all.

The other was quite different. Talking of the head's approach to learning and the problems of providing sufficient stimuli to develop motivation, a member of staff recalls:

> I always remember the head inisting suddenly, that all our children were to be called students. It raised expectations at a stroke. It was incredible.

The deputy says 'that stuck with me for years'. However all this did not raise them quite enough. The head tried very hard to create a sixth form but it never really materialized.

Curriculum expanded further

There were three other developments which affected both the content of the curriculum and the pedagogies deployed. The first was the appointment of a deputy head from outside with the responsibility for pastoral care. The second was the introduction of records of achievement which in effect began a long term staff development exercise. The third was management of equal opportunities.

Speaking of his new responsibilities, the deputy head says:

> It was clear to me however that the pastoral curriculum was almost non-existent and it seemed that various attempts had previously been made to introduce something to the school in some way. It was also clear that that introduction would be of benefit to students but that it would have to be well co-ordinated and managed in some way to be a success.
>
> There was a good pastoral structure in place with heads of upper and lower school, heads of year and deputy heads of year. Thus the team of middle managers was well established and I became the leader of the team as a young and new face with the notion that the school should introduce a pastoral curriculum which was planned, co-ordinated, managed through a taught lesson delivered by individual form tutors. There was some evidence of a taught programme already in existence but it was clear that most tutors felt little or no ownership of the programme. Consequently it became immediately clear that major changes would be difficult to manage ... there was some hindrance. It ranged from a combination of staff working hard in their area of expertise and not putting pastoral curriculum high on a large agenda. There was of course some justification for this resistance since some previous attempts at developments in this area had seemed to fail.

Despite being given a free hand he found developments were slow and only some were successful.

> Those tended to be those where a group of staff took ownership of an initiative and devised and taught the programme themselves. It seemed we could generate some enthusiasm for curriculum change in short bursts but that it would not always last. In any case it did not last for long as a result of government pressure. As demands for evidence of standards and accountability rose higher, so the importance of the pastoral curriculum declined with ever greater demands made on the timetable and the taught period was dropped.

Before 1988 that was a warning sign for what was to come.

However pastoral care came in down a different route via records of achievement. One of the first tasks that the head set his staff was to work out what the Hargreaves Report suggested the school might do. 'Improving schools' published in 1983 (London) was the report of the Committee on the Curriculum and Organisation of Secondary Schools chaired by David Hargreaves. A working party chaired by the deputy head was set up and again was given six weeks to complete its report. That was half term of the head's first term. It considered recommendations which ran the entire gamut of life in a school, added recommendations for school itself and published its report for circulation among the staff in November 1984. The section on parents laid heavy emphasis on home–school liaison, as 'parental commitment is the cornerstone of a school's success', and spelt out what that meant a school should do. It had a section on transition from primary to secondary school which was in line with the head's thinking.

One recommendation was that half-termly units of work rather than full-term units should be introduced to the upper school as a more conducive rhythm of working for growing adolescents, and that schools should develop a form of leaving certificate as a record of achievement which included extra-curricular, out of school activities and personal qualities. The working party was charged with producing an operational plan.

A pilot project was launched for Year 9, the 'doldrums' year as it was referred to during the previous headship. Each of the quotations which follow came from a report on records of achievement (ROA) by the director of studies, issued to all staff.

> Year 9 was included in this scheme in an attempt to inject vitality and give a fresh perspective to work in a year where it was felt that many students began to be jaded and lack a sense of purpose.

The purposes of ROA itself show why that decision was made.

> The purpose of these assessments, as well as being diagnostic and building a comprehensive picture of students' abilities in relation to subject skills, was also an attempt to raise aspiration and inculcate the motive to succeed. We had all recognized the psychological truants in our midst – present in flesh but absent in spirit. Traditionally, most teachers had paid little attention to what students thought of their curriculum. Teachers were there to teach and students were there to learn – a one way process.
>
> Since effective pastoral care is complementary to curriculum development, form tutors were involved in discussion and developing skills of self-assessment with the students in their group.

Anything which might re-enliven school experience after the 13+ transfer for the 'doldrums' year 9 was worth trying to offset the unhappiness for many at losing friends, feeling something of a failure, with an overall feeling of discouragement.

As with all innovations, refinements had to be made. Tensions rose, not least because an evaluation showed an intolerable additional workload for staff.

> Attitudes to assessment were changed and developed, however, virtually by brute force. Individual discussions with students during lessons had enormous

implications for classroom management, teaching strategies and the management of time.

Staff were encouraged not to become obsessed in their anxiety, with the notion that all target setting, all assessment and all feedback had to be on a one-to-one basis. There was continued anxiety in some areas about moving from traditional assessment and implementing teaching strategies which emphasized product rather than process. Course work had to be rationalized to avoid 'piles of work' to be marked, and overloading students with a collection of assignments set by an assortment of departments. As one at the receiving end of ROA put it mildly:

> ROAs occupied quite a considerable amount of time. Sheets of paper (per) pupil, logging their efforts, achievement attitudes, competency and so on ... short of weighing them, we tried everything ... they made us think more consciously of the pupils and what we were doing for them. The problem with ROAs was that if they were to be meaningful – consultation was required. The question was when. During lessons with the pupils on a face to face approach inevitably meant that teaching time was lost. Of course it could be argued that consultation is a means of teaching.

And so it was. Clearly ROAs were doing an important curriculum job. But:

> So there we were working our socks off, reeling from change but the work of formative ROAs was being a unifying, sensible stabilizer. Unlike many of the directives aimed at us in what had appeared to have been a relentless onslaught, at least ROA could be recognized as supreme common sense. Having visited the University of Hindsight, I am astonished that we had managed to stagger through a professional life as educators without embracing the principle of explaining to students in advance what they were going to learn, why and how they were to learn and how they would be assessed. By involving students in the assessment process they are reviewing and consolidating content. Students' self-portrayal and self-appraisal are vitally important educational experiences and give valuable information to the teacher on the effectiveness of the work set and teaching styles adopted. It also required more than ever before, thorough preparation and forward planning on the teacher's part.

So records of achievement is an example, perhaps the first, of a system imposed on schools by central government, which was intended explicitly to be a significant step towards improving the quality of learning in schools. The fact that it led to that kind of pedagogical thinking and reflection in Senacre shows how such an intervention could be exploited where there was energy, wit and will to do so. The working party and the style of collaboration between teachers which flowed from it in seeking to implement ROA was consistent with the overall intentions of the head for developing the school.

And this time Kent education committee gets a credit notice.

It is encouraging that Kent has nailed its colours firmly to the mast in supporting the development of ROA. The county has produced an impressive blue hardbacked folder to contain the summative record.

As with TVEI, ROA offered potential benefits to Senacre which were grasped firmly and converted into higher quality opportunities for pupils' learning.

The philosophy of formative ROA has given us the security and vision not to take comfortable cover but to tackle what has been aimed at us and harness what is good. We know from experience the efficacy of a teacher's ability to share rather than impose. We know from experience that the behaviour that most explicitly demonstrates that a teacher really cares about a student and respects his or her contributions is the art of listening to what a student has to say. We also, as a school, accept that contrary to popular opinion, to teach informally is more difficult than to teach well formally. It requires a special sort of teacher to use informal methods effectively – one who is dedicated, highly organized, able to plan ahead and willing to spend a great deal of time in preparatory work.

But this was not a one shot exercise. How the ROA panned out, how it affected teachers and students was kept under continual review. Another document is headed 'Concerned with the impact of 100 per cent course work on pupils and teachers'. In six pages it goes through short term goals, marking, the factors behind the problem of assessment in a traditional setting, developing self-assessment, peer assessment, ending up with 'Is there life after marking'. Each section sets out the issue, analyses it, uses quotes from students and staff to highlight issues all leading to suggestions for action. There is a jokey introduction:

For records of achievement to become more than a tempest to anger, confuse or at worst drown the good ship 'Senacre departments', the attitudes of the sailors must 'suffer a sea change into something rich and strange'.

Again it was the human face on a fundamental change in curriculum practice. The first paragraph reads:

The major sea change required will be in recognizing the use of formative Records of Achievement as a process, not a product. A process designed to help pupils through their learning experience by discussion on progress, achievement and setting of learning targets. This will necessarily involve breaking down courses into shorter periods of learning to facilitate regular target setting, assessment and feedback. In many cases the work for GCSE has already begun this process but there is still a long way to go. It involves changes in teaching and learning styles with a more pupil centred approach. I don't believe that we have to become obsessed by the notion that all target setting, all assessment and all feedback has to be on a one to one basis. What is essential, is that all teachers accept that through involving pupils in the assessment process, pupils are reviewing and consolidating content. The formative record of achievement to motivate pupils, should give them the incentive of knowing how they have succeeded to date.

That is tackling head-on the pedagogical component in curriculum.

The third area of further curricular expansion was in response to the DES paper, 'The management of equal opportunities'. An internal paper begins thus.

Pupils who have adopted stereotyped roles do not readily recognize the need for change and many teachers feel safer with the status quo. There is a danger of equal opportunities activists being dismissed as feminist. It is too enormously difficult for all of us to step outside our own conditioning.

There was nothing very striking about that. But then:

when we are to embark on any equal opportunities initiative we have to have a clearly established starting point otherwise it will be difficult to measure progress. Data gathering for each project should precede activity. (Option choices, examination entries, jobs obtained by leavers, type of FE sought.)

There was a six-page series of quotes from students documenting their views on equal opportunities and gender differences. They established that there was no feeling among the student body that there was not full equality of opportunity in that all options were open to all. Against that background:

What we have to address is what pupils should know, be able to do and what attitudes they will need to start their post-school lives on an equal – or potentially equal – footing. We have to provide educational experiences which positively influence and act upon the interests of both boy and girl pupils.

Curricular thinking primed with vitality. Its formal provision was being underpinned by far wider considerations. And if some can read the expectations implied as being hopelessly high, by seeking to raise them through carefully worked out policies based on evidence there was the possibility that practice could improve.

Curriculum troubleshooter

By this time, 1988, for the first time pupils were sitting GCSE examinations at the end of a two-year course and entries were full to overflowing. The head records:

> By the beginning of the academic year 1987–8 I felt the school to be in good spirits. Not only were we full in Years 7–9, our reputation in the locality was such that people from other parts of Maidstone were now seeing us as the first choice school. I could not have asked for more from my colleagues. They tolerated this relatively young head, put up with naivety and were usually prepared to have a go at anything asked of them. We were aware that our success meant that other schools were struggling, but we didn't see that as our problem.

What more could the head have asked of himself? But then:

> When, at Christmas time I was asked to visit the area education office for a meeting with the area officer, I was totally unprepared for the news that the authority had resolved that one of the Maidstone schools would close, and that they were going out on consultation over the closure of Senacre

His reaction was as follows:

> On reflection I ought to have seen it coming. Did members (elected county councillors) have up-to-date data on school numbers? I doubt it. There was a sense of remoteness from our county headquarters and I was already too aware that where the county sought to close a school they often did so in the most impoverished part of the town. A sense of least resistance.

I returned to the school, sat down in my office and cried. Even now, fifteen years later, the feelings of pain and injustice burn deep. I had arrived at the school in 1984 and told my colleagues in no uncertain terms that we had to turn the school around or face the reality of closure. Three and a half years later my colleagues had given me everything. We were the strongest recruiting high school in the city and we were marked for closure and I had to tell them. How would they react? Would all that hard work have been in vain? I ought to have known better.

The deputy remembers it, almost defiantly.

> I was there when he broke the news and witnessed the tears, but knew with that head and team of staff around him working so hard and successfully, and with the support of primary colleagues, there was no way that the school would close. I had confidence in this man.

It is hard to read those words without a sense of boiling, furious anger, incomprehension even. Local government officers are not renowned for their sensitivity, nor is central government for that matter. But as an example of crass mismanagement to say nothing of its disregard of educational realities on the ground, it would be hard to beat. But behind that consultation was the possibility of raising huge sums of money with the sale of the school site for commercial purposes. As with the Thameside Scheme it did not seem that educational considerations came first. Now there is a huge Safeway next door to the school. But the authority did not know what it had taken on. The school ran it out of town.

This attempted intervention ran into the ground.

> If my colleagues had shown energy and a willingness to think in different ways in their day-to-day teaching and many had, it was nothing when compared with the efforts they put in to ensure that Senacre would survive. The staff owned the campaign. They developed the logo: Senacre Alive for Education (SAFE) (*see* Appendix 5). It was both an affirmation of what was and what was to be. If the Valentine cards delivered by hand to councillors right across the county was a useful tool to awaken some to the reality of the school, a series of public meetings enthusiastically attended and supported in each of our feeder primary schools gave a very public picture of the support that the school now enjoyed in the community.

As the deputy saw it:

> The campaign was such a force for uniting the staff, students and parents with one aim – to keep Senacre alive.

Radio 4, the chair of governors who was a county councillor, MPs, put increasing pressure on the LEA until it accepted 'that Senacre would continue to provide for the needs of its community'. That was a feeble euphemism for saying 'Right, you've beaten us'. The close connections with primary schools and parents, the strong parent teacher association added weight and turned up the volume of protests and objections being ever more public. Governors had 327 letters of protest to read before making their own submission. At one stage the head was summoned to the area office and warned off. As the head remarks contemptuously, 'a little threat to a condemned man'. It took a year out of his four year headship to escape the gallows. The head, the school itself, its governors, the community had played the authority at its own game and won. It was collaboration which produced the victory.

And that collaboration was the fruit of all the curricular efforts over the preceding four years. There could not have been any idea at the time of what would be the wider consequences of the attempt to shift teaching from isolation to collaboration, of paying such closer attention to transition from primary to secondary school, of putting such energy into developing records of achievement, pastoral care and equal opportunities. But without them it is a fair guess that the Senacre story would have come to an abrupt end. As it is, the story is a fine example of the significance of seeing the curriculum as the embodiment of the school's collective activities in their entirety, as a human endeavour by staff to create and support a place of learning for growing young people.

What fuelled the anger and outrage was the sense that academic achievements were being ignored by the local authority. The head of English had long experience of CSE and served for years as an examiner for GCSE. In retrospect he considers that the CSE grades 1 and 2 achieved by students in Senacre 'would all pass handsomely nowadays with Bs and Cs in GCSE', remembering that at the time CSE grade 1 equalled a GCE O level pass. This happened in a school which was overflowing with students while its neighbouring school was half empty.

But there were plusses for curricular planning as well as all the obvious minuses. According to the deputy:

> The threat of closure helped Senacre to focus on those issues it needed to maintain in order to continue to encourage large numbers of students to apply for admission. It also helped us to think about what issues needed to be addressed for the future but at the same time it distracted us from putting all our efforts into learning and teaching.

There is a delicious double irony in the story. The head's high profile in this very public fight led to him being appointed to a senior post in the LEA. He did not last long. He says 'I enjoyed my three years at Headquarters and was able to play a small part in modernizing a well meaning but confused inspection and support team'. The disdain is clear. His heart remained in schools and he went as head to a large comprehensive in the west country in 1991. But before he did, as a Kent Inspector he opposed strongly and vehemently moves by his successor to take Senacre into grant maintained status. Having saved the school he found it going down a path he resisted. He was now poacher turned gamekeeper. On that he lost as the next chapter will show. But reflecting on his time at Senacre the head writes:

> I am not sure how others will see my days at Senacre. Some may feel that I found a school under-managed and left it over-managed. Looking back I wouldn't disagree. I had to learn to lead and had to overcome those who wanted to carry on in their own isolationist way. ... I had the joy of meeting and working with some of the most able and talented teachers that I have ever met. Together we were at the end of an age. I came into a headship at a time when teachers often taught what they wanted and taught how they wanted. They often worked in isolation and rarely reflected on their practice or worked with one another to improve their skills. By the time I arrived at Plymstock [his new headship] local management, National Curriculum and Ofsted were well entrenched and Senacre would face new challenges of public accountability.

Certainly it was 'the end of an age'. But as one age ended, a new one began. External intervention had provided a critical turning point. The need for government to become an active partner in the nation's education instead of a passive one had been understood well before Callaghan's Ruskin speech. Derek Morrell and other civil servants with HMI as independent advisors, had been worrying for years, knowing that somehow the department had to become involved with curriculum matters but were unclear about how it should be done. In those days, government was very careful of its relationships with LEAs. It was just a long time coming, that was all. From Shirley Williams through to Keith Joseph consultation remained the chosen style of finding ways to effect the changes which were considered necessary. After them it was different.

So this fourth headship at Senacre saw the ending of that style of consultation. Records of achievement allied with the shift from CSE/GCE to GCSE acted in some ways as midwife for the changes which were about to be imposed by central government. Senacre was well prepared for meeting them.

After such an experience it is no surprise to find the head writing:

> The campaign had taken away the better part of the academic year and my momentum in terms of leading the school through the changes it needed ... The school gave me the greatest pleasure and I remain for ever indebted to those who gave me the opportunity to lead it forward.

Curriculum development had thrived. It acted as a troubleshooter when the school was threatened because it was based on a whole school concept which included head, staff, students and parents. That is what gave it the strength to resist and survive. In an interesting way it was curriculum with a different kind of social purpose and a precise target. It enabled the school to accommodate all the interventions which it was about to experience, without being swamped and enveloped.

This fourth headship was also a period when external intervention both actual and potential, did spur on efforts to lift performance. But it did so in an unfortunately paradoxical way. Collaboration between schools was encouraged, even required, as through TVEI. Competition between schools for pupils was being imposed both implicitly and explicitly by the 1988 Act, and through the effect of outside interventions such as parental choice. When league tables arrived they drove competition further. The open question was and remains: How far do competition and its companion choice, serve to improve the educational opportunities available to all students in all schools? This is a highly contentious issue where gains and losses are hotly disputed. The next headship had the same conundrum to deal with.

At the end of the third headship the notional intervention account book would have registered – losses: narrowed curriculum, falling numbers; gains: secure academic structure, distinctiveness of provision for the physically disabled.

For the fourth it would read – losses: imposed contract, denigration of teachers, de-professionalizing of teachers begins, parental choice; gains: TVEI, Hargreaves and ROA, high school morale.

Chapter 6

Curriculum revolution
The fifth headship, Neil Hunter, 1988–95

Opening the discussion

Comment: Your stint there, 1988, the Baker Act. Enter the National Curriculum (NC).

Response: Right.

Comment: So you get that dumped on your head and you didn't even know what you had bought.

Response: That's right.

Question: What did that do to you?

Answer: Not a lot in the sense that most of us signed up to the National Curriculum anyway in theory and principle. We thought that a broad banded curriculum for young people was realistic. It was well on the way when I arrived. There was a fairly full diet, mathematics, English, science, technology was the thing we increased.

Comment: And you jumped on that didn't you?

Answer: Yes, we certainly did in a very big way.

Question: What did you hope it would do to the curriculum?

Answer: It was painfully obvious that to do the things you wanted, you needed revenue, and you needed as many mechanisms as possible to get it.

A different context

And that was the key to curriculum development during the fifth headship. Opportunities presented by external intervention were seized and exploited. It is almost as if the first two headships were exploring and exploiting curriculum opportunities offered by wide independence and with great freedom, while the next two headships consolidated the curriculum, albeit in quite different ways, the second with interesting new approaches but within an increasingly externally defined set of boundaries. As a senior colleague said:

> to put it crudely: the Werner years were a period of ferment and innovation, the Lynch period one of retreat and retrenchment towards the traditional. With Parsons came a further period of innovation, coinciding with the beginning

of a drive at national level to control the curriculum, which eventually would lead to the centralized model we see today.

Following on, the fifth headship saw a return to a considerable degree of independence within fixed curriculum boundaries by capitalizing on local management, the legal status of the governing body, becoming a grant maintained school and then seeking technology college status. It meant there could be curriculum innovation and development of an entirely different kind.

The route to the fifth headship was different too. Neil Hunter had come by way of Borough Road College of Education, teaching science in Bexhill while studying for an Open University degree, a Master's degree at Sussex University, and was a deputy head in Eastbourne, before moving to Senacre as a 42-year-old incumbent.

By the time the fifth headship began, Kenneth Baker had been secretary of state for two years. Like James Callaghan, but for different reasons, he was a man in a hurry. Whereas Callaghan fastened on education as a valuable way of connecting with the general public which might help stabilize his threadbare majority in the cmmons, Baker had the 1987 election staring him in the face and a brief from Margaret Thatcher, the prime minister, to do something about education. In came the National Curriculum. Consultation was over. Diktat was arriving.

Interestingly the National Curriculum bears a strong resemblance to the civil servants' 'Framework for the curriculum' which had been seen as too prescriptive. No doubt some enterprising civil servant found it in a drawer and presented it to Baker as the finished article. It meant however that HMI's framework, which was structured around key learning areas rather than subjects, leaving details for the schools to work out, went by the board. This can only be interpreted as another downgrading of teacher professionalism. Political diktat had indeed arrived.

So from 1988 onwards in short order for Senacre came the National Curriculum, local management, with the financial delegation which was at its heart, and the possibility of becoming a grant maintained school, independent of the LEA. The creation of city technology colleges as independent bodies also outside the authority of local authorities gave a spur to developing technology within Senacre's curriculum and no doubt planted a seed which grew eventually into acquiring technology college status. The first two were requirements. The third was the choice of the head. And round the corner there was the Office for Standards in Education (Ofsted). But over it all hung the requirement to be competitive, which meant naked competition with other schools in recruiting students.

Perhaps equally important, the commitment to technology as a driver for the curriculum shored up the ramparts. By seizing those opportunities for development, Senacre strengthened its position in the increasingly competitive environment secondary schools were forced to live in. The school did well, especially given its earlier difficulties. With an entry of 210 pupils on roll in 1988 when the fifth head took office, but with smaller year groups further up the school, numbers increased to over 900 in 1995 when he left. This was no mean achievement. It was reached in the face of aggressive advertising by other schools. School names and messages were on the side of buses. There were television adverts too. Recruitment had become commercialized.

Half way into this headship, the Kent LEA abandoned its 13+ scheme and reverted to the 11+ selection arrangements. This meant that Senacre changed from being a fully comprehensive school for its first two years to a school with a first year entry without the top 25 per cent of the ability range in an age cohort. The advantage for the school was that there was no disruption to overall organization at the beginning of the third year. The disadvantage was that without the most able contingent in the first two years, inevitably it might be perceived that the levels of pupils' achievement would drop, with the inevitable knock-on effect that the school's reputation could suffer. In the event the school had become so popular and its recruitment so strong, that it remained a 'full' school. There were even 'waiting lists', with parents requesting places, not just for entry but further up the school. Those high numbers were the result of very energetic and carefully planned recruitment strategies with members of the senior management team maintaining a close liaison with all the primary schools in the area. They were able to play on the technological emphasis in the curriculum and there was no doubt that this appealed to many parents. But it was a close run thing. Demographic changes in the Maidstone area notched up the competition between schools.

That success was based on the development of the whole school view of the curriculum, infused with radical curricular changes. But the successful performance of the school stemmed from vigorous and imaginative entrepreneurialism.

However using technology as a lodestar was one thing. Coping with the National Curriculum and everything else which went with it was another. The entire 1988 Education Act was driven by a few powerful ideas:

> Distrust of local authorities and institutions of local government
> Distrust of professional autonomy
> Belief in market mechanisms as applied to the public sector – e.g. education and health.
>
> (Maclure 2000: 247)

That rested on a firm, but unproven ideology, and on government's irremovable conviction that schools were failing.

First there came the new contract for teachers specifying 195 days and 1,265 hours a year. Open enrolment was supposed to create a market, which was of course rigged by continuing control from the centre. Later the citizens' charter made the flaws in the market concept for education more serious. By using his power through parliament to impose a National Curriculum, with Standard Academic Tests (SATS) to ensure that scrutiny of standards made them transparent so that parents had adequate information about the schools their children attended or wanted to attend, while at the same time delegating increased powers to school governors, the secretary of state got the control he wanted while passing responsibility for getting it done to governing bodies. It was a very smooth operation.

The composition of governing bodies had been changed already, reducing the representation of LEA and increasing that from the community. Greater powers of co-option meant representation could be extended. Legal responsibility for every aspect of the school's operation transformed governing bodies. It also transformed the relationship between governing body and the head and the staff. This was what Senacre faced in 1988 as it tried to produce a curriculum which was tuned to a world in which the students and their parents lived.

It was no comfort for the staff that almost at once, the National Curriculum was seen to be grossly overloaded with ten subjects taking between 75 and 85 per cent of the timetable and began to be watered down almost before the details were published and imposed on schools. Additional demands on their professional time were just taken for granted. Nor was there any comfort in stories of the almost theological arguments between prime minister, secretary of state, civil servants, HMI and professional advisors which accompanied the evolution of the National Curriculum. Having worked so hard to put ROA to the best educational use, it is not surprising to find the deputy head responsible for those developments having this to say at a meeting of Kent teachers on the value of ROA.

> Imagine our astonishment and dismay, then, when it was announced that a National Curriculum would be introduced to make teachers, who were obviously such slouches, so inept and so uncaring, accountable; a curriculum structure that seemed by its definition to leave little room for imagination and one which could in its worst scenario severely encourage teachers to take a nose dive into what could have seemed a comparatively secure bolt hole of a narrow and didactic approach when programmes of study are heavily laden with facts which must be memorized and are apparently rigidly prescriptive ... the same anxiety that had been experienced by the speed of light introduction of the GCSE with little consultation and training ... how were we to poke our noses out of this bolt hole with any confidence when it appeared to us that we had already understood ourselves to be totally accountable ... the philosophy of formative ROA had given us the security and vision not to take comfortable cover but to tackle what has been aimed at us and harness what is good.

The hurt is almost palpable as is the outrage and resentment.

> All teaching became highly structured. Syllabuses were chopped up and delivered in very specific chunks. Theoretically everyone knew exactly what they had taught last week and what they would teach next week and beyond. At least that's what all the paper work indicated. The history syllabus for example was a joke, even to a non-specialist. It was virtually impossible to cover it any more than superficially.

That was how one senior colleague perceived it. Not everyone agreed. The art master looked back and said:

I'd *always* worked out a programme that addressed central issues in art and design for the pupils in my charge and I couldn't really see that that was being mentioned did not already apply to my teaching programme.

And then almost wistfully, as a complement to the outrage felt by others:

After all since the introduction of GCSE teachers met in groups at regular intervals – we also went to group moderating meetings so that we could gauge the level of work being done across of the area.

And again for English:

The increasing demands of examination boards and the NC in their search for current national icons of 'transparency' and 'accountability' had determined that by ever expanding 'can do' lists and boxes to tick about each student's response and each piece of work, almost every word would meet some pre-ordained 'target'. Marking became a nightmare. You'd have to read a piece of work for interest, correct it, then re-read it to determine which targets had been met and then note them at appropriate points in the margins.

However there was broad agreement that a large part of the problems caused by the National Curriculum was the speed with which it was introduced. As the head of design technology put it:

Especially from the point of view of design technology, I believe it was introduced badly and with a lack of clarity that inevitably caused confusion … and that little thought appeared to have been given to ensuring that there was an adequate supply of suitably trained teachers. Some who were charged with the responsibility of its implementation were transferred from other areas of the curriculum, sometimes voluntarily, given short full time courses, if they were lucky, and if they were not, part time after school courses on top of their normal teaching.

It is hardly surprising that many a teacher felt de-professionalized. But in 1988 that became the fixed point of reference for the curriculum, and so it was the context for all other forms of curriculum development. Perhaps it was the thrust towards technology which did something to sustain a sense of purpose and commitment which otherwise might have been sacrificed on the altar being built by Ofsted, when it came along, to add to the pressures on teachers.

Like the National Curriculum, changes in the way schools were inspected were a long time coming. The composition of the inspectorate, the purposes and procedures of inspections by HMI had evolved for well over a century. When Kenneth Clarke became secretary of state in 1990 there was already talk about ways of arranging regular inspections of all schools in the system, with consistency across the programme of inspections to ensure standards in relation to the expectations raised by the National Curriculum. Talking of the Citizen's Charter, John Major, by then prime minister said 'I want to turn school inspections into the parents' friend' (Maclure 2000: 304). That was almost like a cue for introducing lay inspectors to Ofsted teams with the risk of giving licence to some to deploy their ignorance during inspections. Such was the suspicion in government of the Department of Education, that to avoid contamination, inspection had to be separated from the education establishment. Links were severed between the inspectorate and the department. Like Baker before him, Clarke too was in a hurry and so the Office for Standards in Education (Ofsted) was established in the 1992 Bill just before the general election. To underline its independence, Her Majesty's Chief Inspector was appointed by and would report directly to the prime minister and merely provide an annual report to the secretary of state for education. It was raw, untested ideology at work.

Henceforth, school inspections were put out to tender on a competitive financial basis. It was outsourcing inspections of education. Ofsted established an approved list of companies which could bid for contracts to conduct inspections. Each had to have registered inspectors, many of whom were former HMIs, lists of team inspectors who were recruited more often than not as part-timers and drawn from across the education service, including LEA advisors/inspectors, sometimes moonlighting to earn money for their own institution, and some lay inspectors. This was the fast changing educational world in which curriculum development in Senacre took place during the seven years of this headship.

Curriculum strategy

The head says

> When I first came I asked the parents what they wanted and was given a clear mandate. They wanted the school to be wide-ability but with a sixth form and an increased emphasis on technology. So I started to move.

The fact that he could do that and felt able to ally himself so positively with parents is a tribute to the previous head's pre-emptive strike over the threatened closure under the flag of Senacre Alive for Education (SAFE). The policy of positively engaging with parents and then binding them to the school during that crisis would prove to be the launching pad for the school's most dramatic development a few years later.

As a deputy head who watched it at close hand put it:

> When looking back on the whirlwind of change and development the outside world and the school demanded, it is difficult to believe how any lesser mortal could have coped.

But for some it all came at a price.

> During this time schools were made competitive, and had to do everything in
> their power to increase their market share of Maidstone's children. This had
> huge impact on staff development, which became extremely insular. We no
> longer shared good practice with our colleagues in other schools and an
> atmosphere of suspicion and rivalry was engendered between schools.

The very words 'market share' conjure up the harsh world of competitive commerce
and industry and tinge the regret, almost with sadness, as that deputy pointed to
the price that had to be paid for some of the consequences of the 1988 Act. Without
doubt that Act contributed much to the raising of standards of individual schools,
as at Senacre, but some of the wider effects were not so beneficial. Some schools
would succeed, some would fail. The social consequences of inducing competition
for many a locality are now being reaped in the whirlwind. And although there is
no way of determining it, it may be not too fanciful to relate the incidence of
failing schools to competition and all that goes with it. How often it is that policy
decisions have unintended consequences.

The deputy head with particular responsibility for the curriculum set out the
major strands which dictated the shape of the curriculum in simple straightforward
terms.

> First was government national strategy for school curriculum. As their plans
> were unveiled the school attempted to change the curriculum to meet
> government requirements.
> The second was an attempt to be a forerunner in any curriculum initiative.
> The third was awareness that the curriculum needed to be attractive to parents
> and students in order to maintain and increase the numbers admitted to the
> school each year.

Making a technology school

The head's words 'so I started to move', meant just what they said. He moved on
information communication technology (ICT). He had a four stage approach to
installing it in the curriculum: first, clarify a problem; next work out a solution;
third test the solution and then modify as necessary. He held that that procedural
sequence could apply to any walk of life. He was not concerned that people did
not understand the equipment, nor wanted to. Being able to use computers was the
key. And he was convinced that parents would see the value of ICT for their
children's working future, and would support the endeavour. Ushering in the future
was his private way of thinking about it.

Within two years the secretary of state, John MacGregor, was in the school
congratulating it on 'scoring a first', as he opened a £50,000 computer suite. What

appealed to him particularly was the ingenious scheme whereby the school obtained a loan from a local business firm called Marley Tiles, which would be repaid by the school training the company's employees at the computer centre which the company was financing. Reporting this in November 1989 the *Times Educational Supplement* gave this story a headline:

Old fashioned barter deal provides latest technology

The next year there was another notice:

Another financial first at Senacre

The first paragraph read:

Allied Anglo group and Senacre High School will inaugurate their exclusive moneysaver club on Wednesday 6 February. The Club gives parents and students access to a stunning range of discounts, insurance, financial and other services for a modest fee.

Technology is not cheap. Buying, replacing, renewing, servicing, money had to be available for a technology programme to be successful. Any legitimate means of finding it would serve.

The school then changed its name to Senacre Technology School. Along the way it opted to become a grant maintained school and in 1994 became a technology college under new government regulations. The school had to raise £100,000 which it did as the head puts it 'by hawking around ... some of it was from expectations of getting their money back, ... very strong PTA at that time – by standards I was used to then, several thousands of pounds'. That enabled the school to undertake a major £100,000 project and receive an additional £100 a year for every student in the school. And about that time the head appointed a business manager, more of which later.

These developments were designed to enable the school to undertake fundamental curriculum change, as the head put it when the school changed its name to 'technology school':

We believe that all students should be in touch with technology both in terms of hardware and through our style of teaching. It is a student centred, problem solving type of approach and we felt that we must nail our colours to the mast. Our proposal was fully supported by the Local Education Authority, school governors, staff and parents, but the message is that nothing else will change. We will remain a school for the community and the change will make no difference to our admission policy.

(*Kent Messenger* 19 July 1991)

That last sentence is a faithful adherence to the parents' wishes expressed at his first meeting with them: wide ability with a sixth form and an emphasis on technology. But his insistence was derived from something else. The city technology colleges (CTCs) introduced in the Baker Act were private corporations to which business was expected to contribute hugely to their cost. And they were to be selective. At different times the head made it clear that Senacre was not becoming a selective school where the opportunities offered by technology to enrich the curriculum were available to the few. 'All our students in touch with technology', was the watchword. So the entire technological thrust was based on a high education principle. The school was there to serve the many and not the few.

That commitment is even more impressive when seen against the circumstances of the school. At various times it was classified as a school of special difficulty and its surrounding area, a culturally deprived area. Statistics for the early 1990s showed that over half of Senacre students were on the special needs register, and second highest in Kent.

The head of aesthetics recalls the head's almost lyrical exposition of what he meant by a technological bias in the curriculum.

> We were all asked to (a) consider how 'technology' (IT particularly) could be used in the teaching and learning of our subjects or subject groups. And (b) (and this was really cute) how we could apply the technology of thought processes to what we were doing: think technologically. In drama I interpreted this as encouraging the use of word processors ... and by analysing more overtly the ways in which we thought, organized ourselves, constructed plots and so on. The changes were quite subtle.

If that was the dream, it was not so easy to realize. The lesson had been well learnt from TVEI; without a coherent general plan of action to influence the system, there was little point in putting money and equipment in schools where the suspicion of the public was that they were relatively low grade courses. As it was, neither the system nor the schools changed significantly in their bias against technology and vocational courses as a result of TVEI. Getting technology to infuse the entire curriculum meant root and branch change throughout the school.

An article in *Managing Schools* Vol. I No. 5 has this to say:

> Senacre Technology School in Maidstone, Kent, has made a determined and singular effort to drag its mode of education into the 21st century. Senacre planned to become a 'technological school' a long time before the government constructed its latest initiative in that direction. It has adopted a radical approach to the curriculum in order to overcome the sort of defences which would reduce technology to an additional bolt-on subject in an otherwise conventional school. In fact, information technology is considered a pre-requisite in all areas of study and so does not exist as a separate subject within Senacre School, and is not an option at GCSE.

That article quotes the head as saying:

> technology is not just an abundance of computer systems but the process by which man uses equipment and techniques to solve real problems. Such a concept of technology can give children the critical problem solving skills they need in our society – attributes that our didactic, academic style of education has clearly failed to deliver.

He saw access to a technological education as an educational entitlement for every pupil and student. The deputy confirms this. 'Central to our thought was that all students should have high levels of skill in ICT'. That does not just speak of curriculum change. It is talking about thorough-going curriculum and educational reform.

The first step was to change the departmental structure to one of seven curriculum areas. They became faculties: communications and creative studies, mathematics, science, modern languages, recreational and physical studies, humanities, design and technology. Each had its own curriculum leader who was responsible for teaching and non-teaching staff. Each had its own budget. They joined the head and deputies as a senior management team. A deputy head was made technology coordinator, so that there was a 'top brass' group to give weight and authority to send a clear message about the change which was about to come.

Not everyone liked it. The head of mathematics shifted sideways with an offer to become head of the upper school and later took early retirement. The head of English declined an offer of becoming head of the faculty of communication without additional pay and resigned rather than grapple with more internal reorganization. He says:

> The rediscovery of my Senacre files reminded me of why I took early retirement at the age of 55. I kept only those pieces which seemed to have special significance for me or threw light upon a particularly fraught chapter in the school's history. But even just reading through these again and reawakening memories of all that perpetual change and strife has been enough to give me a headache.

And thus began the exodus of long serving staff. Early retirement deals led to changes in the leadership in English, mathematics, aesthetics and art.

To implement such a reorganization as a means of harnessing the faculties as facilitators of curriculum change there was a comprehensive programme of staff development. The SMT members took weekend time in seminars to understand and assimilate what it was the head wanted. 'Away days' followed for staff, with the school picking up the bill.

> We did a lot of work on understanding the technological process and then sharing the ideas with all colleagues. It was understood to be a process of

settling on aims, gathering information, formulating objectives, review and evaluation. The drive was for staff at Senacre to understand this and to incorporate the process in their teaching programmes.

The deputy who was technology coordinator underpinned all this:

> the guiding principle in the use of technology is that it will help the children to acquire skills and solve problems presented to them in their general studies. Instead of using IT to collect and analyse meaningless data, they are using databases and spreadsheets on issues which will be relevant to their own lives, or enlighten some area of study in a practical way and lead them on to further areas of inquiry.

All students were expected to become competent in word processing, using databases and spreadsheets. For example, a mathematics and PE project concerned the study of pupils' own health and setting scientific hypotheses which could be tested to see what effect a training programme had on heart rate, lung capacity and so on. Mathematics came to life with that kind of data collection and analysis. Talking of its use in religious education the coordinator says:

> In RE we might set up a database based on books of the bible, their length, period of time covered, historical sources, authors and so on. Data searches can draw out remarkable conclusions.

He goes on:

> The impact had been to focus on the style of learning and teaching. We are giving the students transferable skills which will help them in work or at home.

And what was the effect of all this effort? The deputy head claims that there was a noticeable increase in the motivation of students, particularly among those considered to be slower learners and it struck a chord with parents. He records that staff views changed considerably so that more creative, project based teaching could play its part alongside the didactic, which retained a necessary place in the repertoire within traditional lessons. None of this ran foul of the National Curriculum. Projects were not bolt-on studies or a replacement of normal studies. They were part of them. Rather, it was finding a way of using the National Curriculum as a vehicle for the pedagogical principles to which this technology school was committed.

There are other ways of measuring success. It is important to remember that the 13+ transfer scheme was still in operation until 1992 so that Year 9, that doldrums year, and above were non-selective entry, the wide ability school. After that, pupil entry was without the top 25 per cent of the ability range so the wide ability principle made it harder for the school to meet government targets. Further, the school's location in a poorer part of the town meant that families entitled to free school meals could rise to nearly 50 per cent of the roll. The examination results have to be read off against that background. The school recorded a 25 per cent pass rate at grades A–C in English. Performance in science improved and less than 5 per cent left without a GCSE pass. And that litmus test of success for government, attendance, was up to 99 per cent. The school was full with a waiting list, but behind that full capacity lay something else.

The deputy explains:

> We made a positive decision to establish a sixth form which would be successful. At the time it was small and mostly students retaking GCSE subjects. In order to get rid of that perception of what a sixth former did, revise and re-take, we stopped entry to the sixth form for one year. This enabled us to plan and introduce something which would be successful and would offer qualifications at A level equivalent. Our focus was on GNVQ provision in art, business studies, science and ICT.

So a sixth form was growing. By 1994 there were 140 students in Year 11, sixty-one boys and seventy-nine girls. Eighty-one per cent achieved five or more GCSE passes. Sixty-one per cent attained one or more A–C grades and 14 per cent achieved five or more A–C grades. Those scores came from eighteen GCSE subjects. In addition there were RSA courses in French, word processing, desktop publishing and City and Guilds starting photography. There were also entries for British government and politics, English, French and modular mathematics at A level. There was a BTEC business and finance course. Like everything else it was a problem-solving programme. Each sixth former had a business partner in a local firm where they were given real assignments. This was no work experience. It was intentional learning through experience of working.

There is a nice footnote. It took staff some time to realize that the head's son was taking the business studies course, with a placement for work experience. With ease, he found a job and now ten years or so later is regional manager for an IT firm with a car which leaves his father way behind. Staff, parents and others could not fail to register that as an indication of the head's own commitment to what he was trying to do with the curriculum.

That sixth form could not have existed without the students who stayed on beyond the 16-year-old leaving date. That meant that the curriculum revisions being effected through the pervasive use of technology were not only improving standards but were convincing parents that what the school was providing was what they and their sons and daughters wanted. They too had found their school experience satisfying and they wanted more of it. And it helped to quieten the nagging question of numbers and the targets that went with them.

There is an important feature underlying all that development, without which it might have faltered. The technology coordinator referred to a large programme of staff training and development. Weekend seminars and away days were integral to the preparation for the strategy for change. And right from the beginning the curricular revisions were seen as a collegial enterprise. Faculties were essentially interdisciplinary so that cross-discipline thinking and planning was built into the school's organization. How could it be otherwise with design technology, home economics with textiles, as a faculty of applied technology; or English, drama, music, art, pottery and media studies as the faculty of communication and creative studies, and history, geography, religious studies and business studies as the faculty of humanities? Each with its own budget and responsibility for teaching and non-teaching staff, whether they liked it or not, it was difficult for staff to avoid collaboration. So although there might be regrets that in-service training across schools was more or less lost, there were plenty of opportunities for stimulus within the collegial nature of the school's academic organization.

Curriculum development strategy

In June 1990 the school placed an advertisement for a business manager. *The Times Educational Supplement* carried an article with the headline:

> Executives vie for new school fundraiser's job

Stockbrokers, company managers and top bank executives had applied for the £20,000 a year post. The head was looking for someone with entrepreneurial skills who would attract £100,000 a year to supplement the school's annual budget of over a million as well as paying his own salary. Had John MacGregor been around no doubt he would have declared another first, which it was literally. It was the first time in the country that a state school had appointed a business manager. A deputy head says:

> The day that the news broke of his appointment the rest of the senior team were out of school and I had to spend the whole day answering question from the press. The business manager became a member of the Senior Management team. We would meet in the newly extended head's office round a huge dining table which Neil had found for the purpose.

This was not just a money raising ploy. As well as managing a growing budget, the Business Manager was an educational colleague. An additional element was being inserted into curriculum development. Speaking of his appointment he insisted that his job was not to run round with a begging bowl.

> Our pupils are the workforce and consumers of the future and there is much we can offer local firms. We shall be looking for sponsorship but we will be offering something in return.

But as well as cash, his contacts with local business enabled him to persuade two senior men in business to become school governors. He joined in with local business people to design the business and finance course. He planned with a company called Busy Bee to build a creche as an income generator. And when he presented the prizes for industry links as part of the work experience programme, he said:

> This is not like work experience practised in most schools. Pupils really get to know the companies and some have been offered summer jobs. What they learn at school in theory they put into practice with the companies.

The business manager became an educational promoter. He was extending the concept of work experience which had begun in 1959. In itself that is an important curriculum issue. The business of running a school with quite a large budget was incorporated into the whole school curricular concept.

For the head the rationale for business manager was simple at one of two levels. Either employ a full-time fund raiser to raise more cash or move into aggressive competition with neighbouring schools for extra pupils. It was numbers again and he went for the first. Another bonus was that the deputy head, who had been looking after finances, went back to teaching in the classroom. In the head's view it was a ridiculous waste of a superb teacher that he should be looking after finances. So the head decided to get someone with business interests to take on the finance. In a sense it was a curricular decision.

> But that was not sufficient. If we were looking for someone to keep the books, there were lots of people to do that. What I wanted was someone that was going to pay for their keep and who was always there to raise finance.

What was the purpose and its connection with the curriculum?

> it provides us with opportunities and equipment to allow us to develop the curriculum in ways which we think appropriate. For example, let's take information technology. That is a huge budget commitment. It's not just that we've bought it. You have to have a sinking fund to keep it going because it is the most dreadful drain and burden on the revenue ... students expect faster and faster machines. We were able to produce an environment, provide technicians, provide kit, promote it as public relations to really launch something which was worth while, seen to be high profile and have the youngsters signed up to it. I wanted any student going through a school where I was associated, to have 'an edge'. And it seemed to me at that time the 'edge' which the young people could be offered was ICT. In my terms it was both neutral, and positive. If you were serious about finding an 'edge', technology was a realistic answer.

And how could that be done?

We then went into training for our staff. Those who were good at it had no problems. But actually we either had to appoint people with the skills or train our own existing staff. It started to take place; it was very slow. There was a lot of nervousness and the nervousness was that you were dealing with the unknown and you were putting staff at risk. And the risks were twofold; either you could be seen as the duffer or the whole lot would not work so you were left with a class of thirty and the kit did not do anything. So those were the risks for colleagues. The first risk we tried to cope with by training. The second risk we tried to raise money to have a technician. So if something goes wrong, whistle, someone will come and fix it. You are not exposed with all this kit and you do not really know what the hell you are doing. Don't bother to understand it; just find out how to use it.

Making the curriculum work

It was one thing for the senior management team, expanded as it was to include the curriculum leaders for the seven curriculum areas, to do the blue skies thinking and try to bring it down to earth. It was quite another to try to engage the other sixty members of staff so they changed their ways so as to help realize the intentions of the curriculum renewal. In those circumstances schemes for curriculum support became crucial and assumed a strongly interventionist role from the centre. If students were to benefit from the renewed curriculum then staff needed some tools to help things on their way. Moreover if targets were to be met, then a reliable information database had to be created. And that meant not merely numbers and figures, but trying to understand whatever factors there were which lay behind student performance and what steps might be taken to deal with them.

Continuing professional development became the school's main engine for curriculum development in its widest terms. A 1991 document was headed 'Monitoring the standards of students' work'. Some of it can seem rather rudimentary, but the need was to establish a set of common denominators designed to reach for a common standard of professional practice throughout a sixty strong staff.

The document began with a section on 'The state of books':

It is important to distinguish between those books which are expected to 'travel' and those which are not. In English for example, final drafts of work are placed in a file which never leaves the school.

Presentation of the page came next:

Books/files will show a mixture of homework and classwork. The task may have some bearing on the presentation. Unless drafting is in place, copying will be more difficult to present neatly than an original piece of work. Many students come to Senacre with little, if any experience of homework and therefore have not learnt to present it attractively ... what does an 'untidy' hewn into a page in red pen actually mean in the absence of study skills?

Marking followed on:

> Is the work marked/acknowledged to date? If there is just a tick remember
> there are different purposes for marking.

And the golden rule in capitals.

> There is no excuse, whatsoever for 'work' that has not been acknowledged in
> any way.

It is all blindingly obvious but the document was there as a reference point for the
academic monitoring which had become a requirement. Preparations for monitoring
were meticulous and done on a sampling basis. Tutors were asked to interview the
selected students and complete with them sheets referring to attendance, extra-
curricular activities, merits awarded. Then the interview was to become a discussion
about 'What do you see as your part in a team? Is there one area of your school
work or school life that you would like to improve?'

A sheet covered every subject with columns for teacher's initials, column entries
for work presented, marked/acknowledged, evidence of work in IT and space for
comments.

The students selected for the sampling were to be interviewed by the deputy
head responsible for the monitoring. Each had a letter of invitation, worded carefully
indicating warm personal respect, and conveyed an expectation of standards of
behaviour.

The note to staff about this exercise began with:

> Before half term the SMT will be monitoring the work of these students in
> Year 9 who at 13+ transfer were ranked as being at the top of our ability
> range. This is in response to some parents' and governors' disquiet about a
> perceived lack of expectation in Year 9. As a prelude to this monitoring exercise
> I asked to see the following students.

This is a clear example of the changes wrought by local management and the
legally enshrined responsibilities of governing bodies. Year 9, the 'doldrum' year
had not gone away. Governors got interested, being responsible for the school's
fulfilling of the requirements of the National Curriculum and for the standards of
achievement in the SATs for Key Stage 3. Scrutiny of the school's academic work
was becoming a routine assignment. How the problem of Year 9 came to the
attention of governors is unknown. It was probably a parent governor. Certainly
their anxiety would have been seen as nothing compared with the continuing search
by the school to find ways of motivating Year 9 more strongly. No doubt this
inquiry sharpened the attention being given to Year 9 and as a result monitoring
became more rigorous.

The head was also spurred on in the drive for rigour by the commitment of
parents. Many students who had been offered grammar school places, chose to

remain at Senacre. Doing the best for them was to justify that commitment. It was also a matter of pride for the school in being able to do so.

As the deputy head said:

> The governing body assumed far higher responsibility and had to be part of the decision making process. I found this particularly hard at first. What other profession has to hold itself accountable to lay men?

What was also the case however, was that governors too found it 'particularly hard at first'. There is more on this later in this book.

The exercise led to important findings which were circulated to staff. Among those students selected there were two boys who had gone to the grammar school after the 13+ selection and returned to Senacre, one girl who could have gone to the grammar school and stayed, and one girl whose case went to appeal and lost.

The report recorded students' views of the various topics in the survey. They all were depressed at the fewer merit marks they were receiving. One said 'Merits are much harder to get and it's not fair. The work is harder, I'm working hard but because I'm only average for the group, I don't get any'. This led to a commentary about merit marks and better ways of acknowledging the work of students.

Time spent on homework was a hot topic for the students. A school policy stated that homework should be set for forty-five minutes of work. Students' reactions were varied. 'The homework has become longer, not just the little five minute ones. Sometimes mathematics goes on for 45 minutes'. 'Teachers are more strict about giving homework this year. More is given regularly'. 'We have to spend a longer time and it has got harder. I usually spend between one hour and one and a half hours each night'. But there was a nice twist. The two boys who had been to the grammar school and returned to Senacre, independently recorded that the amount of homework was about the same in each school but 'They weren't as strict there as they are here'. That meant that the policy was working.

Hence the report could include;

> Homework is being set regularly in most subjects. Mathematics was exemplary in this respect. In all cases, from the students I saw, only one subject was timetabled on Monday. Homework appeared to be getting off to a slow start after the holiday in some areas and similarly infrequently set in the week before a holiday. 'None Set', is still the phrase most recorded in the journals.

This illustrates two aspects to managing curriculum change. Any serious attempt to know the consequences of curriculum change, success, failure, modest, either way, needs deliberate action to find out what is happening as a result of changes which have been introduced. Without that there is no reliable means of discovering how to change things for the better. And second, any scheme for the implementation of an agreed policy needs to have built into its procedures a self-checking mechanism to record what actually happened. It is no good asking questions after the event. This is as true for education policies as it is for building bridges.

On the challenges the students were facing, some said that mathematics was much harder. One said that she did not understand science, although she worked hard at it. For English 'more difficult than at the grammar school, we only read there', 'Discursive essays are hard. You have to think about what you are doing'. And then trying to get a feel for what students felt about the move from Years 7 and 8 to Year 9 the report recorded these students' comments.

> Work is getting harder, preparing us for work in Years 10–11 ... Teachers are more strict than in Years 7 and 8 ... Now they make us 'bottle down' to work ... There are more people in the classes than there used to be ... I am a lot more involved. The work is harder than in Years 7 and 8. I have moved up a set.

> There is lots of group work here. People in classes are 'workable with'. At the grammar school clever people did not want to know us. It was as strict there. Nobody wanted to mess around at the grammar school.

> I have become more interested in my work and I am determined to do well. This year I am not mixing with people who muck around and I am getting on with it.

That is curriculum development by basics. Earlier in a staff development document there was a remark to the effect that teachers could not assume that while they knew what they wanted students to learn, students' perspective and understanding was the same. Due account had to be taken of those differences if learning was to be promoted effectively. It is easy to imagine that deputy head mulling over all these comments and listing a series of issues to be dealt with. What shall we do about awarding merit marks? This thoughtful passage in the report reads:

> These high attaining students were 'miffed' by the lack of merits. Could it be that the 'embarrassment' we have assumed students to have on receiving merit marks in Years 10–11 is merely a response to a continued 'wind down' in Year 9 and we have sub-consciously promoted their lack of effect in the senior school?

All this can be interpreted as putting into practice what the head was referring to when he talked about the approach of the school being student centred. This goes way beyond the pedagogical niceties of problem solving in groups in classrooms, or setting data base tasks on computers. It is trying to look at things from the other end, the students' end, so as to be in a better position to work out how they can be helped to learn more. Again this was curriculum development by basics. Syllabus content and teaching methods could be infused with them. And in any case, Ofsted would have something to read.

This was taken further. To check up how records of achievement were working another survey was conducted involving both students and tutors. Using a twenty-five page long National Federation of Educational Research (NFER) constructed survey, ten boys and ten girls from both Years 10 and 11 were surveyed for their attitudes and perceptions. Students were asked if they had chosen to have a one-to-one interview with their tutor, whether they had gone with a friend or two friends and why. They were asked to comment on how they experienced talking about their achievements and their targets for their next year. They were asked to say what extra help they could be given to reach those targets, what sort of help and by whom. They were asked questions to elicit information about the amount of support their parents were giving them. They were asked to give their views as to why attendance in Years 10 and 11 was not as good as it should be. They were asked if there was anything else good or bad they wanted to write about the college, and what was inevitably the most important question of all: they were asked what the college could do to help them think out their futures. There were no surprises there: careers information and guidance, practice interviews, more work experience. Inevitably there was, 'make lessons more interesting' and 'the teachers could explain more deeply what it is we are asked to do so the task is done properly', and help for getting good GCSE results. Many said they wanted more time for the arts and drama.

But interestingly there was 'by educating you about the things you will have to cope with in life that you don't have to cope with now', and 'talk to us about the real world when we have left college, like responsibilities, problems, coping with different situations', and 'the college could help me in the future to behave, be polite, special skills and to get to know and work with other people'. And the licensed wag 'Stop nagging me when I get something wrong'.

As with the previous monitoring, this is rich with information for curriculum planning in the future. It is the same approach. If the students are to be well served, try to get alongside them. Seeing those student attitudes and impressions and what they wanted for themselves in 1993 against the relaxation in 2004 of the National Curriculum requirements, it is almost saying that the students knew what was good for them far better than the Quality and Examinations Agency.

External curriculum scrutiny begins: the first Ofsted

This is where intervention in the curriculum got serious. In 1994 Senacre had its first Ofsted inspection. For any school the first Ofsted inspection was bound to be a traumatic occasion. The way the chief inspector had set about his work with denigration writ large, feeding the press with his highly controversial, even insulting views of schools and their teachers, a significant proportion of whom he considered ought to be sacked, was hardly going to produce a welcoming party for one of his teams. Tension for all, panic for some, anxious anticipation all over, that was the mood when the team arrived. That wariness was heightened by gossip from other colleagues' comments on the quality of the inspectors and what appeared to be inconsistencies in judgements. In 1994 inspectors were not very experienced either.

The contents of an Ofsted report are organized under broad sections: main findings, key issues for action, an introductory piece about the school, aspects of the school, curriculum areas and subjects, and inspection data which includes a summary of the evidence.

The first Ofsted report for Senacre Technology College (Ofsted contract 922/ S4/000802) began by saying that it provided a sound education for most of its students, most because some did not reach the required standards while other did. It qualified that by finding that a good majority reached satisfactory levels, when their ability is taken into consideration. Over three-quarters reached the levels indicated by national standards and a quarter achieved higher standards. Interestingly the least satisfactory were those who had gone through what the deputy head had referred to earlier as the 'doldrum years'.

English was singled out for showing many students had reached higher levels that those required for Key Stage 4. Physical education, information technology (IT), science, art reached the required standards throughout the college, while mathematics and religious education did the same at Key Stage 3, as did history and geography at Key Stage 4.

So at one level everything seemed satisfactory. Nothing much was left out. That was for students' achievement in school. But seen against the national expectation of standards, many were not up to it. There were 909 students in the school. Forty per cent had special educational needs, 28 per cent had statements for special educational needs and 27 per cent were eligible for free school meals.

Seen against that background the disparity between national standards and those achieved by the 909 pupils is hardly surprising. And it points a sharp finger at the problems of providing an appropriate curriculum for a school with such a wide diversity of pupils, working within the constraining boundaries described by the National Curriculum. Because of the rules which inspectors were required to observe, it was the score card of national standards and not the achievements of the students which informed the emphasis in the report when it was written. That disparity and the way it was reported caused grave disquiet and some anger in the school.

Inspectors found that the school was ably led. Governors were involved appropriately and the college had a clear ethos and established values and was an ordered community. Behaviour was generally good and there were good opportunities for the development of pupils' spiritual, moral and social under-standing. The quality of pastoral care was a strength as was the integration of pupils with physical disabilities. However it is no surprise to find comments that sometimes practice did not match policy, that monitoring by middle managers was not as good as it ought to be. Surprisingly a finding was that awareness of cultural differences was underdeveloped. That looks odd, seen against approvals given for ethos and an ordered community.

In the subjects of the curriculum section, inspectors found that the quality of teaching was sound in all subjects, sometimes better, except for design technology, history, modern languages where the quality was inconsistent. The majority of teachers were found to be on top of their subject, created good learning environments and engaged students well. Unsurprisingly, some stuck to the factual recall type of questions and answers. Lesson planning was generally sound. Where it was not, it was to do with bad timing and muddled objectives, over-direction which reduced time and space for students to develop independence and initiative. And notably, inspectors found that throughout the college relationships between students and staff were good and positive. At a different level, it was pointed out that governors and senior staff needed to develop strategies for spreading the good practice in some subjects to all of them. All that seems to read as a sound bill of health, with some curious inconsistencies.

In a more critical vein, the report made two significant claims. It said assessment was inconsistent and was not an effective tool for lifting standards. It also claimed that neither in classrooms nor in the college generally did students have much opportunity for using initiative and taking responsibility for making their own decisions about their own learning.

On the first the school felt that its efforts over the years to create consistency were disparaged and ignored. On the second, one member of staff was incredulous.

> Teaching did change because we tended to encourage the pupils to experiment and find their own interest/material/approach sometimes from central themes or ideas. The work became much more individual and varied but should show at the end research, development of ideas and skills in the chosen media. A sketch book became an important part of the whole process – homework was set regularly, and marked with grades linked to GCSE.

In passing, it was difficult to think of a more discouraging way to make an important point about assessment than leaving staff, who have spent long hours trying to achieve consistency in assessment feeling 'ignored and disparaged!' 'A poor attempt to promote learning by teachers'. Like local and central civil servants, Ofsted is not noted for its use of supportive language.

In this case it was resented and it hurt. It seemed outrageous that all the work spent on consultation and review systems, precisely to develop a sense of initiative and ownership among students, was disregarded. And unfortunately it led to the staff generally thinking that much of the report was bland and obvious, that much of it could be applied to any school, anywhere. The general reaction in the staff room was that the inspection had gone pretty well.

But there were differing reactions to the inspection among senior staff. One deputy head and the head of English thought the inspection had gone as well as could be expected, given the nature of the student population, with its wide range, not only of ability but also of social and economic circumstances. There was always room for improvements so it did not hurt to suggest where they could be made. Their view was that there was nothing much to fuss about. That did not lessen the sense of disappointment that there was such tardy recognition of what the school had accomplished. A head of faculty summed up her reaction to the registered inspector. This seemed like 'an iron fist in a velvet glove'. A strange approach to education.

The senior deputy recalls his concerns at the time. He felt quite confident going into the inspection but had his confidence knocked during and after it. In hindsight, his reactions may have been heightened because of his later experience with the next inspection, but in 1994 they were pretty damning.

> I strongly believe this Ofsted report to be the beginning of the decline of Senacre, because what was said was out of the blue, and I don't think I was so naïve as not to know what was happening. I was shell shocked by what was said and I thought there is something not quite right and that was down to the team. If you had a different team ...

The head used different words but meant the same thing.

> The inspection did not take us forward; it knocked us back. It introduced an uncertainty about what we were doing, which was unhelpful. Against what we knew the school had achieved, however subjectively, there was a sense of personal inadequacy.

He trained a bright sidelight on the point raised by the deputy about the team. The entire team of inspectors was drawn from local authority advisors in East Sussex. All secondary schools in East Sussex were fully comprehensive. It had no secondary modern schools. Nor did that authority have any grant maintained schools within its area. It had fought tooth and nail against them. There was no means of knowing what 'political' nuances 'unconsciously' were going on in the background, but he felt it not unreasonable to comment that on both grounds, in some respects the inspectors were unfamiliar with what they were inspecting. He agreed with his deputy.

Such comments from a successful school, with such a highly motivated staff, merely illustrate the inevitable 'hit and miss' element in Ofsted's operations. Under the present arrangements for inspections it is hard to see how they can be avoided. What angered the deputy particularly was the disparity between national standards against which the school was judged and the actual achievements of the students which represented the work of the school.

> We raised this issue with them several times and the reply was 'we're not here to report that, we are here to compare you with national standards. Our hands are tied behind our back. That is how we have to report'.

Such a lopsided measurement of student achievement in effect downgraded them. Coming from a mild, committed, thoroughly experienced professional, who had been deputy for five years, he made some harsh judgements. Worse, overall, it is a rather frightening indication of the damage which can be done to a school through a well intended intervention. It is perfectly proper for government to do everything it can to raise standards. But there are more ways of checking them and detecting failing schools than the heavy handed treatment doled out by Ofsted. To have an inspectorial regime which was so rigid as to be not supportive of what a school was actually achieving, seems an almost incomprehensible error of policy. And to apply all that to a school, which by inspectors' own account, was doing more than satisfactorily with its students, seems a curious use of inspection. For the next seven years that deputy had to help pick up the pieces.

The 'initiative' point made by the inspectors prompted the school to do even more of what it had done successfully already. An early paragraph of a staff document prompted by the Ofsted report headed 'locus of control', read:

> Our motivation to work however at its basic level is different – that of 'earning a crust!' Such motivation is strong and places our energies and responsibilities securely in the 'need to' (at worst) and 'want to' (at best) categories of motivation.

But then some of the basic principles of curriculum development take over.

> How many of us, at the beginning of Year 10 take the first step of passing ownership to students by making them thoroughly familiar with the examination syllabus? Do they have their own 'user friendly' copy? Do we read it through with them? Discuss it? Give them the opportunity to consider in advance which parts might cause them trouble and which parts they feel relatively confident about.

The document goes on about how to motivate, how to react to the survey which revealed, unsurprisingly, that some students found some lessons boring.

> a prime requisite for combating students' alienation is to make each student feel that he or she matters, that the quality of their work is important as is their behaviour, attendance and attitude.

Again, all are blindingly obvious. But as part of attempts to harness the energies of some sixty members of staff and persuade, cajole them into conducting their teaching according to some basic common denominators, it needed saying. Flat footed Ofsted might be, but the school took its flat footedness seriously, making something positive out of it.

This was all designed to promote learning and teaching more effectively, in the view of the deputy head with the curriculum brief:

ICT and business education were developed in the school and became a strength and attraction to both students and parents. Sciences, mathematics and design technology were also considered as an important core to the curriculum. English was considered vital and for most of my time at Senacre was a strong successful department with effective leadership. It seemed to me that the humanities subjects like geography, history and RE all suffered to some extent and their status as subjects seemed to diminish.

And that is where the curriculum-balancing act was struck by 1995. Ofsted contributed nothing to thinking about the curriculum, and if anything, risked discouraging the very initiative in the staff that they urged should be encouraged in students. Such can be the baleful effect of one kind of external intervention.

Going grant maintained

On 13 December 1991, the *Kent Messenger* carried two headlines on page 11: in heavy black, large print, 'School's head hails opt-out bid success' and in smaller print 'Parents' turn to face a lesson in technology'. The first was a condition of the second. But the interesting, intriguing link between the two is that it was the parents who initiated the moves towards independence and it was no wonder the head said:

I find it very exciting that the move towards grant maintained status was instigated by parents rather than governors. Parental involvement is very important here and this will give parents even more say in what happens to their children.

That had not been entirely straightforward. A governors' report in 1990 includes:

After a thorough examination, Governors decided by a majority vote not to take the step of recommending to parents that Senacre seek grant-maintained status, opting out of local authority control.

But the next paragraph reads:

If parents of students at the school wish to pursue the grant maintained option, they can seek to mobilize parental support for the idea. Ultimately there would be the need for a majority among those parents who vote.

Clearly they did wish and seek. When local management began, Senacre was a pilot school so by 1990 the governors had some experience of the implications of their new roles. In 1990 there were three parent governors, two teacher governors with the head ex-officio, five from Kent County Council and four co-opted members. One can only guess at what went on in the background to overturn the governors' initial decision. In a governing body of fourteen it is an early example of realigning of powers affecting local authorities, governing bodies and parents and staff and hence of the curriculum.

The head adds that the main driver behind seeking grant maintained status was Kent's funding formula. Its per capita calculations left Senacre worse off than grammar schools by a long way. Given the needs of technology in the curriculum that was intolerable. GM status offered a way out of that. Unfortunately the twelve-month long negotiations prevented the school from getting the £250,000 grant during the first year GM funding. In addition the head recalls wryly, it prevented Senacre being the first GM school in the area and so lost an 'edge' in the public's perception.

The head repeated his commitment to what the parents had said they wanted when he arrived: wide ability range and no concentration examination work to the detriment of the less academic sixth form, and increased emphasis on technology. As with the status of technology school, Senacre was to become no specialist school. Referring to that parents' evening, the deputy head commented that the idea behind the evening was to allow parents the same experiences as their children. English, science, recreational studies, modern languages, design and technology, mathematics and the humanities were all there for the sampling. He went on:

> The new 'pupils' quickly found that computers are only a small part of the technology picture. More important is the practical way in which problems are explored ... I think that the evening helped to enlighten a lot of people – the practical approach helps pupils to gain a deeper understanding. When I look at some of the things they do, I wish it was like that when I was at school.

On April 1994 the *Kent Messenger* carried another headline banner.

> School granted status as technology college

That underlined the emphasis in the curriculum on the various uses of technology. It took the school further down the road towards up-to-date learning opportunities which parents were asking it to follow.

What did not feature in those reports was the extent to which that success of the enterprise rested on the shoulders of the business manager. He had twelve months or so to bring his business experience to bear on making the money go round. Everything was in place to cope with the strict control of a 5 million budget in effect turning the school into a self-supporting enterprise. Entrepreneurialism would be at a greater premium.

The deputy head summed up those two developments:

> One of the major initiatives to shape the curriculum was the introduction of grant maintained status and technology college status. This opportunity was

seized by the school because it felt that the status itself would be attractive to parents, that a technological focus would help shape the curriculum in today's world, and it would give us some degree of freedom in making decisions about the future and would bring in a substantial amount of cash to the school.

Governors and the curriculum

The 1988 Baker Act transformed governing bodies from nobodies to somebodies. Their new composition downgraded the LEA. Their legal responsibilities were awesome compared with their previous status. For a start there was financial responsibility. They were required to approve annual budgets, showing income and expenditure from both public and private sources as the peak of the school's financial management. That meant they had to approve staffing plans and levels to ensure that the National Curriculum was covered, all within a balanced budget.

As government initiatives designed to raise standards streamed in with demands for returns to provide evidence of those standards, so did the need increase for governing bodies to scrutinize all aspects of the curriculum. Assessment became a very hot topic both for procedures as well as academic results.

In the year 1994–5 the deputy head responsible for student support and assessment produced a sixty-page assessment document for staff. It had six sections: Senacre assessment policy; calendar for reporting and consultation Years 7–13; report writing; students' and parents' involvement in the reporting process; the national record of achievement, and partnership for progress. Each section had examples as well as guidelines, complete with cartoons produced by the art department. There was a language policy with sections for action by teachers, action for subject areas and whole school policy. It was this sort of detail, laid on classroom teachers which could make the school and its governors feel confident about the reliability of the returns which had to be made. The school was required to produce statistical predictions about student performance at Key Stages 3 and 4 as well as GCSE results. When governors received the Summary of Examination results for 1993–4 and compared them with predictions, again they were tacitly scrutinizing the curriculum.

League tables piled on the pressure. Governors were required to monitor the results of SATS at Key Stages 3 and 4, and GCSE, to read them off against local and national results, and they probed the work of any departments where results did not seem to satisfactory. It was not only that. Every new piece of legislation, every new regulation affecting health and safety, special educational needs, needed documenting for implementation. Records of attendance, ethnicity of students and staff, compliance with equal opportunities legislation, watertight disciplinary procedures for students and staff, policies for admission, behaviour, punishment, marking, assessment, charging fees for extra curricula activities, complaints procedures, all had to be drafted, approved by governors and made available to parents if they were not distributed to parents. This is what local management meant in practice.

It was the workload of record keeping, and making returns so that the school could compile full records which took some teachers to the limit. Furthermore, once the curriculum committee of the governing body got to work, staff could be asked all manner of detailed questions about what was being taught, how it was being taught, and why it was that results were either up or down on previous performance. So the pressures of staff mounted up as governors took their legal responsibilities ever more seriously.

In that way curricular matters filtered down through the entire staff, adding responsibilities for all teachers. Heads of department became more consciously responsible for the work of the department, overseeing record keeping. Heads of year became the main engines for dealing with attendance, behaviour and providing appropriate pastoral care, again all of which had to be assimilated in a data base to deal with returns to government.

There was clear gain in much of this. That kind of scrutiny sharpened the attention of teachers to what they were doing and how they were doing it. Monitoring enabled them to be more aware of their strengths and weaknesses. But the pressures became something of a different order. And when an Ofsted inspection was due it all culminated in almost unbearable pressure for teachers, with the governing body having to answer for its stewardship. But as the head put it: 'A superfluity of bureaucracy in the name of accountability'.

The Ofsted report took them further into the curriculum. The college was required to produce an action plan designed to meet the alleged deficiencies reported by the inspectors. It was produced by February 1995, signed by the head and the chair of the governing body and distributed to all parents, who were invited to a meeting in April 'to discuss the plan in more detail'.

The action plan was constructed around nine issues. Each had the same set of headings: what we aim to achieve, what we need to do, when completed (the self-checking mechanism), staff responsible, resources required and criteria for success. The issues were:

1 The health and safety concerns listed in the main body of the report must be addressed as soon as possible.
2 To improve overall standards strategies must be implemented to share the expertise in teaching and learning apparent in some curriculum areas with others where these are less secure.
3 The assessment policy has to be consistently implemented and assessment information used more fully in curriculum planning and in providing for the individual needs of students.
4 The college must continue to take notice of the code of practice for special educational needs (SEN), especially in production of individual learning plans.
5 Sex education must be provided for the sixth form and the programmes for music and modern languages must be fully implemented in Key Stage 3.
6 The college must make all efforts to improve the attendance of pupils, especially in Years 10 and 11 where levels are unsatisfactory. The registration

system should be reviewed with the aim of improving the access of information as an aid to monitoring.

7   The provision of religious education through the college must meet the requirements of the agreed syllabus.

8   The college must conform to the statutory requirements for a daily act of worship for all pupils.

9   The college development plan should be more concise and have a longer view. The costing of individual targets would provide greater efficiency.

That was what the governors agreed to undertake in fulfilment of their legal responsibilities following the Ofsted report.

Overall it seems fair comment that no serious weaknesses had to be addressed, that the action plan was more of a clearing up operation than undertaking anything new. For the curriculum, the report could be interpreted as, 'press on regardless'. It is little wonder that there was disenchantment at the report's use of national standards of achievement as a yardstick for judging the work of the college rather than what the students actually achieved.

The curriculum story so far

In 1995, at the end of the fifth headship, Senacre had been in existence for thirty-eight years. Its five heads had taken its curriculum from an essentially unsupervised regime with many initiatives and innovations to a highly centralized system with a supervisory regime which amounted to attempted micro management of schools by the Department for Education and Employment, using Ofsted and its contracted inspectors as its outriders. In between those two poles the curriculum had evolved from an exploration of possibilities, through the requirements of an all ability entry under Kent's 13+ scheme into a second phase of innovation and carefully managed consolidation. A strong drive followed to infuse the entire curriculum with technology as an essential learning tool, seizing the benefits of becoming a grant maintained school and a technology college, while negotiating a course through an ever increasingly complex series of bureaucratic demands.

Official intervention on the curriculum had developed exponentially. It began with TVEI as a benign influence, went on with the records of achievement, created new opportunities through the replacement of CSE and GCE with GCSE. Those were affected by the requirements of the National Curriculum, tests at Key Stages 1–4, GCSE examination results. League tables according to targets set by government became the measuring tools for determining the effectiveness of schools through Ofsted. It had been a hectic, hurly-burly time for reacting to intervention. And just as intervention developed exponentially, so did the workload laid upon teachers at every successive stage.

During that time, governors had come from nowhere with nothing much to do, apart from technically having the deciding voice in the appointment of the head of the school, to somewhere where they had a legal responsibility for every aspect of the life of a school and in particular for the curriculum and the standards of achievement. The local authority had changed from a body which controlled the school to an institution used by the department as it found convenient and used by the school if it chose to pay for its services. Parents who took little interest in the early stages had become powerful figures on the governing body, scrutinizing all the various activities the school undertook and settling priorities for future development. Admissions procedures had changed from prescribed catchment areas so that parents were told where to send their children to school, to complicated arrangements for meeting parental choice, which in theory, but not always in practice, meant that children went where their parents wanted them to go.

It all meant that Senacre had moved from being one of a protected species to a threatened species, one that existed primarily on its own efforts to recruit students, educational Darwinism. It also meant that uncertainties about numbers and the narrow room for manoeuvre within the prescribed curriculum placed constraints on any efforts to use home grown initiatives to tune learning opportunities to the needs of the students, as the school understood them. Local professional judgement had been replaced by central government fiat. That was part of the legacy which the sixth head inherited.

However there was another part. The school's success depended on using technology in the curriculum to override some of the constrictions of the National Curriculum. And it could not have been done without the benefits of becoming a Grant Maintained School. A technological flavour was introduced to the curriculum diet. It is an arresting example of how pragmatism can help to realize intentions, even dreams.

One theme runs as an obbligato to the curriculum provision throughout: numbers. The problem of maintaining a full first year entry began in the third headship; the competition forced on schools became a major issue during the fourth headship, which to a large extent was dealt with satisfactorily by curriculum development. And it was curriculum renewal through the emphasis on information technology which contributed largely to the school holding its own during the fifth headship. That was the mechanics of it, but by 1995 the educational question posed in 1988 remained. How far was competition helping Senacre serve its students educationally to the best of its and their ability? That question now probes governments' claims that extending 'choice' ever more widely is the best way to improve secondary education. Doubts remained.

Had there been an intervention account book it would have had many more entries than before. Losses: Ofsted's crudity and inconsistencies, bureaucratic madness, naïve approach to teacher workload, narrowed curriculum, exclusion of teacher initiative; gains: higher standards, sharper staff, local management, grant maintained opportunities.

Chapter 7

Curriculum on the slide

The sixth headship, Allan Deacon, 1995–2000

Becoming head of Senacre in 1995 was no easy assignment. The college had had two outstanding, dynamic leaders. They were no easy act to follow. Becoming a head of a grant maintained school with technology college status was no sinecure either. The targets that went with that new form of independent status were demanding. The amounts of extra funding were declining and were not recurrent and at Senacre there were the requirements laid upon the school as a technology college. Moreover rolls were falling again. There was bound to be a knock-on effect of these developments on the school and its curriculum, but no one could possibly predict the kind of educational environment in which those effects might be felt. Hence there was no knowing what might happen to the curriculum and the innovations brought in by the last two heads.

The curriculum tasks of the three previous heads had been clear. The third head from 1974–84 had to revert to a more or less traditional curriculum to accommodate changes to admission policies introduced by the Kent LEA, which meant running a pre-grammar school regime for pupils in their first two years. Apart from that, changes to the curriculum were modest. Between 1984 and 1988 the fourth head set himself to preserve the school by making curriculum changes which were a calculated attempt to persuade parents that Senacre was the school for their sons and daughters, and so securing a full complement of students. To do that there were a whole host of internal reorganizations and reforms. The fifth head, taking the school up to 1995, built on the success of his two predecessors. By using every financial means available there was an attempt to create a curriculum which was infused with information technology and give it an entirely new direction. Again this was accompanied by wholesale changes, this time not only to the way the academic work was organized and conducted of what had become Senacre technology college, but by a radical overhaul of the administration of its financial affairs.

So for eleven years Senacre experienced more or less continuous change to its curriculum. And because every change affected the staff in one way or another, it was bound to take its toll. Institutions are simply collections of individuals who work to established practices within necessary sets of requirements. Change in institutions is always fraught for some of those individuals who are at the receiving end and there comes a limit to the amount of change they can accommodate. During that period the full range of change had been sustained through strong leadership with a vision to steer by.

In 1995 in the new head's first year, the deputy saw things clearly:

> The issue in the Deacon era was (1) to try to retrieve falling rolls (2) to address the issues raised at the last Ofsted inspection in 1994 and (3) to operate a budget, which was acceptable to the LEA.

Every one of those three succinct tasks posed difficult problems. But it was the second which became almost intractable. It meant improving all the items on the agreed action plan with diminishing resources.

The head's second year began ominously for the curriculum. In October there was a letter from the technology college unit at the DfEE. It began:

> Ministers are disappointed that the school's examination achievements in 1996, particularly in design technology and science, continue to fall short of the standards we had expected to see.

It said that approval for the third year's funding was given 'in expectation that the school will continue to make every effort to make significant progress towards its third year targets'. It ended with what seems like a tactful warning, which in the event was heeded. 'The specification for the second phase of funding is demanding and you will wish to consider carefully before deciding whether to apply'. The college did not apply.

So the sixth head had a very difficult task. Against that background of targets not being met, it was to maintain the sense of direction and enable Senacre to hold its own in a fiercely competitive world. Allan Deacon was an English specialist, like his predecessors John Warner and Margaret Lynch, and had been a successful deputy head of a large secondary school in another local authority. He had attended Gordonstoun, taken a degree in English and had taught in a community school which had highly developed 'outward bound' activities, before moving on and becoming a deputy. His was a very different style, relatively laid back whereas his predecessors had been hard drivers. One senior colleague who was then teaching part time recalls:

> I attended one of two of his assemblies and 'felt the changing pulse' ... he was exceptionally reasonable and logical towards the students, always appealing to their common sense.

And he had a different kind of aura and presentation. As one person remembers: 'he had potential charisma, being of significant build, having a cast eye and wearing a cape and Australian bush hat for his playground duties'.

He found a very experienced, effective senior management team, which had worked together through the two previous headships. They ran the school smoothly through long and very hard work, put huge effort into pupil recruitment, oversaw all curriculum developments, coped with whatever crises arose, especially disciplinary, and had clear reporting lines to the head. They were expecting a lead. It seemed in his first year that the new head was taking stock of his inheritance, and just let things run on. Unfortunately the drive for recruitment slackened during this period and before long the numbers problem hit home hard, with inevitable consequences for the curriculum. The task of sustaining the school and preserving its imaginative curriculum became increasingly difficult, not to speak of meeting the requirements of the action plan which awaited him, following the Ofsted inspection.

The deputy head refers to numbers in these terms.

In my early days at Senacre the intake was 240 students per year. In the later years this dropped to well below 100 students per year. Consequently the major driver in the latter years was not the desire to be innovative but the importance of increasing numbers of students in the school. The need to survive in a competitive market became the most important influence on the decisions we made.

Nevertheless three years later the examination results for 1998 were glowing. The *Kent Messenger* reported:

The dramatic improvement in examination results in Senacre Technology College has continued in the past year. The percentage of students gaining five or more A–C GCSE grades has doubled in as little as three years. This summer more than 86 per cent left with at least five passes so the success goes right across the ability range. The success story continues to the sixth form. There were thirty students in1995 but now there are eighty and the number of courses has doubled. The students are achieving quality results both in GNVQ and A levels. This year there are distinctions in GNVQ advanced and B and C grades at A level. More than half of Year 13 went on to university or higher education.

The article reported that there were more than 200 computers in the main network, many running on Windows 95 and all kept up to date. It reiterated the views expressed by the deputy head earlier that students did not just learn how to use computers but used them to solve problems, and to tackle new challenges and learning opportunities. By then there were five computer rooms with terminals across the college, and the library was the central learning centre with videos, CD-roms and internet connections. The emphasis on the technological strand to the curriculum continued.

The provision for the physically disabled students remained strong. The same newspaper article said:

> The college has a specialist unit for the physically disabled students. The fifteen young people are fully integrated into the life and work of the college and supported by special staff. The site and buildings are fully adapted.

That short paragraph is a tribute to the foresight and wisdom of Margaret Lynch, the third head, who took the initiative in establishing the unit during the school's third headship. All in all things seemed satisfactory. Below the article there was a large block advertisement inviting parents to visit the school for an open evening at one of the half a dozen times when a tour of the college was being arranged.

There were however two factors which influenced those 1998 GCSE results. Those students who scored convincingly in the GCSE had entered the school six years earlier when the school was in full flood of excitement of becoming grant maintained and a technology college. Powerful parental support then made Senacre a first choice school for many, which translated into a strong student thrust to achieve well. At the other end of the ability range a humanities course had been devised to take the pressure off students who otherwise would be entered for five or more GCSEs and for whom some experience of the world of work would serve them better. Six periods a week were taken from their GCSE allocation so they could cover a range of topics: law and order, consumers, local authorities, fire and police services. The number of students rose to fifty on one occasion, and they affected the statistics. But behind those impressive results worries multiplied.

Academic review days

That article referred to academic review days, and therein lay a serious and longer story. It was a reaction to some comments made by the Ofsted inspectors. But in another sense it was an attempt to deal with the numbers problem.

Since Kent dropped the 13+ transfer scheme for grammar school selection in late 1992, attendance at parents' consultation evenings had dropped to about 30 per cent. Unsurprising because parents who are ambitious for their sons and daughters and/or come from homes where education, books and schooling are seen as a vital route to success in life, are keen to know everything they can about the results their children are achieving. School features large on their horizon. Attending consultation meetings enabled them to find out. Many from those kinds of homes no longer came to the college, so a larger proportion of the parental body tended to have lower aspirations for their offspring, for any one of a thousand reasons. The composition of the parent body changed with the inevitable consequences. Numbers attending dropped.

Academic review days were introduced to try and encourage more parents to take a closer interest in the progress their children were making. This was a different way of looking at Consultation. The idea was to give each student targets in every subject, assess them at the end of the term and use them in discussion with parents during the academic review day. Clearly it was a response to one of the criticisms made during the 1994 Ofsted inspection. The deputy head explained.

> I introduced academic review days as an attempt to formalize target setting for students in the school and to get more parents involved in their son or daughter's education. This involved a massive amount of staff development and management.

It worked. The head said:

> These are held between 8 a.m. and 6 p.m. and we are delighted with parental response. More than 90 per cent attend with teacher and student – a strong commitment during the working day.

But behind that lay other concerns which worried the deputy head:

> Target setting was the new concern. The government was keen to measure progress in terms of value added. We began to make more use of NFER data to chart trends and to use an NFER service that predicted individual performance at GCSE ... the GCSE in English was demanding and challenging. League tables brought immeasurable stress to curriculum leaders. They were now answerable to the head and governors for their subject results.
>   'Open days' continued to be a 'big sell' for the school trumpeting its success with an eye on recruitment, rather than the erstwhile pleasant and relaxed occasion when parents could look at the work of the school and their child in particular.

So at the same time as trying to enlist stronger support from parents, academic review days became a tool for not only monitoring individual students' performance but for conducting what was essentially a curriculum review.

Careful preparation preceded the launching of academic review days. A document went out to all staff.

> During the academic year 1997–8 Senacre will be moving away from tutorial arrangements whereby tutors are mainly concerned with pastoral and administrative concerns, to a system where more attention is given to monitoring academic progress and thus there is ultimately a higher profile for tutoring within the school. It is hoped that quality one-to-one tutor reviews will become an effective way of raising levels of achievement.

Subject teachers were required to make an estimated grade for each student, and to use the relationship between it and the target minimum grade as the focus for discussion with parents and pupils about whatever seemed the most appropriate steps to be taken for the student to improve. Report sheets simplified recording for teachers. There was a 'how to do it best' section spelling out suggested ways of exploiting the occasion for the benefit of students and then this.

> Involving students in an assessment dialogue is a simple means of providing a wealth of insight into the impact of teaching – how the individual is coping with that teaching and the impact on him/her. It is important that students examine the way they allocate responsibility for their success or failure – the LOCUS OF CONTROL. PERHAPS THE MOST IMPORTANT OF ALL, BY INVOLVING STUDENTS, ASSESSMENT ACKNOWLEDGES THEIR STATUS AS UNIQUE, INDEPENDENT HUMAN BEINGS – not a faceless component of a homogenous 10E(1) or 11W(4).

Locus of control referred to a comment made by inspectors in 1994. The deputy head was urging the staff to use academic reviews as a chance to try and get students to accept more responsibility for their own studies as well as having a sideways swipe at the instrumental nature of the National Curriculum.

Academic review days were designed to stimulate the interest of parents in their children's learning attainments while at the same time collecting data which would enable the school to meet the returns demanded by government. But implicitly it was yet another dimension to the staff's professional development. Close examination of the curriculum for which they were responsible faced them with the quality of the learning which it revealed. The entire enterprise became a commentary on the quality of teaching, which no doubt is how some staff interpreted it. This was a thorough-going response to the Ofsted inspection but it threw a huge additional workload on staff, already stretched in other directions. But if 90 per cent of parents used the opportunities offered by academic review days, then there must have been some sense of gratification. There ought to have been, because later in the Ofsted inspection in 1999 they were singled for praise.

But it did not stop there. An evaluation followed the first academic review day to check its effectiveness. This was the briefing for the teachers who were involved.

> I was anxious to gain some insight into students' understanding and perceptions of the Academic Review Day at this early stage of the new development. I ask that the form tutors who were kind enough to assist me in conducting the survey, give no assistance to the students in their care other than explaining what the questions meant, if there was any confusion.

The survey had four sections which posed questions for students. The first was, 'Explain in your own words what is going to happen on academic review day'. Responses were typified by 'I talk with my tutor and see if I am good or bad and see if I am having a good time at Senacre ...' 'ARD is about my parents coming into the school and looking at my next steps. They will talk about my improvement and difficulties. These next steps will then tell my parents what my problems are'.

There were several 'I don't know, don't really know'. One cheerfully remarked 'it could be fun for everyone'. Another said, 'I don't know much. All I know is that we get a day off school while our parents come in and review our work and behaviour'.

Responses were as varied for the section 'Are you looking forward to the academic review day?' The last two sections asked if students had any general comments on the targets they had been set and which targets were most easy to meet and which were the most difficult.

Drawing inferences from the students' responses, the introductory note for staff at the top of that last section in the report of the evaluation reads:

> We still have a long way to go in sharpening our target setting procedures. Whatever our present shortcomings, however, the students are enormously interested in and serious about their next steps. Students, like everyone else, work better when they share some control over what happens to them. Students are already 'measuring up' to their targets and the progress they have made in achieving them to date. It is important that all students see their next steps as challenging and are not allowed to be complacent.

Some targets 'lifted' verbatim from the National Curriculum must be made more 'user friendly'.

> Targets must be differentiated – there is a wide range of ability, previous experience and aptitude within each set. Students selecting from a menu should be monitored/guided. Targets must be subject specific. 'To complete homework' will not do. It is the subject teacher's responsibility to *ensure* that each student *understands* the target set. The target should be succinctly expressed.

Thus the evaluation was a means of facing up to the threefold intentions which lay behind academic review days: arousing greater parental interest and sustaining recruitment, acquiring data to use when completing the returns demanded by government and monitoring the effectiveness of the curriculum in promoting learning.

But it is also clear that academic review days were based on an interpretation of the issue of locus control which had arisen from the first Ofsted report in 1994. It was student engagement in the curriculum down a different route and was a deliberate exploiting by the college of Ofsted and so government requirement, using it in the college's own way, to help students concentrate on what they were in the college for and why. Because of the way the questions were posed, it was like a powerful dose of a personal social and health education programme. The emphasis throughout was on the value of getting students to take responsibility for their own learning. It was tuned to meet their growing needs as individual young men and women. Simultaneously and without saying so, it was a means of trying to encourage staff to do the same. For the college, whatever the level of success of academic review days, it was an indication of the seriousness with which it approached its educational responsibilities. Implementation of a scheme like that depends heavily on a clear chain of command, running through top to bottom of the staff, with heads of department in the pivotal position. It was bound to be patchy, weakened as it was by the retirement of some key staff members.

In essentials it was another version of the whole school interpretation of the curriculum. The school was not doing anything new. It was merely the latest attempt to find ways of doing more to promote students' learning. And that is one of the reasons why staff found it so hard to understand, never mind accept, the grounds on which the 1994 Ofsted inspectors said what they said in their report. There was no wonder that the curriculum was in danger of languishing. But even behind all those efforts to use the curriculum more effectively, all was not well.

Curriculum scrutiny deepened

The second Ofsted inspection took place in 1999 (Ofsted contract number 704593). Then there were 757 students, a 17 per cent drop since the previous inspection. Half of them were on the college's register as needing educational support. Forty had statements of special educational need and one-fifth were entitled to free school meals.

Early on, the report referred to the large number of students who came from three nearby housing estates where there was considerable unemployment and elements of social and economic deprivation, with all the challenges that posed for the head and the college. The report also noted that the re-instated 11+ examination meant that 25–30 per cent of each year group attended grammar schools and that the increasing popularity of other wide ability schools in the vicinity of Senacre had contributed to the reduction of pupil numbers.

Nevertheless, the inspectors had the action plan derived from the first Oftsted inspection as a reference document for what the college had been required to do to improve. Against such a background, that was no easy assignment for any school. The Ofsted inspectors wrote a troubled and troubling report. There was little good news to comfort the governors.

The inspectors found in contrast to the first findings, levels in mathematics and science were low and too many students at Key Stages 3 and 4 showed unsatisfactory results. They identified at all levels in the college's organization, poor management and leadership. And there was a general finding that the key issues and weaknesses identified in the first report had not been tackled effectively. That was a very serious matter indeed. So much so that given those deficiencies, the inspectors doubted that the college was capable of making the necessary improvements.

That was a bleak message. Nevertheless inspectors acknowledged the improvement shown in the 1998 GCSE results, the continued good service offered to physically disabled, positive attitudes among students and good relationships between them and the staff, good standards of behaviour, good support and guidance for pupils to ensure their welfare. They found that the curriculum was improved for pupils who previously did not achieve GCSE and that finances were controlled very effectively with good financial management and planning. With all that on the plus side the weaknesses stand out uncomfortably and rather strangely.

There was an even-handed commentary on the governing body. It was supportive, well informed, with a sound structure of sub-committees so that it played its proper strategic role. Despite that, it did not know much about curriculum development which meant it was not able to monitor effectively, and it needed to be more active in pressing for high levels of achievement and so a sound educational provision.

And that seems to be the central cause of the unravelling of the curriculum. One way or another inspectors found that effective management at all levels brought into focus the unsatisfactory levels of learning. There were extensive references to what were considered to be serious weaknesses of attainment throughout the report.

That contrasts sharply with many remarks in the quality of teaching section. There, it was reported that three-quarters of the lessons observed were satisfactory, and very good in about 15 per cent. Throughout the college English was judged good, and mathematics sound. For Years 7–9 teaching was sound with art, history and IT as most effective while geography, mathematics and science least effective. For Years 10 and 11 English, art, history and physical education were most effective and design technology and science least effective. At sixth form level, English and business education were good. Given that the teaching was sound in those particulars, the unacceptably low levels of student achievement as the inspectors judged them, stood out with alarming prominence. Somewhere along the line, it had to be that the drive had weakened for lifting learning attainments through the classroom provision of the curriculum. It seemed that lower expectations all round had taken over.

Curriculum disintegration

For some time the head and the college had been caught in a range of external events over which it had little or no control, facing them with a series of issues, which at the very best of times would have presented a chorus of daunting problems. Numbers of students dropped steadily with disastrous consequences. The demography of the area served by the college changed, so that there were fewer potential students to go round all the schools. This was where the lessening of the drive for recruitment hurt the college badly. Demolition of part of the Shepway estate meant re-housing some families in a different area, which again reduced the numbers of children in primary schools and so they became less effective as feeders.

Demography affected other schools as well. One nearby slipped into serious trouble and was on the edge of closure. Numbers were threatened in another school which was situated in a far more pleasing area and had looked more to rural areas than to housing estates nearer to Maidstone. It reacted to the numbers danger with a very strong and aggressive recruiting campaign which without doubt, took students away from Senacre.

Reduced numbers meant less income. Balancing the budget became a nightmare but it was done successfully, as the inspectors noted. Staffing costs amounted to about 80–85 per cent of the annual budget. Possible reductions in other costs, like curriculum materials, maintenance and in-service training for teachers were so small in comparison with staffing costs that inevitably the school had the horrible task of reducing staff numbers.

Just when a sense of stability could have helped cope with the inevitable low morale caused by these developments, the senior staff were gravely weakened. The deputy who invented academic review days was made redundant within a year of the inspection. Another took early retirement. The third had a heart attack. Others who had served for thirty years had retired already or taken early retirement. So the salary bill was reduced but at a very heavy price.

In these circumstances there were fewer possibilities for promotion and staff, especially experienced ones, looked for posts elsewhere. Enthusiasm declined as some staff did not care for the regime which was developing around them. And so there was a rapid turnover of staff as well. All this was on top of the way the ending of the 13+ scheme had prompted some very good teachers to look for posts where they would continue to teach the top 25 per cent of an age range. And a decimated senior management team weakened further the grip of the head and other senior staff not only on the curriculum but on the general running of the college.

It is hardly surprising for the deputy head who was the curriculum manager to recall that somehow the thrust seemed to have gone out of curriculum leaders, so that there was less energy than there might have been to cope with the gruelling problems of staffing subjects across the curriculum. It was not easy to find replacements at middle level. Staff found themselves teaching outside their immediate expertise. English remained strong as it had been from the time when the school opened. Mathematics was adequately staffed, and in fairly good shape, although the head of department had a dreadful time making do with supply teachers because of long-term absences, so staffing remained a continuing anxiety. Science also remained a continuing problem. But certainly it all distracted attention from teaching and learning. The deputy added another point.

> I did have the feeling though that although the sense of wanting to work and drive was there, it had gone a bit stale so that there was not the same energy and enthusiasm. There was something of the attitude 'Oh I've seen it all before'.

In an attempt to get on top of some of the financial problems, as numbers fell the head introduced a flatter management system at senior and middle level. Inevitably this weakened further the grip on the curriculum from the centre and increased the difficulties of monitoring performance. The staffing problems and reduced student numbers meant it was hard maintaining any direction of the curriculum, whatever the system. With two deputies gone, and one on sick leave, the difficulties of keeping a grip on things were illustrated when a new internally appointed assistant head without significant administrative experience – he had been a head of year – found himself appointed one day, and the next, the only member of the SMT on the premises. As he says, 'it was scary'.

A senior colleague makes the point directly.

> The size of the SMT peaked at head plus four and was reduced by 2001 to head plus one ... meant that the work load of any individual increased and in some cases meant that effectiveness was curtailed. [The remaining deputy] was primarily responsible for discipline and attendance in addition to other things. Was his workload realistic?

Clearly this senior colleague thought it was not. He relates that to loosening of discipline.

> Over a period of time discipline deteriorated to the point where generally staff found it difficult to cope with more difficult students, disciplinary procedures were often ineffective ... there is a direct correlation between increased disruption in lessons and reduction of the quality of teaching. If one is unlikely to be able to deliver a lesson effectively, is there a real point in preparing superb lessons?

And such is the way that things are; fluke pays a part. Successive entry cohorts are always different. At that time it seemed as if there was a deliberately disruptive element which was working its way through the school, and set out to make itself a nuisance during the inspection. It seems that the cards were stacked heavily against Senacre, leaving very few in the hands of the school itself.

The upshot of this sorry story was that the curriculum became something of a lottery, as gaps in the staffing were plugged as best they could be by juggling those available. Teaching became increasingly difficult and some of the learning opportunities for students shrank or disappeared. To the outside world this presented a picture of a college struggling to preserve itself which was hardly likely to encourage parents to enrol their children when they had the option of seeking entry elsewhere. Whatever the college did, the numbers of problems continued.

All this had borne very heavily on the three deputy heads from 1995 onwards. It meant that there had been less time and energy to do what the college had been good at doing: recruiting students. The drive weakened. There was less time for the kinds of pastoral activities which had stood the college in such good stead with parents. Home visits became almost impossible with the inevitable result that in important ways discipline suffered. The sense of team work at the top diminished, and without a strong sense of direction, senior staff tended to go their own ways.

To a limited extent the financial consequences of declining numbers were disguised. Part of the deal for the Safeway supermarket to be built adjacent to the school had been a land swap. Safeway got some land from Kent Constabulary.

The police got some land from Senacre and the college got a field next to its own playing field which was poor land. A developer wanted it and so the school sold it for £680,000.

But that could not ward off the financial difficulties facing the school for long, and it was against that deteriorating financial position that the school had decided against applying for the second tranche of funding for technology colleges. The special funding that went with the status of technology college dried up making a difficult financial position even worse. A combination of declining numbers and the need to meet targets of attainment threatened to throttle the college. The so say market economy was extracting a heavy price.

The governing body and the curriculum

Thus the governors found themselves in an unenviable position when they received the Ofsted Report in 1999. It confronted them with the fact that the college had only just escaped being put in special measures. Their legal responsibilities were clear. They had to produce a balanced budget and ensure that the requirements of the National Curriculum were met. That was bad enough, but when it came to making the returns demanded by the department they had the unhappy task of submitting returns which failed to meet the targets for attainment which had been set. They had to reduce staffing costs while having less means of getting the results they were supposed to produce. And in the middle of all that they had to introduce performance related pay. Even coverage of the National Curriculum was under threat. It was a tragic dismantling, even demolition of what had been so recently a fine edifice.

And as before the Ofsted report required governors to produce school development plans which listed key tasks, targets, and required an action plan to meet them. Progress on the deficiencies from the 1995 report had to be recorded on carefully prepared charts which itemized tasks, activities, completion dates and staff responsible. Performance by subject departments was scrutinized. School attendance figures featured prominently, plotting the various up and downs. Equal opportunities, disability, special educational measures all had to be kept in line with the latest legislation. It was all laid down in neat lines and boxes in a fourteen page document.

But all that which relates to the curriculum directly was only part governors' responsibilities. There were myriad other items for them to attend to. The range of their responsibilities is illustrated by a one term training programme put on for governors by another LEA. Consider these short course headings: the leadership incentive grant; implications for governors of the Disability Discrimination Act; sex and relationship education – developing a policy; school workforce remodelling; the foundation stage profile for governors; new governors – understanding your role and responsibilities; developing a drugs policy; off site activities – governors' role; being a parent governor; working with gifted and talented pupils; how to set a safe budget; governor development; whole governing body development. Those fourteen courses were offered during a single term in 2003. Some were for two and half hours. Others were conducted at weekends. It was a very full programme. Yet there are only two sessions which relate directly to the curriculum. And that is a measure of the problems for governors in trying to fulfil their responsibilities for the curriculum. And over it all, in order to conform with legal requirements, each year a report had to be distributed to parents, giving an account of the school's performance and activities over the preceding year, followed by an open meeting for parents to ask questions or comment as they saw fit.

None of those responsibilities can be discharged without comprehensive information collected, collated and made available to governors by the head and the senior staff. Any new regulations about health and safety or statements on pupils with learning difficulties had to be dealt with while trying cope with the chronic difficulties arising from reduced staffing, declining numbers and growing disciplinary problems. Minutes of governors' meetings show anxieties expressed by a staff representative who urged governors to understand the importance of the support to staff given by deputies and the dangers of reducing them. The frustration shows through in the minutes.

> Although teachers have been criticized for poor teaching, the SMT and the governors must take responsibility for lack of assessment and review which could have added to these problems.

Meantime the LEA had taken note of the deteriorating situation. However it was in a difficult position itself. As Senacre was a grant maintained school, it had had no close contact with the LEA since 1993. Seven years is a long time to be without detailed information about a school which had got near to special measures. It did the best it could. It sent in some of its own advisors to try to help the school manage itself better.

HMI take a hand

When a school is found to have serious weaknesses in an Ofsted report, HMI visits the school periodically to investigate the progress being made. In February 2000 a letter went to the head, copied to the LEA and the Chair of governors, concerning the implementation of the college's action plan following a two-day visit by two inspectors from HMI late in January. The letter ended up by saying that the college had just avoided being put in special measures; that weaknesses, including leadership continued. Securing specialist teaching was a priority, particularly in mathematics. Generally everything needed improving before the next Ofsted section 10 inspection: governors' attention to quality and standards; links between middle and senior managers; standards in teaching; monitoring student attainment; improving attendance. That can be interpreted as meaning that if improvements did not come soon the college would find itself in special measures. Earlier there were references to low expectations by the staff, progress being too slow, an inadequate use of outcomes to improve teaching and raise standards of learning, and a lack of rigorous checking to see if those policies were fully implemented.

On teaching, despite finding that about half of the lessons observed were satisfactory and that some were either good or very good, the problem was that too many lessons were not well planned and were not pitched to match the known current levels of knowledge, understanding and skills within each class, however the students were grouped.

But it all homed on leadership. HMI recognized that the head had managed to change some attitudes, and that was reflected in students showing a greater will to succeed. While that was just about satisfactory, much more was needed to be done to develop a coherent strategy for raising standards and produce the necessary rigour, drive and determination to do so from the head. That was underlining the doubts expressed in the second report about the capacity of the college to achieve the necessary improvements.

That left the governors with a lot to think about. So, too, for the local authority. It acted. In January 2000 it parachuted-in an experienced deputy head, Mrs Sheila Storey, initially as deputy to strengthen the leadership. The sorry story was not over yet. The first Ofsted was satisfactory according to the inspectors and good according to the staff. The second found serious weaknesses, followed by a dire warning from HMI that it was only just on the right side of going into special measures. The threat was still there even though in each case some teaching was recorded as being of a high standard. The numbers problem made sure there was more to come. During those five years, intervention served the college ill: great loss; no gain.

Chapter 8

Curriculum recovered
The seventh head, Sheila Storey, 2000–4

Getting to work

In 1999 there were 757 students on roll. In 2002 there were 576 and in 2004 the numbers still stood at 572. Those were the boundaries within which the seventh head set about recovering the curriculum.

Sheila Storey was installed by the LEA in March 2000 as a deputy to help to steady the school. By May the Chairman of governors announced that the one remaining deputy would not be returning to the college owing to ill health. At the same time he explained that the head was on long term leave. He did not return. In May Sheila Storey was made acting head and from September 2000 she was appointed with a three year contract as headteacher of the college. In the event she stayed until August 2004.

Sheila Storey's route to becoming head of Senacre was as different as could be imagined from any of her predecessors. She trained as a physical education teacher, was awarded a Bachelor of Education degree, taught all of her thirty year professional career in Maidstone, and was promoted steadily, until she became a deputy head. As a result she was no stranger to the ups and downs of Senacre in general, but had little idea of the particulars of what she had let herself in for by agreeing to try to steer the college towards improving its position and performance.

In May 2000 she was without any senior staff and morale was very low among the staff. Even worse she was confronted by a staff with very low expectations characterized by 'What can you expect from kids like these?' The head took that as a professional affront and set about finding ways of changing it. She faced daunting difficulties. As she put it:

> Every stone I lifted had something unpleasant underneath.
> I just had to work with what I had got.

Her principles were clear: putting students' learning first as a way of concentrating minds on teaching. Putting those principles into practice was a nightmare. Without a deputy, she had two assistant heads who were inexperienced and had been internal appointments; essentially it was merely an embryonic senior team. Poor results in mathematics and science meant that the college had lost its technology status and both the strong teachers in the English department had left.

Being on the edge of special measures, the school was banned from appointing newly qualified teachers. Gaps were filled, sometimes by using people without any qualifications at all, and by PGCE graduate students from Canterbury College at the University of Kent (now Canterbury Christ Church College) and students from Stockwell College. An assistant head remembers staffing was so serious that there was no cover at all for staff absences, and he found himself taking 200 students in the hall. The LEA seconded some other senior teachers to fill in some gaps. But again, under those conditions fulfilling the requirements of the National Curriculum, never mind trying to lift standards, was indeed a troubleshooting job.

The head produced for herself a list of fifty-five items under the heading of 'Improvements since HMI January 2000'. That was a year after the second Ofsted inspection. It covered everything from a line management system with a schedule of meetings, through coffee meetings for parents and a school council for students, attendance, increased supervision at break and lunch time, uniform, daily briefing for staff, contacts with primary schools, a fashion show arranged by parents down to a box for complaints about bullying, briefing incoming Year 7, targets for every year, and ending up with 'replacement of the management team' and 'improvements to the staff room'.

That long list of 'can do/will do' items, some accomplished and some yet to be dealt with, gives a glimpse at the style and manner of approach to the task of recovery. The fifty-five items can be grouped crudely into four categories. Twenty-two concerned relationships one way or another affecting staff, students and parents. Several were about communication systems and vitally, one was about improvement to the staff room, and another about connections with primary schools. The next largest group was thirteen items connected with discipline and behaviour. Some were at the rudimentary level of compulsory seating plans for pupils and uniform, while others affected staff with increased requirements for supervision and tighter schedules of meetings. Eleven concerned management at school level. The nine which related specifically to curriculum matters were weighty: lesson observation, a document on teaching and learning styles, curriculum booklet for Year 7, new courses for Years 10 and 11, Easter revision courses, structured study lessons in Year 11.

Her priorities within the strategy for improvement were clear. Sort out the relationships with and between everyone involved, from top to bottom, both internally and externally. Use that as a step towards getting fewer uneven standards of behaviour from everyone within the school. School management items were to provide an overarching structure so that staff knew where they were, and what was required of them for curriculum improvement. It was an all-embracing drive which worked on the principle that it is no good having the most splendid curriculum on paper, unless there is some willingness on the part of students to learn, so that staff can feel encouraged to teach them.

In many ways it was a return to the concept of a whole school curriculum, at an operational level where the component parts were fitted together to form a platform for learning in the classroom. Where the first two heads were explicit about their concept of a whole school curriculum and the fourth and fifth heads used different language for different purposes in the cut-throat recruitment competition, the seventh head used the notion to reconstruct the platform for learning.

The third Ofsted

Halfway through that first year, the efforts were beginning to produce results, but slowly. Seven months after the head was drafted in came the third Ofsted inspection (Inspection number 210753) in January 2001. That report credited the acting head with decisive leadership which provided a sharper focus on what needed to be improved and how to set about it, but it found there was a long way to go. Decline in standards had been reversed and there were the beginnings of an organization fit to provide the service which the college should be providing.

However it was this third Ofsted inspection which put the college in special measures. It found that the teaching of the more able students encouraged them to work hard, that teaching in ICT was good, the provision for the physically disabled continued to be good as was careers education and work experience. But there was then a long shopping list of improvements which were required. All were very familiar items.

The obvious start was ensuring the stability of senior staff and of classroom teachers to ensure continuity in college administration and teaching. The inspectors could hardly say anything more obvious than that. They reiterated the need to lift standards in science, mathematics and English. Generally across the curriculum standards were far too low at the end of Key Stages 3 and 4. Inevitably, attendance and behaviour featured, and of course the curriculum needed to meet fully the statutory requirements. Art, ICT and French got modest seals of approval. But alarmingly, there was no music being taught because the music master had been made redundant.

The story runs right throughout the sections on the different subjects. It represents an extraordinary decline in a mere six years. For example, the report on English identified a whole range of reasons why standards were falling. While literacy levels for reading and writing were just about satisfactory, students could not express themselves clearly, found it difficult to listen carefully, and were hesitant to offer their own opinions. And the report commented on the notable decline from the last Ofsted when students spoke clearly with growing confidence and some imagination.

But there came again one of the difficulties of Ofsted inspections, the straitjacket. English standards were judged to be well below the national average, at the same time that most students' achievements were satisfactory. That cannot necessarily mean that any school or college earning those comments was failing.

However those comments need to be seen against two nagging questions. The first was numbers. By the time the inspectors arrived there were 659 students on the roll, a further drop, so there were fewer staff and the composition of that student body presented the same set of problems. Three hundred and eighty two were on the special needs register and forty-eight had statements. The immediate environment of the college was unchanged.

The inspectors recognized that. But the unhappy reflection is that either the inspectors did not know the history of the school or were unable to use what they knew to help them understand the school they were inspecting. That core catchment area for students was common to all stages of the school's story. At different stages, its arena expanded. The Thameside Scheme, the survival strategy of the fourth headship and the technological emphasis of the fifth headship variously added different student constituencies, which to some extent diluted the problems stemming from the core. By 2000, all those additions were stripped away, leaving only students from an above level of deprivation area. Whether any provision by the LEA before 1988 could have alleviated those circumstances is debatable. It remains to be seen how far the 'soft federation' referred to later can improve the learning opportunities open to students from that area. It is hard to see how competition for student recruitment has served them well.

The composition of the student body meant almost inevitably that there would be a gap between student achievements and national standards. It is all very well to accept that students' attainment on entry was well below average, that the ability profile of students has consistently been skewed towards the lower end and go on to judge that nevertheless given their attainment on entry, most students achieve satisfactorily. That sounds like an institution which is succeeding. It sits ill with the comment that measured against national standards there is low achievement among lower attaining students and a significant number of those with special educational needs. Of course there was, but it sounds like failure.

As with earlier Ofsted inspections, inspectors were in a straitjacket, required to stick to the rigid rules of judging student achievement against national standards so where the disparities show up, credit for school achievements takes second place. Whatever its achievements, the school was judged against averages for national standard. It was a bit like judging cakes in a competition where one had eggs and the others did not.

This points to the very great difficulties for a school given that assessment, in reaching satisfactory standards all round in the subjects of the National Curriculum, even with the very best management of the curriculum to be found. And it raises interesting questions about how to balance what is considered to be a nationally acceptable standard of education with an understanding of what a school or college is managing to achieve in the circumstances it finds itself in. So when the report ran over all that and pronounced that improvements were uneven, one can imagine the head thinking, 'Fancy that. Tell me something new. As if I did not know'.

The report laid heavy emphasis on relationships and attitudes. Some students were keen to learn. Many were not. Since student attitudes to learning are affected by every aspect of college life, relationships between staff, students and parents form the arena within which they learn. It was a familiar story. While inspectors found relationships to be good on the whole, where behaviour was unsatisfactory students lacked self-discipline, talked instead of writing and disrupted the work of other students. Predictably, teachers then had to interrupt the flow of a lesson and so wasted teaching time. And inevitably that sort of misbehaviour spilt over outside classrooms.

In the head's view that was a significant source of the trouble. By the time the next inspection came along she considered that a group of student 'lesson wreckers' who had set out to cause trouble during the last two inspections had left. This eased somewhat teachers' tasks in engaging students in their learning.

But as with that previous episode when a new head found a strike on his hands, this third Ofsted report gave the head the leverage she needed to enable the college to turn itself round. Indeed when she had got the college out of special measures in June 2003 and she was asked if she could have done it without HMI, the answer was an emphatic 'NO'.

So this third Ofsted was an external intervention which was thoroughly effective. But it is important to note that it was seven HMIs who gave consistent and regular help during the recovery period. They were full time experienced professionals. They did not lead Ofsted teams and were not occasional part timers, collected in contracted Ofsted teams.

Curriculum recovery begins

One of the keys to recovery was attitude taken by the governing body. The minutes of a meeting in June 2001 record the chair saying:

> He was conscious that the governing body had been criticized by Ofsted for not being pro-active enough in the past.

As if to underline the point, the head reminded governors that since the college was now in special measures it was the duty of the DfEE to monitor performance against the action plan. Termly visits by HMI would follow.

There are references in the minutes to the way that governors' visits as links to staff and subjects would be organized and briefing papers would be produced to indicate how those visits should be conducted. Monthly meetings took place between governors and the head. The effect of these arrangements was to produce a more coherent and comprehensive scrutiny of the curriculum. As governors became more actively involved, so staff became more actively involved. With regular governors' meetings as the apex of a schedule of meetings for heads of department, and the SMT, monitoring of performance and therefore student attainment became systematic. All this brought the governors much closer to being able to exercise their legal responsibilities.

Staffing became less unstable. Half had left during the head's first year, and replacements began to be recruited. The ban on recruiting NQTs was lifted. The LEA approved the appointment of two deputy heads who were inexperienced and had to be trained. Subject heads also required training. By delegating the chairmanship of subject heads' meetings to the deputy heads and not attending herself, the head strengthened lines for reporting and influence and induced an acceptance of responsibility for what they were appointed to do. Senior staff were given policy documents to digest, prompting them to try to see the college in a wider context. That sounds like a later version of the fourth head's feeling that the school was too inward looking. Some staff left. The change was such that by 2004, the head noted that only four remained of those who were on the staff when she first joined the school in May 2000. As the number grew of those she appointed, so did her ability to pursue lines of improvement and development, which she believed had to be followed if the school was to be released from special measures.

The close attention to relationships was another key to all these encouraging factors. Musing on the reasons for recovery, an assistant head put it down to three factors: better atmosphere; better behaviour; different attention to learning. He commented how much was being learnt about the way people learn and that those understandings were affecting staff members' approach to student learning. He had an interest in multiple intelligence assessment. On attitudes, the college he said felt 'warm', warmer that it had been for some time, reaching back beyond the recent headship. Not that it had not been warm before. He meant an easy acceptance by all of all. His reasoning was an echo of a remark made earlier by a deputy head: that there were disadvantages as well as advantages of having a largish number of long serving staff. At the beginning of his twelve years at Senacre, after several years of teaching experience he said he felt like a beginner all over again, so strong was the influence of a relatively large number of long serving staff. The greater warmth he referred to came after they had gone, so he claimed. Improved behaviour he thought might have something to do with the fact that a teacher was a former student and that some of the support and administrative staff who were former Senacre students served as role models for students who were following them. No doubt that could be influential. But essentially, better behaviour came from the all-round tightening of procedures and practices which was being driven by the head.

As part of the attempt to recover something of its external relationships with the community, closer connections were forged, again at head level, with primary schools, which were to be feeder schools for the college. There was a 'primary schools' visit day. Somehow the head thought that during the previous five years 'the school had closed itself off'. In turn this began to alter the perceptions of the school held by prospective parents. She made a deliberate attempt to correct what she saw as a previous failure which went back to recruitment policies. Unlike the fourth and fifth headships, the sixth had not set out to portray the college as a place where parents wanted to send their children. The seventh did. The withdrawal of the 13+ scheme in 1992 had made that all the harder and upped the stakes for recruiting hard against the aggressive competition for pupils pursued by other schools. The trend had to be reversed and it was. Numbers steadied.

Curriculum regained

During 25 to 26 June 2003, three HMIs visited the college for two days following up the seven visits during the preceding year (Reference. HMI 1819). Their task was to check on the progress made on the six key issues in the governors' action plan, which had been approved:

more stability among senior staff and teaching staff to get greater continuity of management and teaching;
more consistency in teaching and learning to higher standards;
improve support of students who have special educational needs;
improve the student learning achievements in science;
improve attendance;
improve the curriculum.

HMI judged sufficient progress had been made to lift the college out of special measures. Leadership had done it. The head had overcome her inexperience, as well as the lack of senior staff to support her. And she managed this despite the LEA's generous, well intentioned but inadequately planned attempts to rescue the college which in HMI's view created additional complications. They also reported that confusion over the renewal of her contract added to the pressure. That referred to her agreement with the LEA to serve for another year to see the college through to its incorporation in a local federation in September 2004 which will be described later.

Clearly HMI saw that the seventh head had served Senacre well. From top to bottom everything had changed. Management structures ensured the close monitoring of staff and student performance so that the curriculum had come back into its own. Governors' sub-committees added weight to all efforts.

English is always a good test of a school's performance. HMI found that standards were improving. There was better teaching and good organization and consistency within the department. Students were enthusiastic about their English lessons and keen to succeed, worked faster and covered more ground. They were impressed with a silent reading scheme to begin each lesson. Students brought appropriate books. Library borrowings shot up. Reading aloud and written work showed distinct improvement from the previous report. Mathematics and science were improving slowly; ICT was good. More significantly as a test for the health of a school, there was comment on the curriculum as a whole.

In trying to broaden a balanced curriculum which reflected the interests and needs of its students, the college had introduced some flexibility. That together with a student support centre for students in Key Stage 3 who found the traditional curriculum difficult to cope with had already proved its point. The report referred to three Year 9 girls, regular truants who had attended the centre, who took the national end of stage tests. The Key Stage 4 curriculum had more opportunities for work and college placements. It was noted that eight pupils followed a work-related programme because they found regular GCSE courses more than they could cope with. There was a different approach to re-engage disaffected pupils and provide confidence building exercises. There were more vocational courses and courses designed for those who wanted to continue study at sixth form level in other schools in the area consortium to come while retaining the course in child care. All in all HMI found that the broader curriculum was serving the students well. It took the head from March 2000 and June 2003 to do it and from January 2001 to June 2003 to move the school from being designated officially 'in special measures' to being officially out of them.

There is a general point to make here about curriculum control by government. The flexibility on which HMI congratulated the school, was only made possible by the relaxation first by David Blunkett and then by Estelle Morris and later by Charles Clarke, as secretaries of state of the prescriptions which govern the national curriculum. (The Tomlinson Report seeks to introduce far greater flexibility.) An assistant head was clear about this. Allocating five out of thirty periods each week to a general course had much to do with improved attendance. Twenty-three pupils went out visiting public services such as fire and health, public offices on a purely vocational basis. In curricular terms, it is important to note that this is almost identical to elements of the Enterprise courses in the 1960s and 1970s before the National Curriculum was imposed. While it is too early to notice any transferable motivation at work, the assistant head expects to see it. Some degree of autonomous initiative is being returned to schools. Without it HMI would not have been able to make their remark about flexibility.

The head was determined and tenacious and the efforts of her staff were amply rewarded. Perhaps even more important they were handsomely acknowledged by HMI. In part it was based on the team spirit which had been created and the very successful ways the school had managed to train its own staff effectively and create a sense of professionalism where staff were ready to change their style of teaching, and attending courses became a norm. Also it found several teachers with backgrounds similar to those of the students, and a sense of gratitude and loyalty to the institution. Half the staff were either newly qualified or overseas teachers or unqualified teachers.

There was still plenty to do. HMI listed key issues which governors, head, senior managers and staff needed to do to improve further the quality of education on offer. It was all very obvious. Eradicate unsatisfactory teaching and improve the rest. Develop middle managers' role as a tool for improving the quality of learning. Set about improving the teaching and learning in mathematics. Improve attendance, which really means reduce truancy.

No doubt the staff as well as the head agreed and said to themselves 'Well, they would say that wouldn't they? So would we'. But the recovery programme was impressive not only in its comprehensive approach to meeting the need for improvement but also in its execution.

In acknowledging that success, HMI produced a report of a different order from its three Ofsted predecessors and not because this one gave the college good marks and the last two bad marks. The language is different. It is elegant. There is a sensitivity running through the report. Whether it is referring to pupils and their below standard performance in classrooms, or teaching weaknesses, overall there is a sense of sympathetic understanding which touches below the surface. Reading this report, even the weakest teacher, recognizing her/himself on the page, would not feel deflated, discouraged, or abused. There is reproving, of course, but it is handled with professionalism, so that in a curious way encouragement is there as well. This report is an education document. No one could read it without being encouraged to do more. The contrast is stark with the mechanically flavoured reports issued by Ofsted.

This points to one of the most serious problems arising from the present regime of Ofsted inspections with their rigid adherence to national standards. How can the supportive style of inspection on which best practice thrives be resurrected? That is taken up in the next chapter.

Curriculum at risk

HMI's signing-off report was not the end of the Senacre curriculum story but one or two statements in the report did forecast a kind of ending. It claimed that through proposals for working with two neighbouring schools, Senacre was getting useful advice on teaching, management and liason between governing bodies.

Kent had created what it called a 'soft federation' of three schools: Cornwallis, Oldborough Manor and Senacre. Advice on teaching management and liaison might benefit Senacre, but those potential benefits might well be outweighed by the curriculum and other problems brought with them.

Cornwallis School's head was to double as a chief executive of the federation. The other two schools, Senacre and Oldborough Manor, would not have headteachers. They would have heads of school. In effect that downgraded them into subordinates, and on lower salaries of course. The idea was that the two subordinate schools should continue to function separately, while organizing their curricula so that they dovetailed with sixth form studies, whether offered in Cornwallis, Oldborough or Senacre. Necessarily for the two soft elements in the federation it seems that this would mean keeping curriculum developments in line with Cornwallis which has the largest provision at that level. They were also expected to develop a more vocational curriculum. At the same time each was supposed to create some specialization to comply with government policy for secondary schools.

Organizationally, this looks like a dog's dinner. Sixth form provision must be rationalized but this is a cack-handed way of trying to achieve it. Establishing a consortium for sixth form studies makes absolute sense. Each of three schools would then retain their own sense of identity, sustaining the loyalty of the staff and the regard of parents. All that is put at risk by two schools with heads of school rather than headteachers. Without a headteacher, institutionally a school seems half a school. In any case applying to run a school of 600 with such a reduced status may not be attractive. Full blooded integration could have been a better answer. Everyone would know where they were, so could a sixth form consortium with three contributing schools.

None of that would be made any easier by having a head of one school doubling as a chief executive of the three-fold federation. It would be extremely difficult to avoid the impression, whatever the reality, that Cornwallis leads at the expense of the other two, however much care is taken and sensitivity shown. Since the success of the enterprise will rest in large measure on the overall level of morale of all those involved, staff reactions will be critical. The 'soft federation' could turn out to be soft centred.

Educationally it looks risky. Cornwallis is also a technology college. Even though Senacre has lost its status, ICT remains a strong suit in the curriculum, as HMI's report documents. So two out of three institutions have strong ICT provision. That complicates plans to make each a specialist school. Assuming that Cornwallis retained its technology specialism, which is likely as the senior partner, Senacre would not be able to play to its strength: proven quality of learning and teaching, good resources and experienced staff. Were that to be the case it would have to devise something different. Under any circumstances that is a difficult proposition for a school. It means creating a new emphasis on the curriculum with all that it implies about re-deploying staff and resources. For Senacre to do that, having just got itself settled, is a daunting prospect.

Moreover to give a pronounced emphasis on vocational courses as a deliberate public policy is just as risky, given parents' attitudes and prejudices. Whether right or wrong, experience shows that parents are not attracted to attempts to promote 'vocational' as opposed to the 'academic' courses. To have two subordinate schools offering such a curriculum could create another numbers problem, perhaps deterring rather than attracting students. Perhaps Tomlinson's forthcoming report will help things along.

However the justification for this 'soft federation' will rest on its ability to create a curriculum which is responsive to the changes which will continue to occur in the world which surrounds it, and to the needs of the students who come from it. That means tapping the inventiveness of teachers. It also means organizing and managing that inventiveness. Doing that by using a senior and a couple of junior partners looks like an administrative nightmare. Two will look over their shoulders at one. And all will be looking over both shoulders at inter-school transport and how geography will affect student choice not only for entry but selection of sixth-form subjects. As a result, for Senacre HMI thought that more changes, building on its improved curriculum, however desirable, should wait until the arrangements for the federation were completed.

That is sad to read. It meant curriculum 'on hold'. The greater flexibility achieved already in the curriculum could not be taken further. Whatever the results of GNVQs in ICT and science, on what amounted to a test run in 2003–4, further expansion would have to wait. Intentions to extend work related courses to complement a reduced GCSE programme for the less able, as complimented by HMI, were put in limbo. It means that the brakes have gone on the drive for improvement of the curriculum.

It looks as if Kent has done it again. For over forty years it has shuffled around to keep its grammar schools. It made a botched job of the 13+ arrangements, which essentially seemed a device to retain them. It tried to close the school and failed because it had not thought through the educational implications it entailed. And now it has created a federation which seems neither one thing nor another, another botched job. It looks as if, again, convenience came first, education second.

Educationally, Senacre and its curriculum have been shunted into a siding. Instead of exploiting the momentum running towards better things, there would likely be an uneasy pause and the momentum lost. Anyone with ideas might well think there was no point in trying them out. It would not be at all surprising if some looked around to see where ideas might be given a fair wind in another school. Promotion could be very uncertain in a school in a soft federation, without its own head and where there is no knowing how far the entire staff complement of the three schools henceforth will be seen as a whole. The staffing problems which nearly wrecked Senacre could recur. All that is gloomy guesswork. It will need very strong drive to show that it is wrong. Despite all, perhaps Senacre can help to power the drive.

All the rewards and pleasure that came from the successful defeat of special measures within two and a half years, were overshadowed. Staff were uneasy. The sense of security, such a vital element and the foundation on which successful teaching rests, and indeed of the recovery accomplished, had been shaken. The head to whom the staff had given their loyalty was powerless to reassure them. Being demoted was of no interest to her. It is a wretched way to repay them.

All that is for the future and outside this story. In 2004 one side of the story for curriculum evolution from 1957 is an account of hills and valleys, ups and downs, far more ups than downs. With one brief interlude, curriculum development has never stood still. More often than not it was inventive. Just as high enthusiasm characterized the first two headships, quietened and then rose again during the fourth and fifth, so enthusiasm and purpose, as testified by HMI, has ended on a high note with what proves to be Senacre's last headship.

The other part of the story is of how successive heads managed to use their position and circumstances to propel the curriculum in directions which they believed would provide the best education possible within the resources available. An essential part of that half of the story is how they managed to do it under increasing regulation from outside.

Put the two together and there is a rudimentary profit and loss account of curricular development in one secondary school, Senacre, over nearly fifty years. That comes in the next chapter. But here it needs to be said that for nearly half of the forty-seven years of the story, curriculum intervention came in draconian measures. Only in the last few years has the government acknowledged its mistakes, tacitly accepting that it did much to damage to the secondary school curriculum.

Chapter 9

Curriculum roundabout

Profit and loss – the intervention account

It was a forty-seven year curriculum roundabout. It began with unsupervised freedom, excitement at adventurous explorations. The curriculum moved through investing the traditional with the progressive, only to revert to the traditional as required by the LEA, and then to deliberate consolidation for self-preservation, largely induced by parental choice and competition. The government's prescribed National Curriculum came next, simultaneously with the school's imaginative 'reach for the skies' information technology initiative. Then came a falling star, and a phoenix-like recovery, only to be reorganized again by the LEA and disappear into uncertainty in a 'soft federation'.

Now in 2004 ministers have decided to be less interventionist. The Tomlinson Report is billed to recommend what appears to be a return of the initiative to schools for curriculum change. The secretary of state has announced he will support those recommendations even in advance of the final report as part of what he claims is the biggest set of changes to the system since 1944. Ofsted is busy trying to reinvent itself by making greater use of HMI; not quite back where the curriculum started two generations ago, but moving towards it. Many schools can tell the same story.

Intervention for Senacre came first from local government. In 1963 it banned the very successful work experience programme which had been running for five years. That wrecked carefully laid plans for a 'curriculum for engagement' recommended by the Newsom Report. The LEA's Thameside Scheme of 13+ entry introduced in 1975 made life more difficult for 75 per cent of the secondary school population and the schools which served it. Both interventions go into the loss account.

Intervention from central government began tentatively. By issuing consultation documents it tried to manoeuvre local authorities into taking a more active responsibility for schools' curricula. Through the Schools Council with representatives from teacher unions and associations, local government, with HMI as observers it hoped to promote a collective curriculum developer with a national reach as a way of influencing classroom practice.

Both initiatives were in line with the permissive and successful forms of intervention, characterized by the introduction of the Certificate of Secondary Education and the recommendations of the Newsom Report. Imposition was not part of that thinking. All of that goes into the profit account.

Unfortunately progress down those two routes of consultation was too slow to satisfy the Conservative central government, so intervention became direct instruction in 1986, with an eighteen-year run of micro management through tight prescriptions, ending with an acceptance by ministers of its educational limitations and a relaxation of curriculum rules. That is where the secondary school curriculum stands in 2004.

Meantime, when Senacre got into trouble, LEA intervention as a support force proved ineffective. It was HMI who got it out of trouble. In this case the loss entry in the intervention account came from the incapacity of the LEA to intervene effectively in curricular matters and in some ways reflects the reservations of the fourth head when he served as a senior inspector, a clear loss. The profit is the professionalism of HMI.

Seen from 2004 there is inevitability about that curricular progression, given the parallel story of social and economic development. What was not inevitable was the form direct intervention took. There is no doubt that the introduction of SATs was a valuable lever for lifting standards. Equally the conversion of GCE and CSE into GCSE was a welcome stimulus to lifting expectations for Years 10 and 11 students and their teachers. TVEI was a benign attempt at intervention with wholly proper intentions. Nor was there anything wrong with the idea of a National Curriculum, or more regular systematic inspections. So all that too goes into the profit account.

What was wrong was direct intervention stemming from an unproven ideology of crude instrumentalism with a set of contentious assumptions about how to get improvements. Schools and teachers were failures and needed kicking. Bring them into line through a National Curriculum. Link that to targets with league tables. Promote parental choice – another entirely unproven instrument for promoting good quality education. Kicks would then be aimed in the right place. 'Ring fenced' funding for special initiatives would whet schools' appetites. Ofsted would patrol the system to make sure that education behaved itself. The entire ministerial thrust was based on chronic and irresponsible under-funding.

Unfortunately, in looking for quick results in the drive to lift standards, ministers ignored three golden rules. Seemingly definitive measurements often measure what is least important. Institutions do not change rapidly or to order. They succeed where the individuals who work in them are motivated to succeed. The point is made clearly by a senior staff member reflecting on his curriculum responsibilities in 1970:

> The moral was and is that in those far off days of curriculum freedom, what really worked was that which you had a hand in creating and/or framing – and that which you felt confident about, intellectually and in terms of delivery.

Because government failed to find ways of applying that 'moral' to the curricular changes it pursued, this is where the loss figures begin to pile up rapidly. Of course many claim, and it is not easy to deny it, that the government's imposition mentality and its reach for quick fixes meant it did not even try to harness teachers' sense of ownership. Instead between 1988 and 1997 there was unremitting hostility to teachers and schools by the Conservative government, with Ofsted and its chief inspector as a willing agent. Teachers felt bullied. It was no way to get teachers striving enthusiastically for improvements. This is failure, and is entered firmly in the loss account.

From 1997 the Labour government did much to rebuild bridges with substantially improved pay, with different career tracks looking for staff continuity. It sought to reduce the paper load on teachers, recruiting teaching assistants to do so. Teacher appraisal was a step towards professionalism. It increased the funding budgets very significantly. But the department limited its own success by driving hard at targets and league tables, while pushing micro management further and by introducing more initiatives than schools could cope with, while bureaucratically demanding ever more detailed information. The head's complaint stands, 'A superfluity of bureaucracy in the name of transparency'.

There were other flaws. Tests were fine but there were just too many of them at seven, eleven and fourteen. 'Teaching to the tests' became the norm in primary schools and the NC targets, GCSE and AS and A level results pushed secondary schools in the same direction. Some of the most valuable elements in the school experience were crowded out – imagination, creativity, exploration, experimenting, time and space to think, not to speak of music – and everyone, pupils/students/teachers, parents were robbed accordingly. The test mentality is exemplified by the infamous, almost incomprehensible 'foundation stage profile' for reception classes with its 117 items on 134 scales.

At the time parental choice seemed appealing as a way of requiring schools to look to their laurels. But it was a phoney choice in a rigged market. Schools were not allowed to grow or dwindle according to numbers. The proximity rule led to appeals and complaints. It promoted the 'moving house' tendency to be near a school of choice. There is no evidence whatsoever that choice of school is the top priority for the majority of parents. Bizarrely, parental choice led to greater student inequality. Astonishingly, another ideology seems to be driving this further.

Parental choice also led inevitably to arguments about covert selection and appeals. Specially designated schools re-inforced that belief. Ring fenced funding made long term curriculum planning complicated if not impossible. Schools were submerged in paper from the DfES. That is all clear loss.

Those flaws made Senacre's attempts to sustain an engaging curriculum more difficult than it need have been. There are now encouraging signs that some of these flaws are to be corrected. But the most serious flaw was the style of intervention. The Conservative period reduced teachers to technicians, de-professionalizing them, which was part and parcel of a profound distrust of all professions and established institutions. Ofsted merely confirmed that distrust. Its punitive stance guaranteed that in many cases improvements came despite it, rather than from it, as one long serving member of Senacre's staff pointed to the contrast between when he joined in 1961 and left in 1992:

> There was a lot of 'trust' in those days ... by the time I left with all the regulations, targets, league tables and returns, I felt as if I was being paid by the hour.

That is a terrible commentary from a devoted professional with a high sense of vocation. Such a serious flaw takes a very long time to mend. This is loss writ large.

Labour has done something to correct that but restoring a sense of professional pride depends on a sense of professional autonomy and takes time. The loosening of the National Curriculum is helping. It remains handicapped by the Ofsted brief of using national standards as the measuring stick of school performance rather getting a common sense combination of those standards and school student achievement. Under its third chief inspector it is moving towards a more supportive role but with troubling ambivalence. It is important however to remember that Ofsted is not answerable to the DfES. A modest profit gets recorded.

So for intervention, a preliminary profit and loss account shows some and some. The price of the loss ticket comes later. Many schools will have gone through the same cycle.

Celestial Ofsted – interim report

A celestial Ofsted answerable to a lord high promoter of learning, charged with the responsibility for assessing the performance of the Department for Education and Skills might begin its report thus:

Opening statement

Governments' efforts to raise standards are generally encouraging and show reasonable success. To some extent those efforts are hampered by what appears to be a rigid adherence to measurements of performance which omit vital aspects of human growth and development, and which encourage 'teaching for tests' to the detriment of promoting learning. They are further hampered by the alarmingly heavy study load carried by students from fourteen upwards which risks diminishing any sense of enjoyment in learning. It is also noted that the number of returns required of teachers and their very heavy marking assignments leave inadequate time for collegial approaches to raising standards.

There is clear evidence that the requirements of detailed returns for predictions of test and examination results as well as the results themselves promote greater attention to learning and teaching. But it is also noted that such scrutiny can lead to obsessive concern over minor variations in performance. Intentionally or not, this can give rise to discouraging impressions that standards are expected to rise exponentially.

Value for money is satisfactory. But value could be greater if budgetary arrangements enabled schools to plan confidently.

The legal obligations laid upon governing bodies to make annual reports have encouraged improved communication between school and parents, showing marked improvements in the relationships between them. There were also satisfactory improvements in the relationships between schools and their surrounding community, especially where the governing body is active. However the large number of additional requirements laid upon governing bodies risk leaving inadequate time for curriculum matters.

The requirements for the correction of weaknesses are

Central – Office at DfES	Reduce flow of circulars, and returns demanded.
	Cease adding responsibilities.
	Prevent duplication of data.
	Avoid gimmickry in new initiatives.
	Avoid precipitative introduction of reforms.
	Reduce NC requirements to one third of the curriculum.
	Reduce prediction requirements accordingly.
	Devise league tables showing school achievements and improvement for core subjects alongside national standards.
	Continue to search for the best role for core subjects within a rounded curriculum.
	Abandon search for instant perfect transparency and accountability.
Finance	Simplify systems, establish and observe realistic budgetary cycle.
	Abandon 'ring fenced' funding.

Ofsted

For the future	Issue a consultation paper – 'Inspection and support; a professional enterprise', might be a title – based on a comparative cost analysis of the total expenditure by Ofsted itself and the schools it inspects for a one year cycle, set against the cost of increasing the size of HM Inspectorate to staff the reduced programme of inspections. See below.
For the present	Expand professional HM inspectorate and extend its role.
	Replace the punitive with support and consultation.

Reduce half time, part time, and amateur participation. Ensure teams have a majority of serving full time professionals, and none retired for more than five years.

Evaluate team leaders more rigorously before appointment and monitor their performance.

Report on core subjects only occupying one third of the curriculum.

Comment and advise on the other two thirds.

Revise programme of inspections so that short, medium and long can take account of schools' different circumstances.

Replace competitive tendering with fixed price budgets.

Set schools' achievements alongside national standards for comparison.

LEAs

Seek power to replace simplistic 'parental choice' either with a genuinely open market with the risks of over/undercrowding and closure or restore catchment areas with suitable variations.

Schools

Complement the reduction of tests/scores/predictions with refined and more extensive use of teacher assessments.

Reduce workload – see DfES

Devise variations for two thirds of the curriculum to suit local circumstances.

Action plan

Ministers and officials are required to prepare an action plan for the next three years submitted for approval within six weeks. A further inspection will follow in six months to assess progress in correcting the weaknesses. It is further recommended that a committee of inquiry should be established with a twofold brief:

1 To evaluate the effectiveness of the separation of Ofsted from the DfES for promoting a high quality educational service.
2 To investigate the advantages and disadvantages for pupils, parents, teachers and schools of the combination of parental choice and competition.

Loss is entered here with a caveat. The correction of weaknesses could show a profit.

It could be that Mike Tomlinson and David Bell, respectively former and current chief inspector knew what was coming from the lord high promoter of learning. So far they are not thoroughly convincing about the likely answers.

Curriculum lost

A deeper sense of loss lies somewhere else. Seen from 2004, the great sadness about troubled secondary school education, indeed its tragedy, as it moved into the 1970s, is that curriculum development as a deliberate preparation for the majority of the country's young people entering the adult world got stopped in its tracks and Senacre with it. The raising of the school leaving age (ROSLA) was postponed from 1968 to 1972–3. Schools Council projects were being disseminated successfully, and seeded the curriculum more generally. A two year programme for fourth and fifth year pupils was truncated. Precious years of momentum had been lost. And Senacre paid the price.

Unfortunately this was made worse by circular 10/65. It was not Anthony Crosland's demands for plans for comprehensive schooling which made things worse. Rather it was concentrating on institutional reorganization, while neglecting the educational implications. Beyond social and educational aspirations as to what comprehensive education was intended to achieve, there was no forceful drive in the curriculum to realize those intentions, no systematic preparation for how best to meet the needs of the adolescent learners, nothing about what the reorganization meant for day-to-day practice in a reshaped school system.

Derek Morrell, a visionary civil servant, had made it clear in the mid-1960s that some government intervention was necessary to provide an education tuned to the complex social and economic changes the country was undergoing. He saw intervention as a necessity and a responsibility of government to encourage the growth of a democratic society in a fast changing world and could be tackled collaboratively. He was looking beyond reorganization.

But government was still dithering, and went on dithering until 1986, caught up as it was in the unresolved relationships between the department, local authorities, and turbulent teacher unions. It hoped that consultation and advice would effect change, rejecting forms of direct intervention. So it can be argued that government faltered to use its power, at the very time when some direct government intervention in the curriculum could have transformed secondary education more successfully than subsequent attempts. But in the circumstances of the time it is not evident it could have done anything else.

Curriculum cultures

In 2004, 1957–67 seems to belong to a different age, a different culture. That is no better illustrated than by something else; the culture of the Department of Education and Skills itself. Then public developments came from a government office which had a remarkable group of assistant secretaries. Maurice Kogan went off to Brunel University and in time became its Vice-chancellor. Geoffrey Caston left to become one of the two joint secretaries of the Schools Council, later Registrar of the University of Oxford and then Vice-chancellor of the University of the Pacific. John Bankes stayed put and was of critical importance for Schools Council activities. There was Toby Weaver who became deputy permanent secretary. Jocelyn

Owen was an imaginative deputy chief education officer who was a joint secretary and went on to be CEO. And Derek Morrell on secondment was the first joint secretary of the Schools Council. Secondary education for all was only twenty years old and so was the feeling that things could be made better after the 1939–45 war.

In his opening remarks for the 1965–6 Annual Joseph Payne Memorial Lecture, 'Education and change or the College of Preceptors', Morrell commented:

> I am simply an administrator who as one of the Joint Secretaries of the Schools Council has tried to help the education service to come to grips with some of the practical problems created by the pace of change in modern society. (p.5)

His thesis was:

> These demands on the educational system require a curriculum which is much more that a mere covering of subject matter. (p.8)

and

> It (the Schools Council) is first and foremost, an attempt to democratize the processes of problem solving as we try, as best we can, to develop an educational approach appropriate to a permanent condition of change. (p.12)

Sadly three years later he was dead.

In May 1971 Geoffrey Caston wrote an article, 'The schools council in context':

> In nearly four years of work for the Schools Council I have developed strong personal aspirations for it. I want it to thrive because I believe it embodies certain educational values which I think fundamental to the kind of vigorous and compassionate society of which I want to be a member. I will summarise these values in two concepts – pluralism and professionalism.

For pluralism:

> Translated into social and political institutions, it means that there are – indeed ought to be – many centres of influence, and that we should not worry when these conflict.

For professionalism:

> For educators the essence of professionalism lies in the exercise of judgement by individuals of choice and judgement in the interests, not of our employers, or ourselves but of our clients: in this case our pupils.
>
> (*Journal of Curriculum Studies*, Vol. 1, No. 3, 1971)

Think Tanks, smart Alecs and bright young political advisors are no substitute for thoughtful, public servants of that quality. Nor are civil servants substitutes, harassed as they are by ministers to produce instant answers with little time to think. Nor are ministers themselves substitutes, obsessed with the need to produce ever more evidence of satisfactory performance. Concern for society was articulated through their work. Now alas, while undoubtedly that concern continues, it gets buried in bureaucracy, and expressed too often in economic terms. Then no one looked for quick fixes. That was oxygen in the air which made the heart race and sped the mind. There was time and space to breath. Idealism, yes. Practical implementations, yes. No wonder at that stage in the 1960s Senacre felt on the side of the angels as a former head of English comments recently:

> I took down a book called *Growth through English* by John Dixon, 1967. It was like reading the Dead Sea Scrolls or some other ancient manuscript of long ago, all that optimism and energy and belief that teachers could make a difference in the sure and certain knowledge that the curriculum was in their hands to mould how they saw fit.

Another says

> At the time, we as a staff did not realize that we were making changes to learning patterns – they seemed the correct thing to do for 'our pupils'. Looking back in the wider context, it is quite frightening, to me anyway, that we changed so much.

There was a sense of professionalism. Now suspicion, even mistrust has replaced it. Instead of overseeing a system, trying to nurture it, the government has got itself into the position of trying to micro manage classrooms. Government diktat has replaced a 'democracy of professionalism'. Instruction and regulation circumscribe initiative. Ministers have something to answer for. This is an entry of enormous cultural loss.

Curriculum revival for renewal

Revival has to precede renewal. The curriculum problem of our time is to know how to return to attempts to create a 'democracy of professionalism', to enable teachers to revive curriculum for engagement while preserving the essential elements in public accountability. The NC and Ofsted introduced a discipline to learning and teaching nationally which had been lacking. The issue now is how to get an acceptable balance between prescriptions which do not throttle and a relaxation which does not risk incoherence – how to re-establish professionalism.

In its follow up, celestial Ofsted could be looking for revival. It could look for evidence that reduced prescription combined with stronger professional oversight by HMI showed signs of revival. It would seek to satisfy itself that the combination of test/SATS/exam results with teacher assessments, produced transparent evidence that standards were sustained with full accountability. It would look for evidence that bureaucratic demands had been reduced. It would assess the educational effectiveness of reducing core subjects requirements to create an appropriate curriculum. It would consider how far schools were enabled to play to their strengths.

One of the most instructive elements in the Senacre story, and it is bound to be the case with other schools, is the relative effectiveness of home grown and the externally induced or imposed curricula. During the first two headships and the fifth, courtesy of grant maintained status, there was time and space to search for curriculum content and pedagogy, which would deliberately engage young learners where they were, in the circumstances of the lives they led. Whatever success they had came from imagination and innovation which was free to get to work. Days were interesting, stimulating, even exciting for some members of staff, who accepted a heavy workload to do what they believed in. As many teachers were stimulated so were many students, a sure way of promoting learning.

By contrast the Thameside Scheme dictated a style of curriculum which was based on assumptions about where students ought to be, rather then where they actually were, a vital distinction. Unsurprisingly the curriculum narrowed. That meant that during the third and fourth headships there was little room for curricular development, although even if there had been, the struggle for survival in the atmosphere of parental choice and competition mopped up the energy. It was an unhappy example of a local authority paying insufficient attention to the consequences of its administrative and political decisions. Senacre's experience meant in effect this put on hold an engaging curriculum for at least 50 per cent of the school's population.

One effect of the content of the NC was to take the curriculum further away from where 50 per cent of the population actually lived and had their being. The gap widened again. In these terms external intervention reduced possibilities for schools to do what they do best: trying to work alongside students rather than on them. Curriculum renewal can only come when the government allows heads and staff to apply their own skills to resuscitating it. Only then can the gap be narrowed again.

It is notable that Senacre's initiative in widening the curriculum during the seventh headship was made possible through relaxation of the NC, and cited in the HMI's report which took the school out of special measures. The dead hand on the curriculum was lifting.

It seems a fair claim that this curriculum story shows that optimum success for students comes only where head and staff are able to take account of their local circumstances. Since government now sets the curriculum boundaries, it alone can enable schools to do that. If the NC was refined further so that one third was devoted to core subjects, and the other two thirds filled with any assortment of optional studies both on and off campus that the school thought best, curriculum revival might enable renewal to be more than a dream. The curriculum needs to engage the school itself as well as engaging its students. A school needs some sense of feeling that it owns its curriculum. That implies trust in the judgement of professionals. It is part of the price of curriculum revival.

There is another price to pay, taking risks. One of the most baleful influences of the NC and Ofsted is that it forces schools to play safe. There is little room for the maverick teacher. Appointing committees do not like taking risks. There are scores and targets to bother about, where a percentage change can send everyone scurrying for cover. And yet so often mavericks are a rich source of innovation. Of course they are a nuisance, inconvenient even, because they are always trying to buck the system. It is risky. Innovation for development can never guarantee success. But without it there is a different risk: stagnation. Failure can be powerfully instructive but risk is a price well worth paying.

It follows that curriculum as a one size fits all should be abandoned faster. The Senacre experience of four Ofsted inspections is supporting evidence. The use of a revised set of league tables should apply only to core subjects. That implies reposing greater authority in teachers to conduct assessments of student achievements and to relate them to student improvement, using national standards as guides rather than notches on a ruler. League tables should show lists of improvements. Scorecards against pre-ordained requirements which can produce some bizarre results would no longer be tolerated. This would certainly engage teachers, give parents more helpful information and enable government to remain confident as overlord of the system.

Returning something of that authority to teachers, while preserving accountability through a reformed Ofsted, offers a possible route back to the professionalism of a former age. Heads and staff would have curriculum workloads they welcomed, replacing time and energy wasted on bureaucracy. There would be time and space for imagination to nurture innovations. Vocationalism could take its proper place again.

That return of authority would create time and space for true leadership. It would reassert what heads are for: leading learning and teaching. At present a head's leadership means primarily enabling staff to cope with a plethora of demands while developing systems which promote learning and teaching to suit Ofsted, completing returns, maintaining a flow of papers to governors so they can fulfil their legal obligations and then, hoping to squeeze some time for thinking with colleagues. It limits possibilities for leadership to be collegial, to draw on all the strengths of the staff to devise a curriculum for engagement. In part it was those limitations which underlay Senacre's troubled sixth headship. It was overcoming those limitations which was the last head's triumph.

Thinking of those limitations, one senior Senacre teacher put it:

> What I did experience most strongly during my time – 30 years of it was steady erosion of my own standing and self-respect as a teacher and of the profession as a whole.

Returning authority would discourage this kind of reaction from another.

> You remove trust, you threaten honesty and openness. Teachers are ingenious enough to have found all sorts of short cuts to achieve more or less what is demanded, which on paper looks reasonable.

It might return to something like this as described by a deputy head.

> When I went into teaching I felt privileged to be allowed to take on the responsibility. I burnt with enthusiasm, commitment and the joy of having the licence to be creative and to innovate in an attempt to enthuse, motivate and occasionally to inspire the pupils in my charge.

To think like that, feel like that and act like that, there has to be time and space. Sadly, nearly twenty of the forty-seven years of the curriculum roundabout have led the deputy to say: 'Such aspirations seem almost irrelevant today'.

Time and space for true collegial leadership could revive those aspirations and make them real again. It would release imagination and energy for curriculum development which at present is suppressed. It could obey: 'The first rule of leadership is that it is to be shared' (Brighouse and Woods 1999).

What goes around comes around. Enough is enough. At this turn of the curriculum roundabout, education needs to stand up and shout from the rooftops: 'Stop. We want to get off, settle, revive, and renew the curriculum'.

Chapter 10

Reflections: personal and professional

John Elliott
Centre for Applied Research in Education,
University of East Anglia

Arriving

I think of Senacre as an institution in the mind. On a wet Sunday afternoon I arrived as a recently qualified teacher at the gates of Senacre to be interviewed by its first head teacher, Norman Evans. Anxiety welled up in me. There was no one in sight. Had the deputy head, who contacted me to arrange the interview, got it all wrong? After all applicants for teaching posts were not normally interviewed on a Sunday, and this was a religious studies post. The deputy had told me that Norman was off for a while helping train teachers at a college of education. Hence, he was only available to conduct interviews at the weekend.

My previous two interviews were held during the working week and depressing events they were. I received rejection notes in both cases, but was not too distressed. I had not felt comfortable about the schools I visited, as places I might feel at home in. These schools were uncertain about their identity. One was a technical high school in the Thames Estuary, neither a grammar nor a secondary modern but somewhere in between. The other was a bi-lateral school (grammar plus secondary modern streams) in Hampshire. Standing outside locked school gates on a wet Sunday afternoon did not seem like a promising start to my third attempt at becoming a teacher. However, I did not even begin to doubt that this was what I wanted to be.

I had belonged to an amateur dramatic society 'The country players' in Maidstone, before going off to college at the age of twenty-one, and it was that that switched me on to teaching as a career. We were doing an open-air production of *A Midsummer Night's Dream* and when we were off set we crowded into a marquee. There a number of cast members sat marking exercise books. They were teachers. Watching them I thought this might be an interesting career. At the time I was working as a laboratory technician on a nearby horticultural research station. I had left school at sixteen and had no A levels. So university was out for me, but teacher training colleges were still accepting people with O levels. So I applied and received an offer from my thirteenth choice, the City of Portsmouth Training College. I was the last of the two-year trained teachers, qualifying in biology and religious education (as well as being an amateur actor I was on the Maidstone Methodist Circuit as a lay preacher). I went on to do a Supplementary Certificate in Religious Education at Bishop Otter College in Chichester, to upgrade my qualifications where we were taught philosophical theology. It ignited an enduring interest in the subject. At the end of a summer job at the Chichester Festival Theatre, I was invited to go up to London's West end and work as a back-room boy. I did not even entertain it. No, I was going to be a teacher (and at Senacre as it turned out). I suppose the prospect of teaching brought my multiple selves into some kind of liaison: the frustrated academic (researcher, philosopher and theologian) with the actor and the preacher.

Let us return to that interview. Suddenly a car drew to an abrupt halt at the school gates. Two men were inside it, one younger than the other. The younger one, pipe in mouth, got out and unlocked the gate, whilst explaining why he was late and informing me that the older man in the passenger seat wearing a green cap was his father. Well, that was a bit of a novelty too. How many head teachers brought their dads along to interviews for new staff? I was soon to learn as a member of his staff that this particular head teacher was indeed a law unto himself.

We entered into the corridors of what appeared to be a newish and well-kept building. Dad disappeared and I was taken into his son's study for the interview. I cannot remember much about it, except having an odd conversation about the possibility of introducing a stained glass window into the school hall in order to create an appropriate atmosphere for school assemblies. Looking back it may have been that Norman, a public school boy and later housemaster at Bedford school, wanted to bring something of the atmosphere of those elite institutions he was so familiar with to this secondary modern school situated on the edge of a vast housing estate. Anyway in spite of feeling this was an odd conversation, I felt strangely comfortable. This was because it was indeed a conversation and not the kind of interrogation I had experienced in the previous two interviews. The interview concluded with me agreeing to pursue the matter further. I never did, and Norman never reminded me. Getting me to agree was Norman's way of telling me I had got the job, and of ensuring I did not have any escape route. Subsequently, I have always admired the strategies he employs to get people to do things they would not volunteer for. The exception is when I am his victim. Why am I writing this final chapter of the Senacre story? That interview in 1962 changed my life.

I ended my 'career' forty-two years later as Professor of Education in the Centre for Applied Research in Education at the University of East Anglia in Norwich. How did I get from being a non-graduate teacher at the time of that interview in my home county of Kent to being a Professor of Education at a prestigious university in Norwich? The rest of this chapter is an attempt to tell a story about this 'voyage'.

The context: finding my way

At the time of the interview I had never been to Norwich or Norfolk for that matter. In a sense it was all Norman's fault and the climate he created at Senacre, as appears later. It was a climate in which the traditional authoritarian teacher found it difficult to survive. This was partly due to the pupils, many of whom held no great respect for strategies of containment and control. Secondary modern schools at the time were faced with the large-scale disaffection of working-class students, who had failed the 11+ entry tests into the grammar schools, and yet had to suffer the pain of following a watered-down grammar school curriculum. Many of these schools attempted to turn themselves into warehouses for keeping pupils off the streets and out of trouble until they were of an age when they could be released into the lower echelons of the 'labour market'. If they were expected to learn anything inside the warehouse it was 'learning to labour' by complying with systems of containment and control that were not unlike those that prevailed on the industrial assembly lines. I found myself in an innovatory secondary modern school, whose head teacher had decided that his school would not follow the majority. Instead he encouraged his staff to find ways of motivating and challenging pupils to learn by changing the curriculum. Senacre was spearheading the school-based curriculum reform movement in the UK.

Norman did not reinforce authoritarian traits in my personality and those of other staff. He resolutely refused to sort out our discipline problems, and expected us to bear the responsibility. He did not like the strategy of dumping disruptive pupils outside his door. I suspect he would disapprove of one currently fashionable solution to the problem: the creation of special 'exclusion rooms' within schools for disruptive pupils. As a youngish male teacher I had 'difficulties with girls' rather than boys. In my first few weeks one incident should have prompted more reflection than it did at the time. I was 'on lunch duty' and attempting to demonstrate to more experienced colleagues that I was 'one with them', or at least how I imagined 'them' to be. Walking into the hall I saw 13-year-old Doreen sitting on the stage and noticed that she had a ladder in her stocking, which I foolishly pointed out. 'Want to climb up?' she retorted. I rose to the bait. 'If you speak to me like that' I shouted pompously 'I will have you down in the headmaster's study', to which she replied in a flash 'Ooh, lovely'. The same trap that earlier another had fallen into.

So much for my future prospects as an agent of containment and control. I should have learnt from it sooner than I did. I well remember the agony of teaching 4C on Friday afternoons, last lesson, and hanging on until the bell went. I excluded one disruptive girl from the classroom frequently, until one afternoon she charged back with a threat to fetch 'her Dad to beat me up'. I felt totally de-skilled with that class, and resented the time when an experienced teacher burst in and took over control. I was furious with her for taking responsibility away from me. It made me feel even more de-skilled.

It was not that Norman provided no direction and support in handling disruptive pupils. The direction was clear. He expected us to operationalize in our classrooms a pedagogy that was based on 'respect for' rather than 'fear of' pupils. In doing so he did not expect us to be 'soft on discipline' but to exercise it in a way that made pupils feel that it was them rather than the system they were 'letting down'. In his own exchanges with pupils he gave little indication that he perceived them to be 'fearful objects'. While making it clear that he would 'not stand for any nonsense'

he also made it clear that he had high expectations of their capabilities. He expected his staff to model such expectations in their teaching. Discipline was to be used to enhance rather than diminish pupils' self-respect and belief in themselves. Moreover, he saw individual pupils' capabilities as diverse and incapable of standardization in terms of a narrow academic curriculum structured around the traditional subjects.

The support Norman provided for us classroom teachers in making the transition from a pedagogy based on fear to one based on respect, was to give us the freedom and opportunity to engage in curriculum experiments that catered for what is now fashionably called 'multiple intelligences', while at the same time providing a 'space for accountability' in which we were expected to justify our plans and actions to the staff as a whole and to him. There was 'trust' in teachers combined with 'accountability'. I remember having to submit my curriculum plans for religious studies on a regular basis, in a specially issued book. It would come back with comments like 'I think that they will get lost if you persist with trying to engage them with these ideas at such a high level of abstraction'. It was not that he did not expect us to develop an intellectually challenging curriculum, but he required us to think about it pedagogically from the point of view of the learner. I also remember Norman stopping me in the corridor outside the staff room and thrusting the newly established Schools Council's Working Paper No. 2 on the humanities curriculum into my hand and telling me to read it. He was of the opinion that it had a better curriculum vision than that contained in the recently published Newsom Report. The latter's concept of curriculum relevance he felt was too 'low level' and not intellectually challenging enough. He believed that we should not give up on the task of finding ways to engage our pupils with the best in our intellectual and cultural heritage. I agreed with him.

The curriculum issues in the academic areas at Senacre revolved not so much around the objects of learning, but how to reorganize curriculum structures to enable pupils to engage with those objects in a more personally meaningful way, one which connected with their lived experience. Little did I know at the time of that encounter with Norman in the corridor that I would within a few years join the central team of the Schools Council 'Humanities Curriculum Project', under the direction of Lawrence Stenhouse, and become involved in helping teachers and schools across England and Wales to operationalize the ideas contained in Working Paper No. 2. It was written by a senior civil servant Derek Morrell.

Working it out

All that freedom and permission to engage in curriculum experimentation that I was thrust into with colleagues at Senacre, while at the same time being held to account for what we were doing against a criterion of 'respect for pupils as persons', provided the context in which the frustrated researcher in me, the person who had failed to make it into the world of science, found expression. It enabled me not merely to survive in the classroom but to feel comfortable and at home in it with my pupils. I started to research the problems I found there as I tried to move away from an instruction-based pedagogy towards one which fostered more active learning through discussion and project work. I gathered evidence from pupils about their experience of life in classrooms and of the changes I was attempting to bring about to create a better learning environment for them. This evidence was used to inform my judgements and decisions, and to evaluate the actions that flowed from them. Such actions were always treated as provisional and open to continuous modification in the light of evidence. In other words they were viewed as 'hypotheses' to test out in the classroom in conversation with the pupils. In this sense my classroom became a sort of laboratory. This time I was in the role of the 'senior scientist' rather than that of the laboratory assistant. Although I did not then have a name for this form of practice-based inquiry aimed at the development of my teaching, I learnt later that some American academics had called it 'action research'.

The curriculum laboratory

In time the change process in the humanities subjects at Senacre required greater cross-subject collaboration between teachers. We started to develop a new 'integrated humanities curriculum' with discussion-based learning at its core and involving a great deal of project work outside the school in the community. It involved team-teaching, in the course of which we observed each other teach, and on this basis gave each other feedback in addition to that obtained from our pupils. In effect I found myself as head of a newly created humanities faculty leading a process of collaborative action research with my colleagues. In the course of it each teacher had access to three sources of evidence about their teaching situation. There was evidence they gathered, often impressionistically, in the flow of events. Then there was evidence about their pupil's experience of these events. And finally there was evidence gathered by peer observers. Some years later I discovered that some social scientists had coined a term for this process of gathering evidence about a situation from different standpoints. It was called 'triangulation'. An account of it can be found in virtually every textbook on research methods in the social sciences. I have used this method continuously throughout my career as an applied educational researcher engaged in helping teachers to reflect about their teaching. I did not discover it by reading articles and books on research methods. In fact I did not 'discover' it at all. Rather I 'experienced' it as a process we teachers created at Senacre in the course of attempting to change the curriculum for the benefit of our pupils. Teachers in other innovatory secondary modern schools probably also found themselves doing something like 'triangulation' without being aware of the term.

Senacre applied

My five years at Senacre (1962–7) served me well as a member of the central team on the Schools Council Humanities Project. My appointment was once more all

Norman's fault. I had applied for a year's secondment to train as a school counsellor, and been accepted for a course at the University of Keele. One morning Norman called me into his study and suggested I apply for an advertised position on the humanities project. 'But what about Keele?' I asked. He told me that in his opinion counselling was not a suitable occupation for someone prone to introversion like myself. Life on a national curriculum development project would be better for my health. He said that he would take care of Keele and advised me to buy a new suit before I went up to the interview. So I found myself being interviewed for the position in London, and accepting the offer that arrived in the post a few days later. Years later I met the HMI for religious education who was on a national committee for RE teachers. Evidently Norman was a member of the committee. The committee had been worried lest an RE specialist was not appointed to represent the interests of that subject on the project team. This prompted Norman to take action by calling me into his office that morning. I am very glad he did.

On the humanities project I found myself working with a group of people who shared the kind of educational vision I had acquired at Senacre. Stenhouse himself had designed the humanities project as a 'curriculum experiment' for teachers to test in their classrooms. For him 'teacher research' lay at the heart of the curriculum development process. It was one of my roles to support teacher research in the project. I found myself drawing on the Senacre experience as I travelled the country to our 'experimental schools'. Part of my job was to help teachers research the problems of changing their teaching in ways that were consistent with the aims and principles of the project, and the impact of these changes on their pupils' experience of life in classrooms. In 1970 Stenhouse became director of a new Centre for Applied Research in Education (CARE) at the University of East Anglia in Norwich, and moved the humanities project with many of its team there, myself included. Apart from a break of eight years at the Cambridge Institute of Education, the centre has been the base for my work ever since. It became a spearhead, in this country and internationally, for the development of the 'teachers as researchers' movement and action research as an integral component of curriculum and educational change. Although the late 1980s saw the imposition of a highly prescriptive national curriculum, that left little space for school-based curriculum development and research, my base at CARE enabled me to keep drawing on the Senacre experience by working in policy contexts where schools and teachers were given space to exercise curriculum initiatives. For over ten years I worked with schools across Europe to develop new kinds of environmental education curricula through action research, and then more latterly with the Curriculum Development Institute and the Institute of Education in Hong Kong as they attempt to build capacity for curriculum development in schools.

Senacre was one of the early cradles of 'educational action research' and the 'teachers as researchers' movement in the UK. I have subsequently argued that these ideas were not born in universities and other institutions of higher education. They were already embedded in the practices of teachers as they attempted to effect radical pedagogical and curriculum change in their classrooms and schools during the period of the school-based curriculum reform movement. What academics such as Lawrence Stenhouse, myself and others did was to articulate the logic underpinning these practices and thereby develop a language and discourse for disseminating them more widely in the educational system.

A lament

Seen against Senacre, it is deeply ironic that forty years on, following a decade and a half of a national curriculum structured around the traditional academic subjects, policy-makers in this country are now talking about 'personalizing' the curriculum to cater for 'multiple intelligences' and provide pupils with opportunities to direct their learning through a multiplicity of pathways. School-based curriculum development appears to be re-emerging and driving it is a problem that has persisted through all the social engineering that successive governments have engaged in, and through all the devices they employed for driving up standards in schools. The problem remains: of large-scale disaffection from learning. By the time I left Senacre in 1967 I had experienced at first hand the kind of curriculum and pedagogical experimentation that yielded workable solutions to the problem of motivating and engaging pupils in learning. It was an inheritance that has stood me in good stead and sustained my optimism in the face of policy interventions that fundamentally disrespected the generative capabilities of teachers to effect worthwhile educational change.

As I observed these interventions from the perspective I had acquired at Senacre, I knew that the edifice of accountability they constructed – a target and test driven national curriculum, league tables, parental choice, and external Ofsted inspections – would not be sufficient to stem the tide of pupil disaffection. This knowledge sustained me over the years. The standards-driven agenda in schools implied a low-trust model of accountability with regard to the role of teachers. Senacre had given me the seeds of a pedagogically driven high trust model of teacher accountability.

There is a sense in which I spent the rest of my career as an educational researcher working with teachers to develop and articulate that higher trust model. I was flattered recently when I met someone at a conference who told me that he had regarded me as one of the leaders of the resistance to those low-trust policy interventions. I have to thank Senacre for that. But for me it was more than the power to resist that I am thankful for. I was convinced that the time would come when the pendulum would swing back, and now feel at the very point of retirement that it is happening. I can now see my career as helping to prepare some of the necessary groundwork for the return of a pedagogically driven approach to curriculum reform that might stand a chance of becoming more sustainable in the educational policy context than it appears to have been at Senacre. This is partly because policy makers in the UK have gradually learnt that centralized social engineering, based on the belief that governments can devise good means to achieving clearly defined ends and a set of objective standards for evaluating those ends, just does not work for such a complex and value-laden enterprise as education. At the same time they are aware that schools cannot be left to their own devices if they are to measure up to the imperatives of a liberal democratic society and provide opportunities for all its potential citizens to develop those capabilities that enable them in the words of Amartra Sen, 'to choose a life one has reason to value'. If a few secondary modern schools in the 1960s, like Senacre, responded to those imperatives the majority continued to perpetuate their status in an elitist educational system as institutions for the containment and control of those pupils who had not been selected to become members of a meritocratic elite.

Reading the previous chapters I was saddened that some of the colleagues I worked with, and whose voices I recognized, retired on a 'low' rather than a 'high' note. With dismay I read how external interventions put a stop to pursuit of 'curriculum for engagement' and suppressed teachers' creativity. I hope it is of some comfort to realize that the vision we worked for in those early years of Senacre, and the processes we engaged in together, are still alive and at work in the world, whatever happens to the school as an organization and ourselves. We made a difference to our pupils' lives. That fact is still having consequences.

The future for curriculum development

There needs to be a new way of holding teachers in schools publicly accountable without diminishing trust in their creative capabilities. In my view it will involve the creation at local, regional and national level of new political institutions that provide public spaces in which citizens drawn from different sectors in society can freely and openly debate curriculum solutions for the most pressing and persistent educational problems that impinge on their interests. Such institutions would have the power to get agreements that emerge translated into policy initiatives. It would then be the task of the professional educators in schools to experiment with the proposed solutions and generate evidence-based accounts of these experiments, which are externally audited and made available for public scrutiny. Such accounts, generated through action research, would enable the citizenry to give the professionals in schools both developmental feedback, and to receive it from them as a basis for further action orientated public debate. We would have a form of reciprocal accountability between the citizenry and the professionals. The role of government agencies would need to change. Rather than exercising technocratic and instrumental control over the educational experiences of pupils in classrooms, they would facilitate a dynamic and interactive process of policy formation and implementation. This would involve administering and continuously re-adjusting the release and use of the financial and human resources required to support such a process. This is not fanciful. I can point to parts of the world, such as the Far East, where it is beginning to emerge.

Some may argue that we had something analogous in the ill-fated Schools Council for Curriculum Reform and Examinations in the early 1960s. It failed because it became a site of struggle between government and teachers' organizations. It was not sufficiently representative of the citizenry. Perhaps it is time to establish a new kind of Schools Council that opens up a public space for all citizens to engage in action orientated debates about the pressing problems of education in our society.

The lesson

Looking back it seems fair to claim that schools would become more effective places of learning if teachers were given the time, space and responsibility to create curricula designed to meet the needs of their pupils, based on the kind of 'action research' which evolved at Senacre, and combined with an intelligent form of accountability. Teachers and their pupils would be happier and parents better satisfied. Opportunities for teachers' professional and personal development would be part of the job. The professionalism of teaching would be re-established.

Appendix I
Outline syllabus correlating social geography and religious studies (4th year)

Term I – what is man?

Social science and economics

A study of how man's needs in primitive societies affected the social organization of the tribe e.g. Samoa, New Guinea, Australian Aboriginals, Sioux Indian, Navajo. How do animals differ from man in the way they cope with their needs? Compare the social organization of the tribes above with ants or monkeys.

Psychology

a   The reflex system: How does man differ from animals regarding behaviour dominated by the reflex system?
b   Drives and needs: hunger, sex, air, parental security and affection, exploratory, aesthetic, fear, anger, excitement. Drives and the nervous system.

History

a   The theory of evolution – Charles Darwin. The beginnings of Neanderthal, Pekin, nutcracker, handyman, *Homo sapiens*.
b   Ways in which primitive man attempted to control his environment (tools, buildings, agriculture, keeping animals, magic) in order to meet his needs.

Geography

a   Theories of the origin of the universe and life. Big bang theory and continuous creation theory (modern), Babylonian Theory Marduk and Tiamat (Ancient).
b   Ways in which geographical conditions of the earth have influenced the course of evolution.
c   Geography of two of the areas mentioned in the Social Science syllabus
   1   Physical
   2   Natural Resources.

Religious Study

What is the point of it all? (the Biblical doctrine of creation).

Literature: *The Tiger's Bones,* Ted Hughes; *The Outsider,* Albert Camus; *The Bear,* William Faulkner.

The Genesis narratives and their teaching about the nature of man and his environment.

The mythological framework in which they are expressed. The meaning of myth – man's attempt to understand himself and his world.

Compare Genesis mythology with other ancient mythologies e.g. Sumerian, Egyptian and Nordic.

Science and religion – Darwin and the church.

Appendix 2

Humanities course
(4th and 5th years)

12 Periods and 4 O level

English	Social Studies
	(RS) (Social science and economics) (History) (Geography)
CSE Mode 3	CSE Mode 3
Continuous assessment	Continuous assessment and written exam

GCE O level	Enterprise	Sociology O level
2 periods	4 periods	2 periods

Appendix 3
Basic assumptions

1 If possible the staff who are going to put a syllabus into practice should be involved in the framework in which they are going to teach as far as curriculum and timetable goes.

2 The timetable reflects our priorities.

3 New ideas will not solve our basic problems of not having enough staff and facilities, neither will they make our work easier but they may make it more efficient and less frustrating.

4 Rigid subject divisions are not as applicable in our teaching situation as they may be in some other types of school, particularly in view of the fact that Senacre has already gone a long way in keeping up with modern developments in the curriculum. Integrating subject disciplines does not mean that specialist knowledge is less important; on the contrary it becomes more important and more meaningful in the new context.

5 The forty-minutes period made more sense in a situation where subjects were taught separately than in our own situation where sometimes we may need a twenty-minutes session and sometimes an hour session.

6 I think I am not the only one in the school who feels that it may be valuable for us as well as the children if we work together more both by pooling ideas and in having two teachers actually working together in a classroom situation. This has already been done in several departments this year.

7 When one person asks other people to work a new idea, they should if possible, be put in a situation which allows them to 'feel their way into' the best method for them to work the new idea.

8 No member of staff, if he has agreed to work a new idea involving extra work, should be put in a position where there is no line of retreat if new and unforeseen difficulties arise. I wish to back staff in two ways if the new ideas are accepted.

    a Information and material to be available from the Schools Council Humanities Project, the Goldsmiths College Curriculum Laboratory, the Keele University's Curriculum Project and schools who have already initiated this method of working.

b Particularly in a new situation, the more useful adults in the classroom the better and I therefore wish to support staff by bringing in groups of students from universities and colleges of education in whom we have confidence e.g. mature students from Sittingbourne College and students from Stockwell College who have served us well in the past.

9 Any new idea involves a good deal of pre-planning and extra consultation. If possible, staff must be helped by being given time for consultation.

10 It would be helpful to try out some of these situations in the summer term of 1968.

11 The idea may fail simply because those putting it into practice do not have sufficient confidence in it and I realize that I must be careful not to oversell the idea and not to ignore quiet reluctance.

Other sections in the document go on to speculate what this might mean were the ideas to be incorporated in the timetable.

Appendix 4

The curriculum – possible points for discussion

1 How far are you and your department committed to:

   a an integrated approach?
   b a subject discipline approach?
   c a combination of both and why?

2 How far are you and your department committed to a principle of:

   a mixed ability?
   b streaming?
   c a combination of both or a compromise between them, and how?

3 What methods of teaching and learning are employed in your department?
4 What is the specific content or programme, or is there any reason why this is felt to be unnecessary?
5 What are the standards and achievements aimed for by your department?
6 What do you see as the major successes and advantages of your present policy? Are there any particular factors to which you attribute those successes?
7 What do you see as the major failures, constraints and pitfalls of your present policy? Can they be solved? If so how? Are there any insuperable difficulties in your opinion?
8 Have you evaluated your policy and with what conclusions?
9 Have you any long term policies/plans/ambitions for your department?

November 1974

Appendix 5

SAFE newsletter

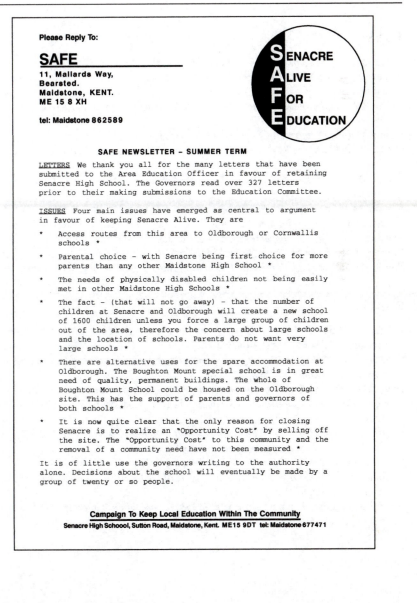

Please Reply To:

SAFE

11, Mallards Way,
Bearsted.
Maidstone, KENT.
ME 15 8 XH

tel: Maidstone 862589

S ENACRE
A LIVE
F OR
E DUCATION

SAFE NEWSLETTER – SUMMER TERM

LETTERS We thank you all for the many letters that have been submitted to the Area Education Officer in favour of retaining Senacre High School. The Governors read over 327 letters prior to their making submissions to the Education Committee.

ISSUES Four main issues have emerged as central to argument in favour of keeping Senacre Alive. They are

* Access routes from this area to Oldborough or Cornwallis schools *

* Parental choice – with Senacre being first choice for more parents than any other Maidstone High School *

* The needs of physically disabled children not being easily met in other Maidstone High Schools *

* The fact – (that will not go away) – that the number of children at Senacre and Oldborough will create a new school of 1600 children unless you force a large group of children out of the area, therefore the concern about large schools and the location of schools. Parents do not want very large schools *

* There are alternative uses for the spare accommodation at Oldborough. The Boughton Mount special school is in great need of quality, permanent buildings. The whole of Boughton Mount School could be housed on the Oldborough site. This has the support of parents and governors of both schools *

* It is now quite clear that the only reason for closing Senacre is to realize an "Opportunity Cost" by selling off the site. The "Opportunity Cost" to this community and the removal of a community need have not been measured *

It is of little use the governors writing to the authority alone. Decisions about the school will eventually be made by a group of twenty or so people.

Campaign To Keep Local Education Within The Community
Senacre High Schoool, Sutton Road, Maidstone, Kent. ME15 9DT tel: Maidstone 677471

References

Books

Blishen, E. (1983) *Donkey Work*, London: Hamish Hamilton.

Brighouse, T. and Woods, D. (1999) *How to Improve your School*, London: Routledge Falmer.

Butler, R.A. (1971) *The Art of the Possible: The Memoirs of Lord Butler KG, CH*, London: Hamish Hamilton.

Caston, G. (1971) *Journal of Curriculum Studies*, 1(3) 50–51.

Cox, C.B. and Boyson, R. (eds) (1975) *The Fight for Education, Black Paper*, London: Dent.

Cox, C.B. and, Dyson, A.E. (eds) (1977) *Black Papers 1969–1977*, London: Maurice Temple.

Keeton, M.J. and Tape, P. (1978) *Learning by Experience – What, Why, How?* New Directions for Experimental Learning, No. 1, San Francisco, CA: Jossey-Bass.

Maclure, S. (2000) *The Inspectors' Calling*, London: Hodder and Stoughton.

Morrell, D. (1963) Joseph Payne Annual Memorial Lecture, London: College of Preceptors.

Wardle, D. (1970) *English Popular Education*, Cambridge: Cambridge University Press.

Reports

Beloe, R. (1960) *Secondary School Examinations Other Than the GCE* , London: Secondary Schools Examination Board.

Crowther, G. (1959) *15–18, Report of the Minister of Education's Central Advisory Committee*, London: HMSO.

Hargreaves, D. (1983) *Improving Secondary Schools: Report of the Committee on the Curriculum and Organization of Secondary Schools*, London: Inner London Education Authority.

Newsom, J. (1963) *Half our Future: Education Between the Ages of 13 and 16 of Average and Less than Average Ability*, London: HMSO.

Plowden, Lady (1967) *Children and their Primary Schools*, London: HMSO.

Robbins Lord (1963) *Higher Education: Report of the Committee on Higher Education*, London: HMSO.

South East Regional Examination Board (1963) *Constitution*, Tunbridge Wells: Courier Printing and Publishing.

Tomlinson, M. (2002) *Inquiry into A Level Standards* (The Tomlinson Report), DfES: London.

Warnock, H.M. (1978) *Special Education Needs: Report of a Committee of Inquiry into the Education of Handicapped Children and Young People*, London: HMSO.

Circulars

8/83 The School Curriculum
10/65 The Organization of Secondary Schools
14/77 Education in schools: a consultative document

Ofsted Reports

Under Section 9 of the Education (Schools) Act 1992, school number 922/541.

Dates of inspection:
31 October–4 November 1994 – contract number 922/S4/000802
18–22 January 1999 – contract number 704593
22–26 January 2001 – contract number 210753
25–26 June 2003, reference HMI 1819

Index